The Dark and Dying Places

Because we're all imperfect

And we can find the ones who see us
perfectly

And that's what love truly means.

~

To my great grandfather, for showing me
who I am,

To Jennifer, Jessica, and Rose,

And to the one who taught me to smile,

You all are perfect to me.

The Dark and Dying Places
Kaitlyn Joy O'Gara

Table of Contents

Prologue:

Woke to an Empty World

Time passes the same wherever you are. A minute, an hour, they all slip past un-noticed until they're gone and all you're left with is the grim reaper in the shape of a bullet or a bus or something else, seeking you out to wipe you from the map.

However, time had broken apart forever ago. In this wasteland, there were few voices, and even fewer people. The spirits of reflections lingered amongst the sparse population of the living. And time no longer mattered. After all, how could it? It simply didn't exist. There was no escape except death. But it is impossible to die here. Unless another has the thirst to kill and you are the only victim within a hundred-mile radius.

The sky was a deathly shade of black, streaked with grey. The ground below resembled that of a desert, but no cactuses lived there. The area was lit, surprisingly, as if there was sun. There wasn't. It was one of those few features of this place that made it impossible to tell if it was good or evil.

It's not like anyone wanted to see what existed there. The lone people that trudged along had sunken faces and thin bodies. Their clothes hung loose on their frail body, and their backs were hunched over. These few living people were mere shells of their past selves, unable to find who they once were.

Some stood, rigid, unable to move from the spot in which they stood. They would occasionally move a hand, as if there was a mirror in front of them, and they were looking at something. But there seemed to be nothing.

It wasn't uncommon to come across a spirit. They looked the same as the living, except their eyes held more life. Who knew that the dead could be more alive than the living?

No words were exchanged between those that still had life. Sometimes voices echoed in their heads, calling them back to their previous lives, but there was never an answer. Rarely, there would be a scream. Someone new had come to this place, and they were scared. They were sad. They were frightened. And soon, they wouldn't be anything. And they wouldn't be able to feel anything.

It came to the point where some begged to die. They would feel that strange ghost of a pull, pulling them back to where they belonged to be. They had a place. But once they reached that place, their eyes went blank. Their mind faded away, and they were even less than the shell of what they used to be. As what could be called time progressed, their bodies began to fade, until they were ghosts that floated there, eyes glinting at the thought of freedom.

There was no returning. Once here, the lives on the other side no longer belonged to them. No one was able to keep a firm grip on their sense of self. Those who could be classified as insane faded slower, but they did eventually fade.

Even the senses began to fade away. The eyes saw nothing but what had once belonged to them. The ears only heard the voices spurring from the mind. The nose smelled smoke, and became so used to this stench that the sense seemed to fade entirely. Touch no longer mattered. There was no one to touch, and there was nothing to touch. And taste had no place here. The lone apple tree that grew was the only sign of life. And the dead never have to eat.

Those apple trees were only there because of the farmer that had come to this side earlier than anyone else. His body is the only one that doesn't look completely dead. His eyes don't work anymore, but if you listen carefully, you can hear his teeth puncture the apple skin. It's the only sound for miles.

And fears spawn here more than anything else. Spiders crawled out of the cracks in the ground. No one knew if they were real, or simply a nightmare. It didn't matter. It still instilled fear in those that lingered here. Sometimes, the sky seemed to be falling, as if about to crush those that lay beneath. And visions of bodies being torn apart flickered in front of the eyes that those that lived.

So maybe it is not right to say that there was nothing to feel. Feeling nothing is much better than feeling fear. This fear drove people past the point of madness. It made their bodies shut down until they were nothing more than a shell.

Those that did find someone else lingering here rarely shared words. But even if they did, it's not like anyone else could hear.

Suddenly, she saw something falling from the black sky. It fell like rain. But rain is a sign of life.

It was the color of a heart. It was the color that used to make people turn, or look back. But now it faded in with everything else. No one could tell that blood was falling from the sky. It stained the ground a darker shade than it already was. It fell onto the flat hair of those that were there, and onto their pale skin. No one cared that something was falling from the sky. Except her.

She lay there, by the apple tree, willing herself away. Her body shook, and she was unable to ignore the blood that dripped from the ominous places above. It mixed with the tears that fell from her cheeks, creating a new color in this place.

A spirit that remained in the apple tree saw the girl. The spirit saw her crying, and feeling fear, and looking very much alive. How did one remain alive in such a dark place?

The girl looked up, and for the first time in however long it had been, she caught the spirit's eye. There was a flash of sympathy in those eyes, and then the spirit was gone. The girl felt that slight tug on her body, and her knees shook as her brain forced her to stand. She screamed out as she took a step, unable to fight it. She was becoming one of them. And there was absolutely nothing she could do about it.

This was no one's home, but it was now where she lived. And it was where she would die. Never again would she see that light that shined through her window every morning. There would no longer be the touch of a loved one or the comforting words of a brother. Everything was gone. And that was the way it was supposed to be here. She had found herself here, and she was one of those that had screamed in fright at seeing this world. That second as she crossed sides was the last time she would experience time passing. For now death was simply expected and welcome. It was never early, and it was never late. It always would be there. And it always would come.

The image of the spirit flashed through her mind. It was only a matter of time before she became one of them. In the distance, she saw the thin outline of what could have been a mirror. And she saw something else.

She saw someone alive. Her brain forced her to move forward until she was standing there, in front of herself. Her hand made the same movements as the person looking at her. Their hands touched, palm to palm except for the barrier between them. The girl on this dark side didn't display any emotion. She couldn't. Not here.

But then the other girl, the one full of life, looked Jacey right in the eyes and smirked.

"You're no longer anyone. You're my reflection. Nothing more. And nothing less."

December
2015

Chapter 1:

Hearts Made of Red Plastic Cups

Jacey's heels clicked along the sidewalk as she abandoned her high school, at least for the weekend.

"Jay, wait up!" Someone ran up behind her, their breath sounding winded. Jacey turned her head, and brushed her dark red hair over her shoulder.

She chuckled softly. "C'mon, slow poke," Jacey teased. Her English accent slipped through, but Connor was all too used to it by now.

"It's a wonder you can walk faster than me in those shoes," Connor muttered, before sending her a wink. Jacey nudged him with her elbow, glancing down at her heeled black boots.

After a moment, Connor interlocked their index fingers, a common gesture for the two close friends.

"You still going tonight?" he questioned, his eyes flickering over to meet hers.

Jacey sighed. "Yes, and I don't understand why you insist on coming. I know how much you despise these types of parties."

"It's—"

"Because you want to watch over me," Jacey finished his sentence. "Why, though?"

"Jay, last time…" Connor murmured before trailing off. He sounded hesitant, his tone filled with palpable reluctance.

Jacey stiffened slightly, tightening their interlocked fingers. She glanced at the cracks in the sidewalk, the sights and sounds of the bustling city dulling as she became lost in her own memories.

Connor hated to even mention it, but it was crucial Jacey remember the consequences of underage drinking.

"Thanks for that," she whispered, unable to look him in the eye.

Connor frowned, ruffling his dark brown hair. "There's no need to thank me. I wanted to help."

She sent him a weak smile, shivering slightly, and not just because of the cold February weather.

"Let's go grab some coffee," Connor suggested, wanting to get her mind off of everything.

If there was anyone Jacey could almost be herself around, it was Connor. She had met him in the later months of sixth grade, and six years later, in their senior year of high school, they were still close friends. Which was contrary to what everyone in their student body thought they were.

Jacey's eyes flickered across the horizon of small shops ahead of them. "Where is the nearest coffee shop?"

"We live in New York," Connor chuckled. "Where is there not a coffee shop?"

He swung a quick left at the intersection, smiling at the familiar green and white logo that awaited them.

"Do you mind ordering for me?" Jacey asked as they stepped inside, gesturing to the restroom as an explanation. Connor nodded, letting his hand fall free by his side as Jacey clicked away.

"What would you like to order?" The blonde waitress smiled too cheerily at him; pen in one hand, and empty cup in the other.

Connor glanced at the menu, eyes scanning it.

"Grande vanilla bean frapp," he said, eyes still flitting over the menu.

The barista wrote the order down, sending the cup to the blender. "Will that be all for you today? Or did your lovely girlfriend want something?" She giggled softly, giving him a small wink. There was an awkward silence, and Connor began to stutter, eyes sliding over toward the restroom.

"She's not..." Connor murmured, before clearing his throat. "A large non-fat latte, extra hot. No foam, please."

Sally, as her nametag dubbed her, nodded, her blonde ponytail bobbing as she wrote down the order in loopy writing.

"Your total is nine dollars and thirty-one cents," Sally said, extending her hand. Connor handed her his debit card, watching it slide across the pad before he retrieved his card, and tucked it back away in his wallet. He trudged away from the counter as soon as the receipt landed in his hand, leaning against the window as he waited for Jacey.

Jacey was staring at the mirror, but not directly at herself. She never really recognized the girl staring back at her. Her hair was dyed red, and was more of an auburn than a red. However, it didn't necessarily look unnatural. The makeup that was layered over her eyes was black and grey, and made her eyes look, well, sexier. It wasn't that she tried to be one of those girls. However, her reputation at Southwood High School wasn't altogether too positive. She brought her fingers to the dark red lipstick that was coated over her lips, staining the tips of her fingers with the crimson color.

She tore herself away from whoever the girl staring back at her in the mirror was, and clicked out of the restroom.

"Over here, Jay!" Connor called from the corner, where he now sat in the booth. He sent her a smile, extending his hand with the latte in it. Jacey sent him a smile, eyes dulled slightly as she slid into the booth, curling her hands around the coffee. She crossed her right leg over her left, back hunched slightly.

"Tomorrow is another one of those days, right?" he asked, voice soft as he tilted his head out of curiosity.

Jacey nodded, eyes flicking down to her wrist. Her eyes traced the scar on her right wrist. "Yeah, it is."

"Why?"

It was a simple question, but it echoed in her mind. She didn't know exactly why. But she knew that it was something she had to do.

"It's part of my life. The part that makes me more American than I am regarding blood. I have to, Connor," Jacey murmured, and frowned at him.

"It's just about patriotism?"

Her frown deepened. "I guess not. It's just...I can't abandon family..."

Connor ran a hand through his hair, moving to touch her hand. Jacey curled her hands around the coffee cup, preventing him from initiating that contact.

"I'm going to come, then," he said after a moment. "Later in the day."

Jacey nodded, tucking a strand of hair behind her ear.

"I'm there for you, Jay. I always am. And you know that."

"I know."

"And I understand how hard it is."

"I know."

"And I'm never going to leave."

There was a slight pause. "I know."

Connor sighed in frustration. Their friendship had been filled with tension recently, and he wasn't sure if the reason he was thinking of was the same reason she was thinking of.

"I'm here, too, you know," Jacey murmured.

"I know."

"You can tell me anything."

There was a pause identical to the one she had made earlier. "I know."

Jacey ran a hand through her hair, glancing at the loopy writing on the coffee cup.

"Need a ride home?"

She nodded, sighing softly.

Connor stood, his plastic cup now nearly empty. "C'mon, Jay," he murmured.

As Jacey stood, her phone buzzed. She took her coffee cup in her other hand, bringing her phone to her ear.

"What?" she asked, eyes narrowing as she gripped the phone tighter.

The caller paused. "Is there a reason I can't call my sister?"

"Sorry, Lakewood. It's been a low day."

"Are you still going tonight?"

"Unless you've changed your mind on letting you go, then no."

Jacey followed Connor to his car, which was parked near the school, not too far from the coffee shop.

Lakewood paused, and blew out a long breath of air. "I'm going to go over the rules again, then, Jacey."

"Why? I know what happened. I know what to do and what not to do."

"Do you, Jacey? Do you, really?"

Jacey slid into the passenger seat, mouthing a 'thank you' to Connor as he shut the door behind her.

"Fine. Reiterate the rules for the hundredth time."

"I will. First, there will be absolutely no consumption of alcohol."

Jacey held the phone away from her hear, making sounds of agreement after he finished each rule.

"Second, there will be absolutely no leaving that house and going somewhere else."

"Yep."

"No sex."

There was a silence, and Jacey's eyes widened.

"Really? You have to double check?"

Lakewood was silent.

Jacey sighed. "Alright, I get it, Lakewood."

"Okay." He paused again. "Love you, Jacey."

There was a click, for he knew not to expect a response from that.

"What did your brother want?" Connor asked, taking a sharp right, and wincing at the unhealthy squeal of the breaks.

Jacey chuckled weakly. "He's overprotective. What do you think?"

"Oh."

Connor ran a hand over the edge of the steering wheel as he made a smooth turn into a parking space outside the apartment complex Jacey lived in.

"Thanks, Connor."

It was silent for a moment, before she climbed out of the car.

He reached for her hand, their fingertips brushing. "Let me walk you in."

Before Jacey had a chance to refuse his offer, Connor was walking toward the door of the apartment complex.

Jacey clicked after him, sighing softly and clicking her tongue.

"Is Lakewood home?" Connor inquired, casually raising an eyebrow out of curiosity.

"Hopefully not," Jacey scowled, touching the phone in her pocket out of remembrance of the conversation that had occurred.

Her friend sighed, pressing the elevator button. "Oh," he murmured.

"What? You know we don't get along," she frowned, stepping into the elevator.

"Yeah, I know." His tone sounded wistful, almost sad.

"What?"

"Nothing. I just said I know."

"Connor, you're a really bad liar."

The elevator stopped on the seventh floor, and Jacey just stared at Connor for a moment, eyes downcast.

"Fine. Don't tell me."

Jacey swept out of the elevator, twisting the doorknob of number seven hundred and seven. She didn't even wait to hear what Connor had to say as she slammed the door behind her.

Connor slowly walked up to the door, his hands in his pockets as he stared at the golden numbers on the door. He couldn't tell that Jacey was looking through the peephole on the door, watching him stand there. Part of her wanted him to knock, and to come in. But part of her couldn't help but push him away. She didn't want to watch him walk away. However, he seemed to be pulling away, wanting to be a part of something else.

She watched him raise his hand, as if to knock, and her heart soared slightly. Her high hopes soon crashed as his hand dropped suddenly.

It was silent for a few moments, as boy stared at the door, and girl stared through the door at boy.

"Jacey, that you?" Someone called, followed by the sounds of chips crunching. Unwillingly, Jacey tore herself from looking at Connor.

"Yeah."

Lakewood came around the corner, a bag of chips in his hand as he leaned against the frame of his bedroom door.

He was wearing an old faded sweater from New York University, with old jeans that were fraying. Lakewood's glasses were askew on his face, even though he didn't need the thin rimmed-wires most of the time. Unlike Jacey, he had gotten the tanner genes, and his skin contrasted hers in a way that made it look like they weren't even related. Lakewood's hair was a light brown, like how Jacey's looked before she had dyed it. His hair was slicked on his head, which he pulled off in a manner that made him look professional.

"Where's Connor?"

Jacey bit her lip to prevent herself from looking back at the door. She didn't even know if he was still there. "I don't know. He dropped me off and left."

Lakewood tugged on the ends of his sweatshirt before nodding, eyeing her.

"Is that what you are wearing for the party?"

Jacey shook her head, glancing down at her leather jacket and dark jeans. "No."

"What are you wearing?"

"Why do you care?"

"Because there are guys out there. Ones who aren't like Connor."

"This is stereotypical, Lakewood. Just let me have fun tonight."

"And last time you just had fun, you ended up almost getting arrested."

Jacey opened her mouth to respond, but then closed it, her jaw set. Her eyes brimmed with tears.

"Why the hell does everyone keep bringing that up?" she asked, her voice dangerously soft.

Lakewood sighed, glancing down at the floor. "Because it defines your actions."

"It doesn't define who I am!"

"Doesn't it?"

It was silent for a moment, as Jacey thought about what her brother was saying.

"Jay--"

"Don't call me that!" Jacey yelled, her voice cracking as she clicked angrily over to her bedroom. Lakewood caught her arm, and Jacey stared at the ground, determined not to meet his eyes.

"Jacey, I'm just being careful. Leroy always said--"

Jacey shook her arm free, glaring past him. "You have no right to talk about him."

Lakewood dropped his arms in frustration, storming into his room to finish his essay.

The house grew silent as Jacey stood there. She paused before slowly clicking over to the door, peering through the peephole. She didn't know why, but she had expected him to still be there. Slowly, she opened the door, staring at the empty space before her.

"Jay?"

Jacey jumped slightly, the door shutting behind her with a click. As it locked, she sighed, before looking down at the boy curled up against the wall.

"You're still here?" A small smile rested on her face as she sat against the wall next to him. He leaned his head on her shoulder.

"I couldn't just leave after that."

Jacey smiled, glancing at the elevator. "I'll be ready in an hour."

"I'll be waiting," Connor vowed.

Chapter 2:

Fairytales Always End

Jacey glanced at the papers scattered on her desk. She stood up, walking over and scanning them. Some were essays from her advanced placement literature class, and others were music sheets. She picked up one with many markings on it, sliding onto the piano stand next to her desk.

The piano was white, and it wasn't the newest piano. It had been her Uncle Leroy's for almost all of his life until she had gotten it from his will. She sat on the matching bench, her fingers resting on the familiar keys. Glancing once at the music sheet, her hand began to dance amongst the black and white.

Music was the only thing that made sense anymore. Her eyes softly closed as she continued to play, the music filling her and bringing her to a place of piece. Colors danced under her eyelids as she played, and she felt this wave of emotions. The image of her Uncle Leroy flickered once, and then was gone.

The song softened as she applied pressure to the pedal on the left. Her fingers were just as fast, but more delicate as they played higher notes. Her piano teacher, Miss Ellie, was the only person who understood her. Now that Uncle Leroy was gone, she was the only person left. She came every day except Fridays to listen to Jacey and teach her what Uncle Leroy loved so much.

Jacey kept playing, losing herself in her own melodies and memories.

'Why can't I play like this?' the young three year old pouted, looking up at her uncle.

The uncle laughed. He took her hands, which were curled except for the pointer finger, and outstretched them properly on top of the piano keys. 'Because music is gentle, and your hands need to dance across the keys.'

'Music can't be gentle!' Jacey said, her eyes bright as she laughed along with him.

Leroy smiled softly, placing his hands next to hers. They slid amongst the keys gracefully.

'It's so pretty,' the girl whispered, as if afraid to break the silence created by the music.

'Close your eyes. What do you see?'

Jacey shut her eyes tightly, and the music began again. Her vision skipped with reds and purples. A vibrant emotion filled her, and a small smile played on her face.

'It's called love,' Leroy murmured to his niece. 'That's what you are feeling.'

The younger girl opened her eyes as he spoke and the music ended. 'Like what you feel for Auntie Kathy?' She remembered them always saying 'I love you' to each other. It was a nice word.

'Yeah. Just like that,' Leroy smiled at her.

Jacey thought for a moment. 'Will I ever love someone like that?' she asked, looking at him, confused.

Leroy nodded. 'See, you'll love a lot of people in your life. But when you find the one you want to *love all your life, you'll know. You'll feel like you did during that song.'*

'I'm going to find someone?' The little girl looked surprised and in complete awe.

'Of course,' Leroy smiled, retracting his hands from the piano. He looked to the side, where Kathleen sat on the couch. She smiled at her husband, and then looked at Jacey gently.

There was a loud sound as a car door slammed shut outside. 'Jacey! Time to leave!'

Jacey quickly stood, hugging her uncle and aunt. As she moved to leave, she ran over, hugging her uncle one last time. 'I love you,' she murmured.

'I love you, too, Jay. I always will,' Leroy rubbed her back before slowly releasing her, letting her run outside to her parents.

Jacey sighed, slamming the door shut behind her. She was grateful she was going, but her brother could be an ass sometimes. Jacey leaned against her door when she shut it behind her, eyes glancing at the dark sky. She had been at volleyball practice until six, and how it was about seven. People started getting their around then so the police didn't get too suspicious.

She slid off her leather pants, pulling on the ends as she hopped on one foot to get them off. After the brief war with them, she tossed them into her laundry basket. Her loose blouse slipped off with ease, and that followed the pants into the laundry basket.

"What am I going to wear?" Jacey murmured to herself. She opened a drawer and pulled out ripped fishnets. Her father didn't even know she owned them, and he would have killed her if he knew. She slid them on, and then tugged her way into a tight strapless dress. Combat boots were pulled onto her feet.

Jacey looked at herself in the mirror. She looked like nothing she had ever seen before. Her hand picked up the eyeliner, and she stroked it on in a thick line. After, her hand moved to grasp the red lipstick, smearing it onto her lips. Her reflection looked nothing like her. She reached a shaky hand up to the mirror, pressing her hand against her reflection's hand. "Who am I?" she whispered.

There was a soft buzzing, and Jacey tore herself away from the mirror to grab the phone lying on her bed.

'Auntie? Why won't he wake up?' Jacey looked at her aunt, who was sitting in the chair next to him. She was unable to comprehend a coma with her seven year old mind.

Kathy sighed, smiling sadly at Jacey. 'Uncle Leroy is lost in his own dreams. But he is still the same person he was. That's why he's still with us. He's going to get better as soon as he stops dreaming.'

'Really? How does he stay who he once was like this?' Jacey glanced at the frail man in the hospital bed.

'You know your uncle. He's the strongest man I have ever known,' Kathy glanced at him fondly.

Jacey followed her gaze. 'You really love him, don't you?' Her voice was small as she kept her eyes on her uncle.

'Of course,' Kathy whispered. 'I live to love him.' Her voice shook as she grasped her husband's hand.

Jacey held the phone to her ear loosely, avoiding looking back at the mirror. "Hello?"

"Jacey?" someone whispered.

She smiled slightly. "Get somewhere where you can talk, Callie."

"Okay. Give me a second."

It was silent for a little over a minute before Callie spoke again. "Okay. Sorry about that."

"Why weren't you at school today?" Jacey asked, cradling the phone in her hand as she sat down on her twin size bed.

Callie sighed. "I had another episode."

"Where was Trent?"

"Taking care of me so my dad didn't find out."

"I'm sorry, Callie Cat..."

Callie chuckled weakly, voice cracking. "They still can't figure out a definite diagnosis."

"Still schizophrenia?"

"Well, that's what they think it is. But I'm so young that they think it might be something different."

Jacey readjusted the phone in her hand, lying down. "This is getting ridiculous."

"I know."

"Come back. I miss you."

"I know…" Callie trailed off, and Jacey could hear soft whispers.

It was another moment before Callie spoke.

"I understand. I swear."

It sounded like she was talking to someone else.

"I swear," Callie screamed, and Jacey's face contorted with worry. She hung up the phone, clicking the second speed dial number.

"Trent? It's Callie. She's in her closet," Jacey was breathing quickly. Callie's twin didn't respond. The phone clicked, and the line went dead.

Jacey touched the piano, catching her breath.

Hopefully, this wouldn't turn out like last time.

Chapter 3:

Walls of Silence Hide the Pieces of Me

Darkness twists around the world like a silk ribbon, creating a cloud of ink that shadows a person's thoughts, and shrouds their mind with lies and deceit.

It's still light out. The dead still linger. The living still die. Being here for so long doesn't mean things have to change. After all, it's quite obvious that this side is just as barren as it was when I first saw it.

But I'm not dead. I don't know why I've been able to hold on. Out of all people here, I was the weakest. The one doomed to die.

He should have shot me properly. He hit me in the shoulder. Idiot.

She hasn't been around in a while. But it's not like spirits have a schedule.

I think she's a spirit. I'm not quite sure.

It makes no difference.

She's dead anyway.

And it's my entire fault.

I can't think straight anymore. My mind is a blur of her and apples.

I think I'm the only one that still eats.

My hands are cold, but they still hold that small and steady pulse.

Is it good that I'm still alive?

Or should I have died long ago?

To be honest, I don't remember what I even look like.

I don't know what color my eyes are.

Or what color my hair is.

Or how tall I am.

And some days I forget my own name.

I only remember it when she calls it out, aloud.

It's the only sound I ever hear anymore.

Her words are the only things that matter.

I haven't seen anyone.

I don't want to see anyone.

Sometimes, I feel like screaming just to know I'm still alive.

But I'm scared to discover the answer.

My thoughts become more jumbled as what I think is time passes.

Food is not a priority.

Not here.

I feel like I am pieces of what once was.

Surrounded by walls of silence.

I'm not like them yet.

The key word being yet.

I still am holding on.

Somehow.

I think it's because of her.

Her name is the one thing I do remember from who I used to be.

And it's the name that sparks something inside of me.

I think it's called an emotion.

I can't tell if my conversations with her are through my thoughts or if I do speak.

I don't even recognize my own voice anymore.

A while ago, I tried counting days but it's impossible to tell when the suns sets.

Especially when there is no sun.

Maybe it would be better if it was dark.

The light makes this more of a hell.

Because the frail, hunched bodies of the living are so visible.

I don't think I sleep much anymore.

And if I do, I can never tell how long.

It's not like it matters.

The nightmares are almost better than reality now.

There are so such things as peaceful dreams here.

I don't remember what I used to dream about.

Maybe I dreamed about myself.

I mean, who I used to be.

Can anyone see me?

I want to leave this side.

I want to go back to what I used to have.

She tells me that I was great.

That I was loved.

What is love?

I don't think I remember.

She says it's the color red.

What does the color red look like?

She says it's beautiful.

What's beauty when all that is here is a hellish, barren wasteland?

She says it makes even the weakest man want to live.

What person would want to live here?

She says I will feel it again.

What do her words mean when I have already gone mad?

She says she loves me.

How can she feel such an emotion?

Out here?

Where nothing lives.

I guess there's an exception to every rule.

But part of me wants to tell her that she's crazy.

Part of me wants her to leave.

But some part of all of me knows I need her to stay.

Because she might be able to teach me this idea of love.

And I might be able to live again.

I might once again see something beautiful.

Yet, even that hope is fading.

There's a sudden scream.

I guess someone new has found this side.

And they're just as scared as we were.

As I was.

I don't want to be part of them.

I'm living.

They're dead.

I see it in their eyes.

They don't see anything except blackness.

They aren't human anymore.

But maybe that's what happens to even the best of us.

She has never touched me.
I want to hold her.
I want to feel warm again.
She tries to tell me who she is.
But I don't know if I want to know.
I don't know if it will make a difference.
The world 'family' echoes through the air once she says it.
And I think I feel something.
It's a beautiful thing, she says.
She says that family is love.
Is family the answer to getting out of here?
Then she smiles sadly.
But I don't hear her next words.
For all I can focus on is her smile.
How is it so bright?
How does it live in the land where everything is doomed to die?
I tell her it's cold here.
She says that she is sorry.
She feels sympathy for me.
But who wants to feel sympathy for someone doomed to die?
I guess she has nothing left either.
We have each other.
But as I look at the black sky streaked with grey, I doubt her.
I doubt that she exists.
I doubt that family exists.
And I doubt that love exists.
Because all I have known is coldness.
All I remember is waiting to die.
And there is no good in false hope.

There is no saving those who are already doomed.

I'm in hell.

That's the only explanation.

And nothing can get me out.

Not her.

Not family.

Not love.

She tells me not to give up.

But maybe she needs to as well.

Maybe we both need to stop holding on to nothing.

Because in hell, there is no return.

There is no love.

And in that moment of realization, I feel something.

But it's not love.

It's absolute fear.

Chapter 4:

Always, Forever, and Never Again

'What about the people we don't love for all of our life?' Jacey looked at her Aunt Kathy, furrowing her brow.

Kathy smiled weakly. 'We love them until we don't love them anymore. Then they go on and find someone else.'

'But isn't that mean?'

'No,' Kathy reassured the young girl, flipping through the stack of hospital bills. 'It's how love works.'

Jacey frowned, glancing at her fourth grade math homework. It seemed much harder than love at the moment. 'Have you ever kissed another boy?'

Kathy nodded, absentmindedly smiling at Jacey.

'So we just kiss boys until we find one we love a lot?'

The aunt chuckled, dragging her nail through the opening of an envelope. 'That's one way to put it,' she murmured, frowning at the bill.

Jacey knew that she was simply trying things out. She wasn't the slut of Westbrook High School. She was simply trying to find love. And failing miserably. It's not like love had worked out for the people in her life. Her parents were divorced. They wouldn't stay together. Not even for her.

She slipped past Lakewood's room, and clicked over to where the front door was.

"Nice...dress. Is that a dress?" Lakewood bit back a chuckle. He was sitting on the counter, casually munching on sandwich.

Jacey glanced down at her strapless top/dress/thing.

"Change."

Jacey glared at him.

"Please."

It took all of her willpower not to snap back at him. She, instead, stalked back to her room.

Lakewood finished his sandwich as she walked back out, wearing a strapless top and leather pants.

"Satisfied?"

"Yes. That was quite a delicious sandwich."

Jacey rolled her eyes, picking up her phone and clutch before walking out.

"Be home by midnight!" Lakewood called as the door slammed shut.

Connor was leaning against the wall outside her door. He was still wearing his grey hoodie with dark blue jeans. His eyes were bright as he smiled at her.

"Hey, Jay..."

Jacey smiled at him, tucking her phone in her pocket. "Sorry about making you wait. I could have just met you there."

"How? You only have your permit."

She stuck her tongue out at him playfully, clicking over to the elevator. She didn't even bother to mention Lakewood as a possible option as a chaperone. Connor knew better than to suggest it, as well.

"What time did you brother call curfew at?"

Jacey coolly called over her shoulder, "Two."

Connor pulled out his phone, scrolling through texts. "I thought it was midnight."

She raised a brow at him. "Have you been *texting* my brother?"

He shrugged, avoiding her eyes as he tucked his phone away. The awkward elevator music made the ride especially more painful.

"Let's just have a good time," Jacey sighed. She ran a hand through her wavy hair, turning to look up at him.

"Of course," Connor murmured, flashing her a small smile.

Jacey lead him out of the elevator, awkwardly holding open the door for Connor.

"I forgot to tell you something," he said with a wide grin.

"What?"

"I got my acceptance letter from University of California, Davis."

Jacey spun on her heel, and couldn't help but squeal, "Oh my god!" She threw her arms around his neck, and he laughed. Connor hugged her back.

"So, I will be beginning my chemistry bachelor's program this fall."

"In California?"

Connor pulled back, nodding slowly after a moment. "Yeah. I mean, I got accepted to University of New York, but..."

Jacey bit her lip. "I know how much you've wanted to go to USD. Don't give it up."

It was silent as they walked to the car, getting in.

"But you're going to a college here."

"But it's your dream."

Connor paused, sliding into the car after a moment, and looking at her sitting in the passenger seat.

"Connor, I understand where you're coming from. But, maybe it's best."

"If you love something, set it free. If it doesn't come back, it was never yours in the first place," Leroy murmured, looking at Jacey.

"Why is that your favorite saying?" Jacey looked up from her kindergarten worksheets, eyes wide.

Leroy chuckled, sending her a warm smile. "It's true. If you love something, set it free. Because it if comes back, it was meant to be." He tapped Jacey on the nose, and she giggled.

"That rhymed!" she laughed, setting her crayon down.

"Indeed."

"But what if it doesn't come back?" Jacey asked with a small frown.

Leroy paused. "Then you have to learn to live without it."

Jacey looked out the window as they pulled up to the house. The faint bass of the music playing in the house was heard from the car.

"We can go back home," Connor suggested.

She shook her head quickly. "Let's go."

Connor got out of the car, going over to the passenger side and offering her a hand. She took his hand, and he didn't let go. Her hand remained loose, though, as he held her hand.

"Jacey!" someone called from inside. Connor ran his free hand through his hair, looking up at the throng of people inside.

"Hey, Kalani!" Jacey waved back, pulling away from Connor to give Kalani a hug.

"I'm so glad you're here!" The girl giggled, nudging Jacey. "We got some fun planned out for tonight."

Jacey raised an eyebrow with a smile, slipping inside the crowd of people. Connor followed at a safe distance, looking displeased with everyone around him.

"Come on, down to the basement!" some guy called out to the room. A few got up, and went down the steps, giggling and slurring. Jacey looked around, clicking down the steps to the basement. She arrived upon a group of people who were starting to all sit in a circle.

One of the guys smirked at her. "Truth or dare, Jacey. Wanna play?"

"Of course. You know me."

Usually, Jacey got lucky in truth or dare. No one ever dared her to do much, for she usually picked truth. It was something she was very happy for, for sometimes truth or dare got...interesting. She sat down, in between Sean and Liam.

"Rina, truth or dare?" one of the girls called out.

The young girl who had been chosen giggled, coughing slightly. She was swaying a bit, and it was obvious she had had too much to drink already. Her black hair was tied up in a messy bun.

"Truth!"

The girl who was deciding the truth to give Rina smirked. "If you had to make out with one of the guys in this circle, who would it be?"

It was a relatively easy question for this round of truth or dare. Rina looked around, making eyebrows at Dallas.

"Dallas," she said quietly, breaking out into a fit of giggles. The girls around her laughed as well, eyes wide with amusement and embarrassment.

Rina looked around the circle, eyes landing on Liam. "Truth or dare, Liam?" she called out.

Liam smirked, leaning back on his hands. "Truth." He knew better than to accept a dare quite yet."

"If you had to choose one girl to see...nude..." Rina giggled nervously, "who would you pick?"

The boy's eyes traveled along the circle, and most of the girls turned a dark red. After a moment, he shrugged.

"Jacey."

One of the guys whistled, and Jacey rolled her eyes, nudging Liam with a small laugh.

The game increased in foolishness, as well as immaturity as the members got more and more drunk.

"If you could have an affair with one of the teachers who would it be?"

"Trade shirts with the person next to you."

"Kiss her on the cheek."

"Smack her butt."

"Who do you like?"

"Who do you want to have sex with most?"

"Have you ever seen anyone nude?"

"What is your turn on?"

"Spend two minutes in the bathroom alone with him."

"Call your dad."

"Have you ever slept naked?"

"How many times have you had sex?"

"Have you ever cheated on someone?"

"Who would you spend seven minutes in heaven with?"

"Hottest girl at our school?"

"Cutest boy at our school?"

"Kiss her."

"Jacey!"

Jacey looked up at Ryan, her eyes displaying panic for a second. He was one of those kids who wasn't afraid to make anyone do anything.

"Truth or dare."

She inhaled.

"Dare."

"Spend seven minutes in the closet."

She exhaled.

"With Liam."

He smirked.

Everyone giggled and chuckled as Liam raised an eyebrow. Slowly, he stood, and Jacey had no choice but to do the same. She walked over, walking in the closet and watching Liam as he shut the door behind the two of them. Someone locked it from the outside.

"Hey," Liam laughed slightly.

Jacey rolled her eyes playfully. "Hey." She knew Liam. The two of them got a long, and were friends. This wasn't a problem. Seven minutes, and they would pretend something had happened. Even though nothing was really going to happen.

"So..." Liam laughed awkwardly.

She laughed softly, deciding to give him at least one thing. "C'mere," Jacey said, pressing her lips against his for a moment.

As she pulled away, Liam wrapped his arms around her waist, as if he had lost himself in the kiss. Jacey was careful as she stood there. He took a step forward, as if to get even closer, and her heel hit the wall, making a loud crash as something else fell.

Liam moved his lips to her neck as there was a knock on the door. It took a moment for Jacey to recognize Connor's voice coming from the other side of the door.

"Jacey, don't do it. Just stop."

His voice was a murmur, so no one could hear but her.

Jacey pulled away slightly, looking up at Liam. "What are you doing, Liam?"

"It's seven minutes in heaven. I'm making heaven."

She sighed.

"Liam, c'mon. We've known each other for two years. It's a stupid game."

"But I have heard so much..."

"I'm not a slut, Liam."

Her voice was sharp, and poisonous as she looked up at him.

"I'm not," she repeated.

"I..."

Jacey sighed. "Let's just pretend, okay?"

"Oh...okay."

It took a moment for him to unwrap himself from around her."

"Sorry," he murmured.

Jacey touched his cheek. "It's not your fault."

The door unlocked as she smiled at him, pressing her lips once more against his. The person who unlocked the door smirked. The two didn't say a word as they sauntered back to the circle, under the watchful eye of the entire circle. Like hawks, they fed off of the dying. But in this case, it was that they were feeding off those whose reputation was dying.

"What's a prostitute?" Jacey sounded out the last word, stuttering over it.

Leroy inhaled sharply. "What? Where did you hear that?"

The young first grader looked puzzled. "I hear some older girls at my school talking about it. What is it?"

"It's," Leroy started, "a person. Someone who doesn't care about their dignity, typically."

Jacey looked confused. "What's dignity?"

"It's like pride, Jay. Think of it as something that makes you proud of who you are. It is what makes you look at yourself in the mirror and like who you are on the inside."

"But can't a prostitute be proud of themselves?"

Leroy paused. "No..."

"Why?"

"Well, it's because they like to throw themselves around to random people."

Jacey ran a hand through her long hair. "But maybe that is what makes them proud."

"But, by other people's standards, that is something that shows a lack of pride, and something that means you aren't a good person."

"Why should other people's expectations even matter?"

Leroy's eyes widened. "I never thought of it that way," he admitted.

"Why not? I just think that maybe those people are proud of what they are and who they do. Maybe they," Jacey paused as she remembered the words her Uncle had used, "throw themselves to people because they want people to see how proud they are. Maybe they just don't care about what other people think."

"You know, sometimes I forget that you're only 6," Leroy laughed, his laugh echoing throughout the small bedroom.

Jacey smiled proudly. "So is being a prostitute a bad thing, after all?"

Leroy's face went a bright shade of white, realizing what he had just conceded to. "Well, really, you shouldn't think of it as a good thing for you. It isn't meant for such smart and kind girls."

"Oh..." she frowned. "Could anyone be a prostitute?"

This conversation was beginning to worry Uncle Leroy. "Well, yes. But not many are. Mom can tell you more about this when you're in high school. Trust me, you will understand it a lot more when you are a teenager."

Jacey paused thinking. "Maybe so..."

"So, how's spelling?" Leroy changed the subject with a bright smile at his niece.

"Thanks for that," Jacey murmured to Connor as they sat down on the couch.

Connor titled his head, confused. "What?"

"For telling me to stop. To be careful."

"I didn't."

Jacey shrugged, confused. She looked around at the party guests, most of whom were drunk or high on drugs. A couple grinded in the corner, while two more coupled were making out by the front door. There was a path of wrinkled clothes that had been left in a path before reaching a locked bedroom door.

"An hour left," he murmured to himself.

"Can't wait to leave?" Jacey teased weakly.

Connor nudged her with a small laugh, and her vision spun only slightly. He didn't seem to notice.

"Police!" someone screamed. The entire throng of people looked up, fear flashing like the red, white, and blue that flashed in the windows. Connor grabbed Jacey's wrist, sighing. This had to happen at every party, didn't it?

Jacey stood, tripping over her heels as she tried to follow Connor.

He turned on his heel. "Jacey, what's going on?"

She felt her head spin as she fell backward, her vision going black, and the door slammed open.

Chapter 5:

Spoiler Alert: She Breaks the World

There were voices nearby, unless she was imagining things.

Come play, one of the voices taunted. *I want to cut your pretty little face, and use your blood as syrup on my pancakes.*

"Stay away from me," she said, her voice almost a whimper.

But we love you, Callie, it coaxed. *We want to stay with you forever.*

She scoffed so she didn't seem so scared. "You don't love me."

I love you. I want to come to you. Let me back in, it pouted.

"No."

The voice snarled, unable to calm itself. *I will be let back in. I'll rip out your heart with my cold hands, and eat it whole. Even as it is still beating.*

Callie couldn't help but shiver. She touched her chest, right over her heart. The beat sounded weak, even though she felt like her heart was pounding.

See, it laughed. *I can do it, and you know it. Look in the mirror, Callie. You'll see a dead girl walking.*

"I'm not going to look in the mirror again," she murmured, looking down at the laminate flooring.

But why? You're becoming a magnificent girl, Callie, it chuckled derisively.

She touched her face, keeping her eyes open, so she could always see the light that streamed in from the windows and landed on the wooden floors.

It was silent for a moment. *You're not going to live through the year, Callie.*

"Who says that?" Callie snapped defensively.

Everyone. The doctors, me, and...your parents, it said, as if rolling his eyes.

She paused. "My parents don't say that." Her voice rose at the end, as if questioning that very fact.

Even you question that, it said, and it was almost as if it was smirking.

"Shut up," Callie's voice was small as she shut her eyes tightly. "Shut up. Shut upshutupshutupshutupshutupshutup—"

Someone's arms looped around Callie as she screamed those two words, and she desperately tried to fight her way out of them. It was as if someone was saying something to her, for she could hear muted voices. But the voice sounded like it was coming from past a wall.

"Let go of me!" Callie shrieked, and whoever or whatever was holding her stroked her hair, shaking her. Slowly, the voice became more audible.

"Callie," it whispered. But it wasn't a creepy lull. The voice was sympathetic, and kind. She felt like the voice was familiar.

"Callie Cat, relax. It's me," the person, or thing, said. At the sound of her nickname, she turned in their arms, and saw the face that made her collapse with relief.

She buried her head in her twin's shoulder. "Trent, I—"

Trent stroked her hair, hushing her softly. "It's okay, Callie Cat. It's okay."

"I almost looked in the mirror—" she sobbed. He didn't respond; all he could do was sit on the bed with her, holding her tightly. After a few moments, she began to collect herself, sitting on the bed next to Trent.

"It's all okay, now," he promised, looking at his twin.

Callie gave him a weak smile. "Yeah. Thanks." She tucked a strand of dirty blonde hair behind her ear, looking down at her fingernails. They were the longest they had ever been, which wasn't saying much. Usually, her mother would cut them down so that Callie couldn't scratch herself. This time, her mother had been out of the house more often, so Callie was alone more often than not. And this was not always a good sign for someone who imagines voices.

Trent glanced down at her nails, biting his lip. "I should cut your nails soon," he commented. He reached out a hand, taking her right arm and pulling up the jacket sleeve so her could see the bare skin. Small little marks littered the pale skin, and it made Trent shiver softly. He tugged the sleeve down, looking at Callie.

She sighed. "I don't mean to do it." Her voice was merely a whisper.

"I know, Callie Cat. I know."

It was silent as he stood, running a hand through his hair. It's almost noon. Can you change into your robe so we can weigh you?"

Callie nodded, and Trent went out of the room, standing outside the door to give her privacy. She only let Trent weigh her, mostly because her mother would have a panic attack, and her dad would yell. It was one of those things that she had to keep secret. Just between her and Trent.

She shed her clothes, and slipped on the robe. The quarters that rimmed the inside pockets weighed the robe down, and she sighed in satisfaction.

"I'm ready, Trent," she called out softly.

He slowly walked in, his eyes looking her up and down. He walked up to her, and bit his lip, reaching into her pockets.

Callie gave him a deadpan look as he removed the quarters that were always there. Then, he walked over to the small weighing station. She followed him, stepping on it.

"You're five feet, three inches still," Trent reminded himself. The scale printed out the number and Trent sighed.

"What?"

Trent scribbled in the book. "101.2. That's two pounds down from yesterday."

"It's a 17.9 BMI, though," Callie protested, as she looked at the BMI window on the scale. "That's not bad."

"It's not bad," Trent paused before agreeing. He put the book away. "Why don't we go out today?"

Callie's eyes lit up. "Will Mom let me?"

"I'll find a way to convince her," he promised. "You get dressed. My treat."

He flashed Callie a smile before walking down the steps.

Kamille was in the kitchen, putting away the dishes. She rubbed a plate with a black towel, whistling softly.

"Mom, can I take Callie out?" Trent asked, sitting on a stool across the counter from her.

She looked up, frowning. "Why?"

"To eat," he said.

"What's her weight right now?"

There was a pause. "101.2"

The plate she had been drying fell to the floor, and shattered instantaneously upon impact with the cold wood that was on the floor.

"It's not that bad," Trent murmured.

"She was 110 last week!" Kamille said, running a hand through her hair. Trent got up, slowly kneeling by his mother to pick up the shards of the plate.

He picked up a sharp triangular piece. "Coming home from rehab certainly did change a lot."

"Maybe she should go back," she murmured, wiping her eyes.

"Why? It'll happen when she gets back."

"She might never get better. So maybe she should just stay there."

The pieces of plate that Trent had been holding fell to the ground, breaking into smaller pieces. "How can you say that?" His eyes flared with anger and protectiveness.

"Because I can't live like this!" Kamille shouted, her eyes brimming with tears.

"I can't live without her!"

She ran a hand through her hair. "It's not like she is sane."

"She's your goddamn daughter!"

Kamille didn't know what to say. So, instead, she snapped, "Don't curse in front of me."

"Don't try and hospitalize Callie!"

"Why not? Maybe it's the best for her. It's the best for all of us."

Trent bit his lip. "It's not the best for me. And I don't think she would like to be neglected by her own parents."

"We're not neglecting her! Don't you dare talk like that to me. I care about her, and that is exactly why she would be safer in a hospital."

"That's batshit!"

Kamille set her jaw. "I don't want it to be this way either," she murmured. Both seemed to have forgotten about the shards of glass.

"Then why are you trying to convince yourself otherwise?"

She shuffled past the shards of the glass plate, sitting down on the ground, leaning against the cabinet. "Because I signed the papers this morning."

Trent felt his chest deflate as he stumbled backwards.

"She leaves tomorrow."

Each word was like a stab in the heart. He breathed heavily, "Don't do this. Cancel it. Please."

"I can't discharge her until the sixth month time period has passed. It's the rule for this place."

"What place?"

"North Albany Asylum."

"She's not crazy! A mental illness does not define someone as crazy!"

Kamille bit her lip. "Think about it, Trent. It's something that made her a danger to herself and the ones around her."

"I have symptoms like her! Lock me up, too, then!" His mind was reeling, and his vision was tinted with red.

"But you don't act crazy! The medicine works for you more than it does for her..."

Trent pressed his back against the counter. "I can't believe you did this. What did dad say?"

"He signed the papers, too. He agrees," Kamille ran a hand through her hair. "I'm sorry you're upset..."

"You just signed the papers to send my sister to a mental asylum. I would say upset is an understatement," his voice grew dangerously quiet.

She paused. "She'll be happy."

"You're a fucking liar."

Before Kamille could protest that fact, or scold her eldest son for cursing, he stormed out of the kitchen.

Callie was in her room, oblivious to the hell that had just been reiterated to Trent. She was putting on eye shadow, humming softly. The brush swept over her eyelid. She was quite good at this, especially considering she never used a mirror.

Trent was outside, calming himself down. If he was panicked, Callie would know, and she would have a panic attack. Her undiagnosed condition made it hard to know exactly what was okay and what a red line action was.

He wasn't calm, but he could feign it as he slipped into their room. "Ready, Callie?"

"Mom said yes?"

Trent thought about that for a moment. After all, she hadn't said no. "Yep. C'mon. A whole day; it will be just the two of us."

Callie smiled brightly, standing up. Her strapless bright blue dress matched the color of her eyes. As she stood there, it was impossible to tell that the beautiful, mature seventeen year old in front of him was supposedly mentally ill. Her butterfly wedges made her a bit taller than she was. Yes, she was a bit skinnier than the average teenager, but still. Her face was pale, and Trent knew that no matter how else people saw her, she looked amazing to him.

"Ready?" Callie smiled and laughed, walking over to Trent. He smiled, nodding at her before walking out of the room.

"Grab your purse!" Trent called over his shoulder to remind her. After a moment, when he heard her footsteps, meaning she had come up behind him, he began to walk down the stairs.

Trent didn't look at Kamille, who was cleaning up the plate. He walked past her, eyes set straight in front of him.

After all, Kamille could clean up the shards of the plate with a broom, but she would never be able to do the same with the now shattered pieces of his heart.

Chapter 6:

If Only I Had Died

I don't really think of anything anymore.
All I ever see is her.
And I don't think that it is healthy to keep seeing her.
But who really cares if it is healthy.
She is trying to teach me to be strong.
But who cares about strength?
A thousand questions pop into my mind when I look at her.
Why is her hair such a vibrant color?
Why do her eyes look so dead?
Why do I smile when I see her?
She tells me that I need to remember.
I know what she is talking about.
But I have taken that memory and locked it behind a wall.
It's in memory prison.
Insidious.
That's what this place is.
Insidious means treacherous.
I wonder if I shouldn't be strong.
I keep seeing those damn spiders.
Fucking spiders.
It's such a cliché fear, but it is a legitimate one.
I mean, just look at the way they crawl.
Or how they stare at you and dart away.
One is crawling toward me.
It looks as big as my hand.

What the fucking hell?
I never understood these spiders.
Why are they alive?
And if they are alive, why are they here?
I hate them.
They deserve to die.
She laughs at me when I say this.
I don't know why.
Why is it funny?
Spiders are not funny.
Some people are worried a spider bite would kill them.
Maybe I should let one bite me...
Her face is outraged.
As if even suggesting me dying angers her.
It's not like I really want to live here.
Or be here.
Why am I here?
Oh.
I remember that fucking mirror.
That's all I remember.
But that doesn't make sense.
It's not like any of this hell makes sense.
She says I won't be alone.
Of course.
Because she is here.
She tells me that it's not because of her.
Great.
Maybe she is a psychic.
That's almost as creepy as a spider crawling.
She rolls her eyes at me.
I think I know what to call her.
Not her name.

For that is something sacred.
Something I am saving for when I am in the
deepest hell.
Sister.
That's the word.
I ask my sister if she is dead.
She doesn't respond.
Sister.
It's a nice word.
It rolls off my tongue.
It sounds so alive...
I wish I was alive.
Am I?
Damn.
Who knew I would end up questioning this.
Batshit mirror.
I do wish I could see my reflection.
So I could know who I was.
Or who I used to be.
I feel like I am missing something.
I'm scared to find out if I am dead or alive.
I think it would be better if I was dead.
I don't want to be alive.
I am scared to live.
Is that something strange?
She tells me it's not strange.
At least for this place.
Maybe I'm a freak in the other place she
speaks of.
She says that world has color.
Like red.
I want to see red.
I want to see color.

But I don't want to be alive.
Is that weird?
I don't think so.
Sometimes, I close my eyes, and will myself to fade away.
But she always stops me.
Goddamn sister.
She says she loves me.
And that is why she can't let me fade away.
I think she expects me to say I love you back.
But I don't know how to speak here.
Or to say such pure words.
Words that are purer than her own name.
That surprises me.
Her name is so pure.
It makes me want to fade away.
I want to fade away together.
But she is scared.
Scared of what comes after.
Comes after what?
She doesn't tell me the answer.
In fact, she doesn't say anything.
Something falls down her cheek.
It's called a tear.
That word I know.
But I don't know why.
She doesn't seem afraid of anything except fading away.
Why are you crying, I ask her.
She tells me that she cries for the same reason I cry.
I cry?
I didn't know that.

I thought maybe it was just me being dead that made me not cry.

She quickly responds by saying that I am not dead.

How does she know?

Maybe I am dead.

And she is just too scared to admit it.

She glares at me.

I wish I understood her.

I wish I understood all of this.

Sometimes, I think about my life.

But I don't know if right now qualifies as my life.

Because I really am hoping that I am dead.

I want nothing more than to be dead.

Because if I am, than I have nothing to fear.

I can fade away.

And fade happily away.

And, right now, that sounds better than anything.

Better than having a life.

Better than having a sister.

Better than having a family.

Better than having love.

Actually, I don't even know if that is true.

Could love be that sacred?

Or am I just kidding myself?

What if I'm not dead?

Maybe I can find love.

And then I can be happy.

I think happiness is worth being alive for.

I really do.

It's something I want to feel every morning and every night.
She smiles when I say this.
And I like how she smiles.
Because she looks happy.
But if I am dead...
Then there will be no happiness.
Then I just fade away.
I don't know which one to prefer.
But as I weight the two...
I can't help but hope.

Chapter 7:

Where Would You Like to Be Buried?

That damn heart monitor was going to end up driving him absolutely insane.

As Connor sat by Jacey, who was lying in the hospital bed, he flinched at every beep. One of these times, he was going to drive a screwdriver through it. But, at the same time, he reminded himself what each beep meant. It meant she was still alive. It meant that she was still breathing. The doctors had told him she would need surgery for the condition she had. And he had five minutes before her heart surgery.

She was in a hospital gown, looking extremely casual and vulnerable, especially given all the wires that surrounded her.

Connor touched her cheek, looking at Lakewood. He was standing over her, eyes red from lack of sleep. Although he would never admit it, it was pretty clear he had been crying. With her dad on a business trip in England, and her mom in Hawaii, it was quite a solemn night. The doctors had gotten the faxed note from Richard Adams, who had custody of Jacey. The note allowed for surgery, and left most decisions up to Lakewood, since this was an emergency. He would be back tomorrow, early in the morning.

The room was silent, and Connor was dreading the moment that the doctors would come in and take her away.

The heart monitor was slowly beeping, and sometimes it felt like the beeps were too slow. Connor was too tired to focus on anything other than the worry he felt and the beeps.

Beep.

He worried that the surgery would fail.

Beep.

He worried that she wouldn't recover.

Beep.

He worried that she would be different.

Beep.

He worried that there would be complications.

Beep.

He worried that this would affect her health.

Beep.

He worried that she would die.

And that last one almost killed him inside.

Three doctors and four nurses came in, ushering Connor, in his daze, off of the bed. Lakewood just watched with sad, scared eyes, as his sister was rolled off to surgery.

One of the doctors and one of the nurses stayed behind. "We already explained everything to Richard, but we wanted to let you know what was going on."

Connor nodded. He missed the beeping now.

The doctor introduced himself as Doctor Conrad, who had gotten his license from John Hopkins University. The nurse stayed silent, flipping through a clipboard with a large stack of papers.

"Miss Adams has a unique condition dubbed aortic valve stenosis. In this condition, the aortic valve is stiffened and has a narrow opening. Because of this, the valve does not open the way it should, which increases the work of the left ventricle when it pumps. Sometimes, people will this condition experience the valve not closing properly, which causes a leakage. This leakage is known as aortic regurgitation. But, in her case, she has aortic stenosis. So, rather than the leakage, she has the issue where the valve cannot open easily. It is an insidious condition, and that is why we are conducting valve replacement surgery. We will take a replacement mechanical valve, and replace the malfunctioning one. This surgery has an eighty-five percent success rate. We are fairly confident Miss Adams will be fine, and that this surgery will fix her condition."

Lakewood winced at the eight-five percent. "Why does she need this surgery? Isn't there some other method?"

"It's a minimally-invasive surgery to replace an aortic valve. We would replace it with a tissue valve, but given her age, we chose the mechanical titanium valve. The biological valves only last for ten to twelve years. However, because of this, Miss Adams will have to take blood thinners for life."

"So she'll be fine?" Connor asked, running a hand through his hair.

The nurse looked up from her paperwork, nodding. "She should be fine. We're going to keep her here overnight, of course. And she should stay here for five to seven days."

"Can you explain what happens during the surgery?" Lakewood asked, sitting down in one of the chairs of the now empty patient room.

The doctor nodded. "So, she received the general anesthesia, so she will not feel any pain. The surgeon will make a ten inch long cut along the middle of her chest. His will allow him to separate the breastbone so he can see the heart and aorta. During this whole procedure, she will be connected to a heart-lung bypass machine. Miss Adams' heart will be stopped during this procedure, and then this machine will do the work of her heart while it is stopped. Once the new valve is in and working, the surgeon will close her heart, and turn off the heart-lung machine. He will place catheters around the heart to drain the fluids that build up. Then, he will have to close the breastbone with stainless steel wires. It will take about six weeks for the bone to heal. The wires will stay in her body, and the bone itself will take about six weeks to heal."

"How come we haven't known the condition was serious until now?" her brother asked, looking confused.

"Well, her records show that she, her family, and her family doctor have known the condition existed until now. There have been recent changes in her aortic valve that caused major heart symptoms. These include angina, which is chest pain, shortness of breath, and syncope, which is a fainting spell similar to the one that occurred tonight."

"Why is this surgery so sudden? Doesn't that increase the risks?" Lakewood seemed to be voicing all the concerns that Connor had.

"Originally, she would be informed of this surgery two weeks before hand. But, because of the heart murmur that occurred when she got here, we needed to take the immediate precautions. Of course, the risks of general anesthesia exist and include infections, breathing problems, and blood clots in the legs, but those are rare. The dangers of surgery are heart attack, a stroke, heart rhythm problems, incision infection, kidney failure, memory loss, loss of mental clarity, poor healing, and pose-pericardiotomy syndrome."

Connor's eyes widened considerably. "That's a lot of risks."

"There is only a fifteen percent chance of any one of those occurring," the nurse promised.

"What happens after surgery?" Lakewood asked quietly, uncomfortable with the long list of risks.

"She will spend tonight and tomorrow in the Intensive Care Unit, and the catheters will stay in her chest during that day. Three days after surgery, we will remove these tubes. She will have a tube in her bladder to drain urine, and an intravenous line to deliver fluids. After two days of the ICU, we will move her to a regular hospital room until she is stable enough to go home. She will receive pain medicine to control pain around the surgical cut. A temporary pacemaker may be placed in heart if the heart rate is too slow after surgery. And she will need to undergo a program to make her heart stronger."

"So it should be a smooth ride after the next day or so?" Connor asked, hopefully.

The nurse nodded. "The mechanical heart valve we are surgically implementing does not fail often, and has a low risk of blood clots. She will, as he said, need to take aspirin or warfarin for the rest of her life to keep her blood thin. This surgery, aortic valvuloplasty, is something that should be successful."

Connor sighed.

"You two should get some sleep. The surgery could take anywhere from two to five hours," the doctor said, placing his pen in his white pocket.

Lakewood took his turn to sigh. "Can someone come get us when the surgery is complete or nearing completion?"

"We'll wake you when we are ready to move her to the intensive care unit," the nurse promised. "I'll send someone in."

Connor was grateful Lakewood had said 'us.' He got to stay and support Jacey.

The nurse pointed to the door. "Let me take you to the operation waiting room. You can wait there and relax until Miss Adams is out of surgery." Lakewood nodded, standing up and following the nurse as she walked out of the room.

The hospital was alive with activity, even for this late at night. Doctors rushed around, and nurses were on the phone by the waiting desk. Connor could hear a woman crying from inside one of the rooms they passed.

As they entered the operational waiting room, Lakewood found it occupied by a nurse, a man, and a janitor who was cleaning what looked like blood off the tile on the far side of the room.

"Here you go. The nurse on duty will wake you when we are about to move her to the ICU," the nurse bobbed her head before scurrying out of the room.

Lakewood sat down by the window that overlooked Long Island. It looked quite wonderful, but an air of misery clung to the clouds. He touched his hand to the window before closing his eyes.

"You should get some sleep," Connor suggested quietly, sitting next to him. Lakewood sighed, nodding. It took a mere moment before the soft snores could be heard from Jacey's older brother.

Connor glanced at the clock, eyes widening at the fact that it was three in the morning. He sighed, leaning against the window. He stole a glance at the sleeping Lakewood, and shoved his hands in his own jacket pocket. It had been too long of a night, and it was about to get longer. Hopefully he would sleep somewhat.

But he was extremely worried about Jacey. There were time when he saw her dead when he close his eyes. Often, because of these visions, he didn't want to close his eyes. He was afraid these would come true. Often, Connor discovered that these visions were something he couldn't get rid of. He just had to hope that they wouldn't come true.

Lakewood looked so peaceful, sleeping there. And he wished he could look peaceful too. He wish he could look like a calm individual. But his eyes were rimmed with red, and his entire face was pale and sunken. His worry had taken over his entire body. It was quite scary, in Connor's opinion.

Two minutes passed as Lakewood watched the nurse on as Connor watched the nurse on duty. But, He found that the nurse was someone who wanted to be there. She kept getting up to offer the man sitting a few seats down some coffee. She seemed to have a genuine care for the people there. She would glance at Connor and Lakewood every so often, and Connor would send her a weak smile in return.

The man stood up, murmuring something to the nurse on duty. She checked her watch and nodded. Something was happening soon. She clicked open her e-mail, and Connor smiled slightly at the smile that came over her face. He watched as she walked over to the man. He could hear some of what she said, and the words 'the surgery was successful' were very clear. He smiled wider than he had in a while. Hopefully, he would those words soon. Hopefully.

It was now very lonely without the man there. The worry clung to the walls of the grey room, and made Connor feel more trapped than ever. He was trapped because of the surgery, and his own emotionally messed up heart. The room's walls seemed to be crushing Connor. He shut his eyes, willing away the crazy delusions as he hoped for sleep.

"Mr. Adams?" someone was murmuring. Connor opened his eyes, wondering why the nurse was waking Lakewood now. He had been trying to get to sleep, and the nurse wasn't helping. Connor nudged Lakewood, looking past the nurse.

The clock read seven in the morning. His eyes widened. It had been four hours, the surgery might have been completed!

Lakewood's eyes shot open, as if he had been expecting the nurse to come soon. He sat up straight, rubbing his tired eyes.

"It's time to go to the ICU," the nurse murmured. "She'll be moved there shortly." Lakewood nodded, standing up. It was obvious that nothing was going to get in the way of him and seeing his sister.

Connor followed, ignoring the cries of the hospital so early in the morning. He looked at the tile floor, and at the pairs of feet just ahead of him. The intensive care unit was only a bit away, and Connor didn't know if he was nervous or excited. He supposed it was because his best friend was either going to be perfectly fine, or would be dead within the hour.

CHAPTER 8:

GIFT OF CRYING

The intensive care unit was alive. Even compared to the hospital, this place was buzzing with activity. Nurses sprinted from room to room, and Connor heard many a heart monitor. He looked up, and to the left, only to see a man sitting in bed with a blackened face. His skin was peeling off, and red flesh was visible beneath the burnt skin. His fingers ran over his face, scratching off huge chunks off black flesh.

Connor shivered, choosing to look at the back of the nurse as he walked. The nurse took a sharp right, entering one of the empty rooms. There was no bed inside the room yet, and Connor bit his lip. There was a large number of monitors inside. He remembered the beeping of the heart monitor, and willed for the beeping to come back.

"She's coming," the nurse told them, and they stood outside the room, looking through the glass. Lakewood gripped the railing on the wall tightly as a bed was rolled into the room. Only her face was visible as they stared through the glass. There was a loud beep as they began to connect wires to Jacey. Her face looked extremely pale, and it seemed to lack life. One of the nurses slid an IV into the back of her hand.

The nurses were murmuring to each other, and they pulled back the blanket on top of her.

He inhaled sharply at the layering of gauze, imagining what laid beneath it. Lakewood seemed to be breathing three times as fast as normal, and Connor realized that he was probably panicking at the amount of gauze, and the paleness in her face. She looked to vulnerable amongst the wires and machines that surrounded her. Connor kept his eyes on the heart monitor, watching its slow but steady rhythm.

Two nurses remained behind to turn on some more machines and double check her vitals. One of the last doctors to leave ushered Connor and Lakewood into the room. Lakewood went in first, walking slowly.

"Just be quiet. She'll be asleep for a while longer. We'll wake her up in a bit," one of the nurses said quietly, clicking a button on the heart monitor.

Lakewood sat on the foot of her bed, covering one of her hands with his. He used his left hand to touch her cheek, eyes brimming with what he denied to be tears.

"Jay…" Connor murmured suddenly, looking at Jacey.

Her brother bit his lip, running his thumb over her cheek. "I'm sorry for everything," he whispered. "But you have to make it through this."

Connor looked up at the heart monitor, and quickly noticed that her heart beat was much slower than it had been before the surgery. He bit back that thought, sitting on the opposite side of the bed as Lakewood.

"She's doing relatively well for after surgery," the nurse told Lakewood, as if trying to cheer him up. "Her heartbeat is slower than we would like, but it's stable."

Connor nodded, looking at Lakewood.

The nurse nodded back slowly. "I'm Julia, her nurse practitioner. I will be running most of the tests and will be in contact with her surgeon."

"Can you thank the surgeon for me?" Lakewood asked suddenly, looking up at Julia.

Julia paused, as if she wasn't used to hearing that from people. "Of course. I'm sure he will appreciate that very much."

Lakewood sent her a weak smile before looking back down at Jacey. "I'm going to call dad," he murmured, squeezing Jacey's hand gently before slipping out of the room with much reluctance.

He held the phone to his ear as he looked at Jacey through the glass. The phone was picked up almost instantaneously.

"Lakewood? What's going on?" Richard's voice was clouded with worry.

"She just got out of surgery. They say she's fine so far, but her heartbeat is a bit slower than they would like."

His father sighed in frustration. "Damn business trip. I'll be there in a few minutes. I took a taxi from the airport. Who else is there?"

"Mom isn't here," Lakewood answered, knowing that was why he was asking.

"Okay. Good. She probably doesn't even give a damn about—"

"I know."

Richard paused. "What room is she in?"

"Room twenty-two of the intensive care unit."

The phone clicked as Richard hung up.

He worked for the government, which meant he usually was out and about. Lakewood didn't know much about his job, mostly because of the confidentiality agreement that his work had. He was employed by the Central Intelligence Agency, and that just sounded like a job that was mean to be shrouded in secrets.

Connor waited for Lakewood inside the room, watching Julia's every move.

"I take it you and Miss Adams are very close," she said, trying to lighten the damp mood.

"Yeah. Known her for over six years," he replied, looking down at Jacey.

Julia clicked another button. "She's going to be okay. I'll do what I can to make sure she is okay."

"Okay."

She sent him a friendly smile before scribbling on her clipboard.

Connor looked at the breathing tube that was helping her breath as she lay there.

"We're going to wake her up," she murmured. "Can you move back?"

Lakewood heard those words, and slipped inside. "You're waking her?"

Julia nodded, motioning for one of the doctors to come inside. Slowly, they began to mess with the machines and tubes; especially regarding the IV she had in.

To Connor, it felt like forever. He closed his eyes, listening to the beeping once more.

Beep.

He hoped she would wake up.

Beep.

He hoped she would be okay.

Beep.

He hoped she would have a stable heartbeat.

Beep.

He hoped she had a working aortic valve.

Beep.

He hoped she would have none of the side effects of the surgery.

Julia leaned over Jacey, opening each of her eyes in turn with a gloved hand, and shined a light in each eye.

Jacey slowly was coming to, and her hands slowly reached up. Her heartbeat began to race as she clawed at her throat, trying to breathe.

"Jacey, it's okay. Don't panic, we're here to help you." The doctors brought her hands down from her face as she struggled.

It nearly killed Lakewood to watch the doctors stand over his sister, who was panicking.

She kept struggling, making a low guttural noise.

"Jacey, I need you to listen to us. We're here to help. We can only take the tube out if you calm down. I need you to calm down. It's helping you breathe." Julia nodded, looking at Jacey carefully.

It took a moment before Jacey put her hands down, even though her heart was still racing.

"Can I explain what's going on? There's no need to panic, okay?" Julia asked, and smiled slightly as Jacey nodded. "You're in the intensive care unit. You had open-heart surgery because your condition, aortic stenosis, caused you to have a fainting spell, and was going to end up causing heart failure. We replaced your aortic valve with a titanium one, and so you should be perfectly fine after this is all over."

Jacey brought her hand, and the doctors all tensed, until she touched her chest, looking at Julia quizzically.

"The surgeon cut open your breastbone. We used wires to put it back together, and those wires will stay with you. It should heal up nicely. You also have tubes around your heart to drain excess fluids, a tube in your bladder for urine, and an IV for fluids, okay?"

After a moment, Jacey understood. She nodded, and then pointed to her breathing tube, looking at Julia again.

"That's to help you breathe. We can take that out in a couple minutes or hours, depending on how long it takes for your lungs to begin functioning normally. You're going to have to tell us when it feels like you can't get any air, okay?"

Jacey nodded again, looking around. She saw Connor out of the corner of her eye, and her eyes lit up. Then, she caught sight of Lakewood, and, as much as she despised her brother sometimes, she felt happy he was here.

"I'm going to stay in here, but I'm going to let your visitors talk to you," Julia said, watching the doctors as they filed out of the room, murmuring to each other.

Connor approached her, sitting on her bed. "Jay..." his voice cracked as he smiled at her. She brought her hand to his face, cupping his cheek. He smiled.

After a moment, Lakewood couldn't bear to be away any longer. He came up behind Connor, and Connor quickly moved away. Despite the small twinge of disappointment in her eyes at Connor moving away, Lakewood sat down, taking her hand and running his thumb over it.

"I'm so sorry, Jacey..." Lakewood murmured, eyes brimmed with tears again.

She frowned, sitting up slightly and wincing. After thinking for a moment, Jacey motioned as if she was writing. Connor's eyes widened and he fished in the purse he had been carrying for her, handing her a notepad and a pen.

What are you sorry for? She wrote.

"For being a jerk."

Don't be. You're here now.

Lakewood smiled sadly, eyes bright. "Really?"

You're my brother, you idiot. Of course.

He chuckled softly, and Jacey brought her hand to his eyes, wiping away a lone tear.

Where's Dad?

"He'll be here really soon. He flew back home."

Jacey smiled, and then wrote, *where's mom?*

"She said she would try and come."

Her smile faltered slightly as she nodded.

"I'm sorry, Jacey," Lakewood murmured.

S'okay.

"Jacey?"

She looked up, eyes growing wider than ever as she saw Richard Adams enter the doorway. More than anything, she wanted to scream 'Daddy!' and run into his arms, and be held tightly. But all she could do was lie there and smile like an idiot.

Her dad came up quickly by her side, looking at her. "I'm so sorry I wasn't there for you, Jacey. I came as soon as I could and I tried—"

Jacey touched her dad's hand. She didn't have to write anything.

"I'm going to go talk to the surgeon and the doctor, okay? I'll be right back, I swear." Jacey nodded as her dad left.

Her dad didn't have the best record when it came to showing up. He flaked sometimes, or made an excuse that he was working. But he was there for her when she most needed him. After all, since Leilani, her mom, was never there, she needed to rely on someone. And this was one of the only times that Jacey actually seemed to be having a good spot in the relationship with her brother.

Her chest constricted slightly, and she felt her chest heave, as it tried to breathe. She made a low guttural sound, and Julia turned on her heel. Her face didn't flash with any emotion as she hit the button on the side of Jacey's bed, and two doctors came in.

Lakewood jumped back, wondering what the hell was going on. He couldn't see anything because of the doctors.

"They're taking out her breathing tube," Connor said, smiling slightly. "She's going to be fine."

He smiled slightly, trying to watch what was going on. After what could have been several seconds, or several minutes, the doctors cleared away, carrying tube parts and bloody scissors. Julia wiped Jacey clean, sitting on a stool by her bed.

"Try to make a sound using your vocal chords. Not talk, just say a sound."

Jacey made a small 'eh' sound, wincing slightly. Julia took out her stethoscope, placing it on Jacey's back.

"Breathe in."

She did so.

"Breathe out."

Julia nodded. "You're breathing is stable, and your lungs don't seem to have any fluid in them. I would say you will be able to mostly talk within the next twenty-four hours."

"You're a tough cookie, Jay," Connor joked, flashing her a smile.

Jacey chuckled silently, rolling her eyes.

Lakewood smiled. "I'll be right back, okay?" He had noticed Richard walking down the hall, and smiled. "Connor, come with me."

Connor looked up at Lakewood, somewhat confused before he saw Jacey's dad. "Oh. Okay."

The two left the room, smiling slightly at Richard as he walked inside, looking at Jacey.

"They tell me you're a tough cookie," Richard said, and Jacey smiled, remembering what Connor had said.

I guess so, she wrote.

Richard sat on a chair by her bed, placing one rough hand over hers. "You're going to be okay," he said. She wasn't sure if he was trying to convince himself or convince her.

I guess, she wrote again.

"It will take a good five months for you to heal," he said. "At least, that is according to your surgeon. He seems like a pretty nice guy."

Yeah, he is. I remember talking to him right before they put me under.

"Do you remember any of what happened before hand?"

I remember passing out. I woke up, and he was leaning over me. He told me I was going into surgery, and they had to put me out immediately.

Richard nodded. "Do you know why you passed out, maybe?"

No, I just remember feeling dizzy, and I my chest felt really tight.

"Were you home or where were you?"

Jacey didn't write anything for a moment, looking up at her dad. *I was with Connor.*

"With Connor where?" Richard asked, raising an eyebrow out of suspicion.

A party.

"Again, Jacey?" He sighed, biting his lip.

I didn't get drunk. I didn't do anything bad. I swear.

Jacey was looking up at him with scared eyes, chest tight, but not from the surgery side effects.

Richard paused. "Okay. Well, there is no need to discuss that more. Let's just...not take about it."

Jacey nodded. *How was your business trip?*

"It was going pretty well. But I'd much rather be here," he admitted, buttoning the top button of his suit.

I missed you, Dad.

Richard felt his heart skip a beat. "I missed you, too."

You're not going to leave again, are you?

"I don't plan on it."

She looked a bit disappointed as she tapped her pen against the notepad.

"I really meant it, Jacey. I don't like leaving you either."

I know. You say that a lot.

She started to cross that out, but Richard stopped her.

"It's true. There's no need to hide that from me."

"Really?" she whispered.

His eyes widened, and Jacey looked at him, confused for a moment.

"You said something, Jacey! I knew you were healing. I just knew you would be okay."

Jacey smiled, looking at Julia. Julia was watching as she fidgeted with the monitors. For a nurse practitioner, she was extremely friendly, and was very kind. Rather than have an emotionless expression, she was full of life. It was a nice change.

The cold ICU room usually was covered by an air of depression, sickness, and death. Jacey was grateful she got to move out of there in one or three days. It made her stay a lot less depressing.

"I wonder where you're brother got to," Richard mused, shrugging. "So, how's Connor?"

Dad, I know what you're doing.

He feigned innocence. "I was merely asking!"

Don't do it. Don't say it.

"He's a good guy."

Yep.

"And he is super nice."

Jacey rolled her eyes, not even bothering to reply to that one.

"I just think that you're seventeen. You need to stop having these flings, and start actually trying to get involved in a deep relationship."

Why?

"Don't you want to get married? Don't you want me to walk you down the aisle to your true love so that you can have a happily ever after?"

There is no such thing as a happily ever after.

Richard paused. "Then make it exist. I know you, Jacey. You can do anything you set your mind to. I believe in you."

No one has loved me.

"Why are you so against love?"

Because love is scary! It makes you vulnerable.

"That's why you have to trust the person who you're with. It is trust that will protect you and make love a good thing. Jacey, don't throw the idea of love away just because your mom and I split. We weren't right for each other," Richard sighed.

I know. You always say that.

He frowned. "I mean it. You and Uncle Leroy always used to talk about who you were going to grow up and get married and have a happily ever after."

But that was when I was a child. And now I'm older.

So"? Richard asked,. "Just because you are no longer a child does not mean that you cannot still live out that dream. What makes you stop trying to live out that dream?"

The fact that people leave people.

"Well, just because you have insecurity doesn't mean you are unlovable," Richard pointed out.

But no one would want to put up with me. I'm a burden.

Richard shook his head. "Don't say that. You are a gift, a joy, and a delight. One day you're going to find someone who will stay by you. You will be able to tell them all of this and they will agree and they will smile and they will love you."

How do you know that?

"Because you are a wonderful girl. I know that there is someone out there who will understand what it is like to be insecure. And they will want to accept you," he promised.

But what if I never find them,? What do I do then?

"You will. Jacey, don't worry about love. Leroy always told you about love. He told you how amazing you are and how wonderful you would grow up to be. I know how proud he would be if he could see you now."

You really think that?

"Of course. Why wouldn't I? Jacey, don't discount yourself. Teenagers have a rough life, and they have trouble. But you will overcome that and you will succeed. I just know you will. Please believe me. I know I've broken promises or made excuses about a lot of things. But this is a promise I will always keep."

Jacey smiled at her dad.

"Hey, Jacey!" Lakewood was grinning like an idiot as he walked in. Connor and him were carrying an extremely large bear.

"Get well soon!" Connor said, winking at her as they at the bear down on the foot of her bed.

Jacey laughed, and they were able to hear some of her laugh as she hugged it.

Thanks, guys. You both are awesome.

Richard sent Lakewood a thumbs-up, and smiled widely at Connor.

"We figured you could use a pal," Lakewood smiled crookedly.

Julia was watching carefully, making sure the bear didn't cause any problems. She was smiling, though, laughing a little bit. It was one of the best things she had seen in the intensive care unit.

I'm hungry.

Julia saw the note, and sighed. "I can give you ice chips, but nothing solid yet." Jacey sighed.

"It's okay. I promise unlimited hamburgers when you get home," Lakewood laughed.

Everyone seemed to be in such an amazing mood. Lakewood was laughing, Connor was smiling, and even Richard looked extremely happy. Julia noticed this happiness, and wasn't sure whether it was a good thing or a bad thing. After all, there was no guarantee that she would be okay yet. It was only hour one. There were no definite answers yet.

Richard glanced at his phone, eyes widening. "I have to take this. I'll be right back, Jacey." He squeezed his daughter's hand before exiting the room, clicking the button on his blue tooth.

"Why are you calling?" Richard snapped, angry at the caller ID.

Leilani sighed. "You don't have to be so snappy. I want to know what's going on with my daughter, Richard."

"Well, if you cared, you would be here for your daughter."

"You know I can't come," she said, sounding tired.

Richard laughed derisively. "That's a fucking lie. I can't believe you. She just had emergency open-heart surgery, and you aren't even bothering to show up."

"Don't be so angry with me. It's not my fault I'm in Hawaii."

"I was out of the country. But I came back home immediately because I care."

Leilani sighed once again. "How is she?"

"So far, fine."

"See? That's exactly why I didn't feel the need to come. She is fine. Therefore, there is no need for me to be there."

Richard bit his lip to prevent himself from cursing again. "She had heart surgery, Leilani. A mother would be there for their child."

"It's not like you're always there for her."

"It's not like you're ever there for her!"

"At least she knows that she can count on me! At least she knows she can call me!"

"And when's the last time she bothered to call you?"

Leilani paused. "A few months ago."

"You don't even know one damn thing that is going on in your own daughter's life. I can't believe you. At least I try."

"I have a life, too! A life I have to live, and worry about!"

"She is part of your life, Leilani. You are her mother. Don't even try and get out of that one with excuses," Richard said, narrowing his eyes.

Leilani paused. "I'm not that one that screws with her mind using excuses, Richard."

"Shut the hell up. At least I'm here."

"You know what, screw you. I can't believe I used to fucking love you. You're such an ignorant asshole."

The line clicked dead as both Richard and Leilani hung up on each other. Of all the rare conversations they would have over the years, that had been one of the worse ones.

Jacey had been watching her father through the window. Her mother made her disappointed sometimes. As Richard came back in, Jacey interrupted Connor and Lakewood's laughter to write, *Why isn't Mom here?*

"The airport in Hawaii shut down temporarily. There are no planes to Long Island," Richard said. He was practically lying through his teeth. Sadly, he was all too used to lying to his only daughter. But what was he supposed to say?

Lakewood knew exactly what Richard was doing. But he didn't have the heart to tell Jacey he was lying.

What happens now?

They all looked at the note, and then at one another. For a moment, all was silent.

Julia saw the note, and sighed, knowing the answer she was about to give was incredibly vague, but also incredibly truthful.

"We wait."

February
2016

Chapter 9:

101 Uses for Bent Spoons

Callie sighed, twirling the plastic spoon around her hand. "When I was twelve, I broke a mirror. Now, five years later, I have come to understand the meaning of the saying, 'Breaking a mirror is seven years of bad luck.'"

Justin adjusted his baseball cap, tilting his head at her. "I break mirrors all the time." He laughed softly, "I can burn them, too."

She laughed with him at this statement, finding it incredibly truthful. "What does a burning mirror look like?"

He saw silent for a moment as he thought, racking his brain for the mental image. "If I remember correctly, it's like dripping silver."

"I want to see that," Callie murmured, propping her arm up beneath her chin. From her seat on the bench, she could see a few scattered patients.

Justin glanced at his hot chocolate. "You want it? They always give me this damn dark chocolate crap."

"Sure," Callie said, dipping her spoon inside the cup and twirling it around.

"When are you going to get of this hellhole?"

She paused. "I don't know if I am ever getting out, Justin."

His jaw dropped. "But you're not even a danger to society!"

"I'm a burden. And my parents classify me as a danger to myself."

Justin slid onto the bench next to her. He thought he understood, but wanted to make sure he had the right idea. "May I?" he asked, trying to gently grasp her arm. Callie watched as he took her arm, tugging her sleeves up like Trent had done three months ago.

His eyes didn't reflect any emotion as she tugged her sleeve down to cover the littered scars and marks.

"Told you..." Callie murmured.

He frowned. "I don't think you're a burden, though." He tapped her on the nose before moving to sit across from her again. The two nurses were strolling around, watching everyone. One nurse kept their eyes on the two of them, wary because of the fact Justin had gotten awful close to her for their standards.

"It's almost time," Callie said, changing the subject. The digital clock behind the plexi-glass wall informed them that it was nearly noon.

In fact, just as she said that, the bell rung, signaling that it was time.

The nurse with the clipboard clicked to the plexi-glass wall, leaning against the counter. Everyone knew the drill. Once your name was called, you would go up, take your medicine, and sit down. Simple as that.

"Caroline Winson," the nurse said, looking at the girl whose hair covered her eyes.

Callie glanced down, tuning the nurse out. She pulled her spoon out of the extremely hot chocolate, eyes widening. The spoon had actually curled and bent in the scalding liquid. Smiling slightly, she tucked it in her pocket, on the tear inside the white tank top beneath her coat.

"Callie Wells," the nurse repeated, sounding slightly irritated. Callie's eyes widened as she walked over, holding out her hand for the three blue pills.

She curled her hand around them, and started to walk away.

"Callie, wait. Take your pills now."

She paused. This was new. This was strange. Why did she have to prove she took her pills?

The nurse handed her a cup of water, and Callie swallowed the first one, hiding the other two on the sides of her jaw. Slowly, the nurse raised her hand, bringing her hand to Callie's face and pressing her jaw. The pills slipped up from their hiding places, resting on her tongue.

"Swallow," the nurse said, sighing softly. Callie had no choice but to do just that. That moment of silence led her to walk in shame to where Justin sat.

"What the hell was that about?" Justin whispered to her as Andre Corren was called up to take his pills for dissociative identity disorder.

Callie shrugged as "Justin Thompson" was called up.

The pink pill was inserted in his hand, and he swallowed it without the water, stalking back to the seat.

"Annabelle Jordan" was called up for narcissistic personality disorder.

"I don't understand why I even have to take medicine," Justin scowled.

Callie glanced up absentmindedly. "Huh?"

"I mean, medicine doesn't stop me from loving what I love," he continued.

She nodded, realizing where he was coming from. "They try everything here."

"Well, why did they make you take your pill in front of them?"

"They must have found out," she murmured.

He paused. "Have you been stashing them?"

Callie looked down guiltily.

He held out his hand. "High-five, girl. That's pretty ballsy of you."

She paused before laughing, slapping her hand against his. The nurse's head turned suddenly before she relaxed, calling up the last boy in their section, "Cody Barrenstead", for sadomasochism.

"I want to get out of here," Callie murmured to no one in particular.

Justin paused, tilting his head as he looked at her. "We will. I promise."

"How can you promise that?"

"Because I want to burn this place down just as much as you want to get out."

Callie tilted her head. "We're in this together."

He nodded, sending her a smile, his eyes flickering like a flame. "Most definitely, Miss Wells."

She smiled. "You know, I found a use for a bent spoon."

"What?" He chuckled, confused.

She pulled out the bent, white spoon, which concealed two blue pills. The ones she had part way swallowed before regurgitating and hiding them.

He whistled softly as she re-hid the spoon. "You know what else you could use that for?"

"What?"

"For eating the spaghetti tonight."

"Or drinking soda."

"For brushing your hair."

"For decoration."

"For telling time, like a sundial."

"For poking people."

"For kindling."

Callie faltered at that. She smiled, though. "You know, Justin, you're pretty cool guy."

"Really?"

She nodded.

His proud smile was etched into her memory as they were dismissed for small groups.

Callie found herself mechanically walking to the circular table, sitting down. People filed in and out of the room, and she sighed.

The psychiatrist sat in the large chair opposite of Callie.

"How is everyone doing today?" she smiled sickly sweet at each of the six teenagers in turn.

Cody's eyes were half-hidden underneath his beanie as he stared dagger at Doctor Seely. Lauren was glancing down, not wanting to meet anyone's eyes. Annabelle was brushing her hair, glancing into a pocket mirror. Gregory was kneeling on his chair backwards, unable to sit still. Justin was simply sitting relaxed in his chair, as if he didn't give a damn. And Callie looked at Doctor Seely with an equally sickly smile.

"Let's get started, shall we? Let's talk about emotions first. Annabelle, why don't you start us off?"

Annabelle giggled, and Callie cringed. "Well, when I looked at myself in the mirror just now, I was overcome with pride. Because I realized I looked better than every single one of you."

Doctor Seely seemed unfazed as she nodded. "How about you, Lauren?"

There was no reply from the girl.

"Gregory, would you like to share with us how you feel?"

The undiagnosed child shook his head forcefully.

"Justin, could you share how you feel?"

Justyn straddled the seta backwards as she said that, nodding. "Yeah. Why not. Well, when I woke up I felt angry because I had been having a really nice dream and I didn't want to wake up. And later today, I realized that I have been feeling a new emotion that I have never felt before."

"And what is that?"

"Happiness."

"Why did you feel happy?"

"Because, throughout my life, people have looked at me weird, like I was a danger. It was as if they couldn't stand being near me because they were so scared. And today, I realized that I actually had a legitimate friend."

The word friend was not lightly thrown around here.

"Who?"

"Callie."

Gregory looked at Callie suddenly, eyes wide. Even Lauren glanced at her momentarily, and Annabelle looked slightly pissed off.

Doctor Seely's face curved into a soft smile. "That's wonderful, Justin."

She didn't bother to ask Callie how she was feeling.

Because she didn't want to know.

Annabelle was glaring at Callie still, and Callie caught a small glimpse of the mirror she was holding. She let out an unruly scream that made Gregory cringe and nearly fall out of his chair. Justin saw the mirror and grabbed it, getting ready to chuck it. Doctor Seely stood up, yelling that they should all be quiet. Lauren rocked back and forth, edging her chair away from Doctor Seely, who was probably losing all sanity she had had.

"It's okay, Callie," Doctor Seely tried to comfort her.

Justin chucked the mirror and it fell into pieces below where it hit the wall.

Amber smacked Justin on the shoulder. He grinned guiltily to her, and Doctor Seely looked at him with a glare of disapproval.

Doctor Seely called over one of the nurses.

"Justin, Callie, why don't you two go to the white room so you can calm down," she suggested.

The nurse grasped both of their wrists, and Callie screamed at the touch. But they were forced into the room anyway, and the door shut.

Callie screamed at the pain in her head, as if someone was compressing her brain. Justin knelt over Callie, glancing down at her with extreme worry.

"Callie, what do you need?"

She sobbed hysterically. "Get him out! Out! Outoutoutout—"

Justin realized she was talking about the voices. Slowly, he pulled her close to him, stroking her hair as she sobbed into his chest.

"I want it out," Callie hiccupped, feeling weak and vulnerable.

He held her tightly. "I got you, Callie. Don't be afraid. I'm here, okay?"

"Okay," she murmured, gripping his shirt tightly with one hand.

Justin glanced at the one-way glass, the small square that told him they were watching. Those bastards. Did they even care about her panic attack?

He reached into her jacket, pulling out the spoon and hiding it under his hand. He used it to brush her hair, laughing softly. Callie caught a glimpse of the white plastic. She smiled at him as he placed it away, glad he knew how to cheer her up.

It seemed like forever that they waited in that box of hell, waiting to be released. When the door did creak open, Callie slowly trudged out, glaring at the nurse. She trudged down the hallway, and Justin followed her.

Just as she was about to go in her room, Justin caught her hand and pressed his lips against her cheek. Callie blushed and clapped her hands over her cheek, eyes wide and bright.

And that's how it was for the next week. They stole those small moments when they thought no one was watching.

On February fourteenth, Justin was smiling widely at Callie before small groups. She had seen the two bent spoons taped into a heart by her door. But now all he could do was smile widely.

He brushed his hand against hers as they exited small groups.

He kissed her cheek before lunch.

He squeezed her hand after lunch.

He touched her cheek during snack.

He put an arm around her shoulder before outside time.

And right after dinner he walked up to her, pressing something against her palm. She looked down, seeing the chain and heart locket charm that was there. Clicking open the locket was a picture of him. How he had managed to do this was unimaginable. But she smiled widely, tucking it in the tear of her tank top.

Out of everything Callie expected to remember from her stay in this hellhole, she never dreamed that that locket would stay with her for the rest of her life.

The question remained, however: How long did she have left to live?

Chapter 9:

A Simple Remedy for Insignificance

She never expected heartbreak to be this painful.

Of course, Jacey's heart hadn't been broken emotionally.

No, her heart had literally been broken.

And now, three months later, she was healing. The scar on her chest was still there, and had not begun to fade away quite yet. Her chest didn't hurt anymore, and she no longer fainted.

Every day, she would wake up, take an anti-coagulant pill, and then go about her life. It's just that now, she wore a bit more modest clothing to hide the scar from her aortic valve replacement surgery. There was no need for people to see that.

She still bantered with her brother, and she still hung out with Connor, and her Dad still broke promises. It was like nothing had changed. The only thing that differed was the new friendship between her best friend and her only brother. They hung out when he came over, and Jacey personally found it quite odd.

It was on the day before Valentines' day that things slowly began to change. And Connor was the only one who was able to see it coming. It hit them harder than the surgery.

Connor was in the local drug store on that very day, twirling a debit card in his hand. He wasn't sure what he was doing here, to be honest.

By that, he meant that a card usually sufficed for Jacey on Valentine's Day. After all, they weren't dating. But, he found himself in the aisle nevertheless, unable to escape the rows of stuffed animals and candy hearts.

What was he doing here? Material goods were never something Jacey seemed to care about. He didn't want to do anything to disrupt their friendship. That would be stupid. But, he wanted to do something for her to encourage her through the program that was helping her strengthen her heart.

"Can I help you find anything?" the saleslady asked, and Connor turned toward the girl, eyes widening in surprise.

Her nametag read 'Sally', and she was in fact the girl from the coffee shop all those months ago. Not wanting any recognition on her part, he paused.

"Yeah. I need a gift for a friend tomorrow," he said, voice quiet.

Sally nodded. "What type of friend?"

"I've known her for six years," Connor said, shrugging. He was at a loss.

The girl bobbed her head, eyes scanning over Connor. He didn't think she would even remember him

"Should I even get her anything?" he asked Sally.

The girl paused. "I'm not just saying this to get you to buy something, but I think you should. I mean, you've known her for so long that it is really worth it. You should."

"Then what do I get for a girl with insecurity?" he asked, running a hand through his hair. "Something to show that I care."

"Well, that depends," Sally nodded her head. "Do you want to stay friends with her?"

Connor inhaled sharply, choking on his own saliva. Sally didn't say a word; she just stared at him with wide eyes. "I don't know," he faltered.

"Okay, well, I say you get her something that will allow her to always have around her."

"Like jewelry?"

Sally nodded. "But make it thoughtful."

His eyes lit up.

"I take it that you've got an idea."

He nodded. "Thanks, Sally."

She smiled. "It's nice to see you, again." Sally clicked away before Connor could even bat an eyelash.

He drove away from the drugstore, stopping at the hospital.

"Can I buy a medical bracelet?" he asked the lady at the counter of the gift shop.

Surprisingly, she actually had one. After a swipe of his card, he rushed out of the store, his mind set on what he was going to do.

Connor barely slept that night. He wasn't sure what she would think. It was one of those things that could make or break their friendship. At least, that was what he thought.

It was Lakewood that answered the Adams' door at approximately seven thirty-five in the morning.

"Hey, Connor," Lakewood yawned, punching the kid on the shoulder.

"Don't you have school?" Connor asked, slipping into the kitchen.

The older boy shrugged. "I wanted to stay home with Jacey today. Make sure she's okay. She is going to have a pretty hard program this morning, and I wanted to be there."

Connor nodded, pouring himself a large glass of orange juice. "How long until she's home from her heart strengthening?"

"An hour and a half," he remarked, running a hand through his sleepy hair. "I'm going to shower. Try not to burn the house down."

The young teen laughed. "I can't promise anything," he called back as Lakewood shuffled down the wood hallway.

Connor walked over to Jacey's room, entering it for what must have been the third time. He rarely got to see her room, or her piano. He slipped open the backpack on his back, placing a rose on the pillow. He wasn't sure if he was doing this right or if he was doing anything correctly.

That was all that he needed to do for now. He sat down on her piano bench, yawning slightly. There was a recorder by the piano, and he clicked play.

Connor's eyes widened at the melody streaming through the recorder. It was soothing, and sweet, and made him dream of happy things. He had heard her play before, but not for a few months since the surgery.

Once Connor clicked the recorder off, the room fell into this strange silence.

He stood, opening the piano bench and shuffling though the books with strange notes and symbols.

It felt cliché when he pulled out a small black book. He recognized it from when Jacey was writing in it a while ago.

Her diary.

"Of fucking course," he sighed. He had to be the one to find out where it was. Slowly, Connor opened to the most recent tabbed page.

Well, humans make mistakes. And this was definitely one Connor would remember.

The diary was written in red ink that reminded Connor an awful lot like blood. He was about to put it down until his own damn name popped up on the page.

That was when Connor realized there was no way he couldn't read it.

Dear Journal,

My heart hurts.

Not the titanium piece that now is inside.

Not because of the wires that surround it, covering my breastbone.

It's because of Connor.

I don't really understand what's going on with us. I feel like he's slowly slipping away from me. It's so confusing. Valentine's Day is in three days, and he'll get me the same little card, and I'll smile because I love it. But then I'll cry myself to sleep again. God, I'm so pathetic sometimes.

See, Uncle Leroy always told me that I could do anything and love anyone and be loved by anyone. I'm starting to think he was wrong. Mostly because if Connor, who knows almost everything about me, can't love me, who can?

I feel like how Callie feels sometimes. She was sent away because she was a danger to herself and a burden. I'm a burden, too. I am not exactly sure why I am here, or even if I should be here. My reflection doesn't even look like me. I can't recognize my reflection.

I don't know if the program is helping me. My heart literally hurts, and taking medicine every day is something that scares me. What if I forget it one day?

Well, that's it for today.

I don't really want to talk about myself anymore. It's a bit too, well, confusing.

I love you, Jay. Stay strong...

Connor's eyes were as wide as they had ever been as he glanced at the end of the entry, which had a lip stained kiss. He flipped through the rest of the entries, all marked with that same kiss.

Jacey always seemed like she knew who she was. Like she could look into the mirror and smile and smirk because of how wonderful she was. Why was this a problem for her?

Connor did love Jacey. He had known her for six years, and knew most of her secrets. He knew she was afraid of blood, and would pass out at the sight of it. He knew that her hair was a dark mix of blonde and brunette, not actually red. He knew her eyes were hazel, and that she was scared of being rejected. He knew that her mother practically left her at the age of four, and that her dad tried and failed to be there for her. He knew that her brother was someone who she rarely got along with. He knew she loved volleyball, and was disappointed with her condition. He knew how scared she was of divorce, and of love. He knew she didn't trust many people, and that she thought people always left.

But he was never going to leave. Connor had always told her that. But, for some reason, Jacey was always suspicious. As if Connor would dash out as soon as he could.

He did love her. He wished more than anything that every day he could hold her and tell her how wonderful she was. But he would never be able to.

As he glanced at the rose on her bed, and the bracelet box in his pocket, his heart started to break. She could love him for all the years to come, and he wouldn't be able to say a damn thing back.

The thing was, if he somehow managed to actually find the balls to say anything, it would be ruined. She wouldn't accept him. There was no way she would still love him.

Because he hadn't fallen just for Jacey. There was one other face that kept popping up in his mind.

Lakewood.

There was no way she could love someone who was bisexual.

Right?

CHAPTER 10:
CRAFTING CHAOS

Jacey sighed as she strolled in, sweating slightly. Her tank top was sticking to her because of the heat. She was breathing heavily, and it was expected after that rigorous heart training. It took a lot to make sure her titanium aorta worked well.

"You took your medicine, right, Jacey?" Lakewood called out. He rounded the corner, wearing a towel around his waist as his wet hair caused water droplets to drip onto the floor.

She sighed. "Thanks for reminding me." Walking over to the cabinet, she took one of the anti-coagulant pills, swallowing it whole. It got stuck in her throat for a moment, until she shoved it down with a swig of tap water.

Lakewood opened the fridge, glancing inside.

"Go put on a shirt and shorts, you weirdo," Jacey rolled her eyes, shivering slightly.

He shut the fridge. "What? You don't want to look at my muscles?"

"Wait, since when did you get muscles? I remember you being so skinny that your ribs fucking poked through." She sighed yet again.

Lakewood mock-pouted. "Awh, come on, sis."

Jacey paused at what he called her, turning to look at him as if he had just spoken in Russian.

Now, it was Lakewood's turn to sigh at his sister's hatred look, turning to go slip on a shirt and, possibly, pants.

Connor had heard Jacey come home, and finally got the guts to go to her once all ahd gone silent. He passed the half-naked Lakewood in the hall, and Lakewood waved, mouthing, 'Good luck.' His mind went blank as he concentrated, stepping out of the hallway and into the kitchen.

"Hey, Jay," Connor said, smiling slightly at her.

Jacey looked exasperated as she smiled at him. "Hey."

"I have something for you," he said, smiling a bit wider.

"What card did you get me this year?" she tried to joke, but it came across as disappointed, because she thought she knew what was going to happen next.

Connor tried to brush off her response, laughing softly. "Cards are too old-fashioned. You deserve something better."

Jacey looked at Connor, trying to shove her hopes down her throat. "You're too sweet…"

He handed her the black box, and as she opened it, her eyes started to water slightly.

It was a medical bracelet, like the one she had, but this one wasn't for emergencies in case she was in public and something happened.

'In case of tears, call Connor Tarrentine.'

That was the inscription on the inside of the bracelet. On the outside was four simple letters.

'Love.'

Jacey dropped the box, the bracelet in her hand. She didn't meet Connor's eyes. Instead, she slowly shut her eyes, sprinting away.

Connor paused; worried he had done something wrong. He slowly bent down, and picked up the box. Placing it on the counter, he sighed. For the next few moments, he trudged around the kitchen, sitting at a stool.

"Smooth," Lakewood called out.

Connor nearly fell out of his seat.

"Yeah, I kind of saw that whole thing," he admitted sheepishly. He was wearing a men's tank top and jeans, casually lounging on the couch. "Go talk to her, dude. Never let a woman cry alone."

The teen nodded, slowly walking to where Jacey's room was. His brain tried to stop him, but his right hand ended up knocking on the door. There was no reply, so his hand opened the door, and his feet dragged him inside.

She was sitting on the edge of her bed, bent over. Her red hair covered her face, and Jacey was shaking slightly. His feet drug him to the bed, sitting him down by the girl.

He batted a strand of her hair. "You look so sad," he frowned. He made an exaggerated sad face himself, looking at Jacey sadly.

"I am," she chuckled weakly, hiding her face.

"Why? Did you not like the bracelet? Was it too much?" He paused. "Should I have gotten a card?"

Jacey couldn't help but actually laugh slightly at that. "It's nothing to do with the bracelet, or the rose, or the lack of a card."

"Then what's wrong?" Connor asked. He batted a strand of her hair again. "Why won't you look at me? I want to see your face."

She sighed slightly, wiping her eyes beneath her hair before she sat up completely. Jacey rubbed her eyes a bit more, yawning.

"So, Jay, what's going on?"

There was a long pause.

"Jay, you can tell me."

"You won't care about what I am going to say."

Connor paused. "I have always cared. What makes you say I am going to stop caring now?"

"Because I know you!" Jacey looked away. "I'm being ridiculous."

He placed his hand on her shoulder for a moment before retracting it. "Jay."

"Fine. But don't blame me when you leave."

Connor bit his lip.

"I love you."

There was a silence.

"God fucking dammit."

There was another silence.

"I fucking knew this would happen."

Connor looked down.

"Go ahead. Leave. It's not like you ever tell me what is on your mind."

He sighed.

"Can't you fucking tell me what's on your mind? For once?"

"It's usually blank."

She paused, faltering. "Do you really not have anything to say or do you think you have the wrong thing to say?"

"The latter."

"I've never known the difference between former and latter. Which one?"

"The second one," he smiled weakly.

Jacey paused. "After everything I have ever said in past six years, and how you have stuck by me, you should know that you can say anything around me."

"It's complicated, Jay."

She sighed, covering her face with her hands out of frustration. "Dammit."

"Fine."

Jacey looked up.

"I'll tell you."

She looked at him.

He looked at her.

"I'm listening, Connor," she coaxed.

"I don't love you."

Those words felt like insidious radiation chunks as they tumbled out of his mouth. He felt like a wretched person. It was as if his soul had turned black with those four words, and was as if his heart and crumpled and torn itself to shreds. His eyes deflated of any happiness. The four lies that were cast out of his mouth shredded his teeth, burning his tongue as it flew to hit Jacey smack in the face. The four words then snuck their way past the titanium, crushing the heart. Deflating it.

Jacey had always thought she knew what was happening between them. She just had wanted him to admit it to her. But apparently, she was wrong. She stood, the shirt she had changed into matching the color of his heart before it was charred by the lies. She snaked the purse over her arm.

"I need to go for a walk."

She left him there, sitting on the bed. The front door slammed loudly, causing the frame to shake slightly.

Lakewood peered inside. "What the hell did you do?" His eyes were wide as he looked at Connor.

Connor paused. "Your rule was to never leave a girl crying alone. I have a new rule."

"What's that?"

"Don't ever lie about love."

Lakewood nodded, running the rule through his mind. "Why didn't you stop her?"

"Huh?"

"When she said she was going to take a walk, you should have stopped her from doing so. You should have grabbed her arm or followed her or something."

Connor sighed. "I didn't even think of it."

"Well, you should."

"Where would she be now? Or heading to?"

Lakewood turned away from the doorway. "You'd know the answer to that question best out of the two of us."

He paused, realization dawning on him.

"Told you you'd know," Lakewood called over his shoulder, smiling smugly. He knew even without seeing Connor's expression.

Connor didn't bother to look at Lakewood. He grabbed his phone, and the rose, before going out of the door, shutting it gently behind him.

In fact, this time, he didn't even take the elevator.

Connor was a blur through New York.

He rushed down the stairs, into his car, and sped off.

It felt like it only took the time it took him to blink once to arrive at the memorial.

The memorial looked more magnificent, yet dark, than it ever had been. He could see a small figure kneeling by the first tower that was hit.

Connor knew why she was here, and he knew that she would be here. After all, this was where her Uncle had worked. This was where he was before he fell into the coma.

He slowly approached Jacey, biting his lip uncomfortably. His feet shuffled along the cement.

"Uncle, I don't know what I'm doing anymore. I'm seventeen, and people think I'm such a slut. Connor doesn't love me back. I told you no one could love me. It's impossible. People leave. And now Connor's leaving. Uncle, I need you..." Jacey was murmuring, eyes shut tightly as she bowed her head.

Connor stood next to her. "Who said I was leaving?"

She didn't jump, for she had recognized those footsteps. "I'm an idiot."

"No, Jay, you're not."

"I thought someone could love me back."

His heart twisted. "Someone will. I promise."

Jacey scoffed slightly, eyes still closed. She knelt, placing one hand upon the memorial.

"Jay, you're uncle knew someone would love you. I know it, too."

She didn't respond.

"I mean it, Jacey."

"I've told you everything. You know more about me than anyone else, and you can't love me back. I put up this damn façade every day, and no one notices. People like the fake me. I hate the fake me. The fake me is stupid, slutty, and lost."

Connor paused for a long moment. "Then be the real you."

Her voice softened as she whispered, "I don't even know the real me anymore."

"I know who you are."

"And you don't love me."

It took all of his willpower to lie, "Me not loving you just shows that I'm not the right person for you."

"Then who is?"

They both looked at the memorial, listening to the water ripple. "I don't know."

"I can't do this anymore, Connor."

"Do what?"

Jacey looked up, as if there was a hundred and ten story tower standing above her. "Live. Breathe. Breathing is no longer worth the effort of expanding my lungs."

"Jay, I need you to breathe. So you can find the right person."

She stiffened. "You don't need me."

"Loving you and needing you are two different things."

"It's scary to need someone! I need you and I love you. But I zip my mouth and don't say any of it because I knew you didn't feel that way and I knew it would screw thing up. I thought we would last, at least for now. I thought I had found something special. I thought this would be better than last time."

Connor knelt by her, a few inches away. "I don't know what to tell you. You are special, and you need to understand that you are a magnificent person. You don't deserve scum like me. You deserve a Prince Charming who is going to sweep you off your feet."

"Who says you aren't that Prince Charming?"

"I say that."

Jacey sighed, squeezing the edge of the memorial's wall.

"I wouldn't say that unless I meant it, Jay."

"I know."

"Then why do you still look sad."

"Because you mean it."

Connor bit his lip. "Please don't give up, Jay..."

Jacey looked at him. "What reason do I have not to give up? I don't even know who I fucking am anymore. What use is a fake life covered by a façade?"

"Because you'll meet someone who loves you for you. They will get to know you."

"And then they'll leave me just like how you're leaving me?"

"No," Connor said instantaneously. "Who said I'm leaving?"

"It's kind of obvious."

"I'm not."

Jacey bit her lip, looking down at her other hand. "Why not?"

"I'm not leaving because I care."

She shook her head. "That's not what I meant."

"Oh."

"I meant, why don't you love me?"

It sounded so pathetic. But she looked so vulnerable there. "I don't know, Jay. I should."

She turned away, and it was silent for a moment. His phone buzzed, and he barely glanced at the caller ID, eyes widening in confusion.

"Why are you calling me?"

"It says, call in case of tears."

His heart shattered like a mirror hitting the ground. "Jay..."

"It's fine. People have left before."

He sighed. "Are you asking me to leave? Because I want to stay."

"Do you want to fucking mess with my heart again?"

"Of course not. I never meant to do that."

She scoffed, eyes brimming with tears, "Sure, Connor. Sure."

He looked at her. "I care about you. Isn't that what matters?"

"What does caring mean to you, Connor?"

He thought for a good moment about this. "Respecting someone, accepting their flaws, always standing by them, and defending them."

"Why would you care?"

"Why wouldn't I?" he challenged, before biting his tongue at his snappy voice.

Jacey ignored it as if it didn't make a difference to her. "Because just look at me. I'm a slut who got drunk at a party. I have horrible grades in most subjects, and everyone cares about how I look rather than who I am inside."

"You're not a slut. And all people make mistakes. You have five A's and one C. Don't try and fool me."

"How can you act like you know me when I don't even know me?"

Connor looked at her. "I have known you for six years. I don't care about the façade. I know you have insecurity, and I accept that. Everyone feels like they aren't perfect. I know your deepest fears and your most prideful dreams. I know your biggest accomplishments and your worst failures."

"Then why are you still here? If you know all the bad things, why haven't you walked away yet?"

He looked at her. "Because those bad things do not define who you are as a whole person. Because you are a mixture of everything, not just the bad, and not just the good."

Jacey bit her lip, moving to hug him. He wrapped his arms around her before she ended up being the one to pull back.

"I'll be back, okay?"

Connor looked at her. "Okay." He moved to kiss her, just to brush his lips against hers, but she turned, and his lips awkwardly brushed her cheek instead. There was no eye contact until she looked back before entering the restroom.

Jacey had needed to get out of there so that she would be able to think. But it was quite hard to do so. She never could tell what was going on with the world, or with Connor, or with herself.

She sat on the counter, glancing at the mirror. The girl looking back smiled sadly, and Jacey looked down. When she looked back up, she tried to fake a smile. She slowly curved the corners of her lip upward, shaking slightly at how much energy it took just to try. As she sighed, feeling as if she had failed, the girl in the mirror smirked at her.

What was supposed to be her reflection had smirked. Jacey stared at the mirror, confused as hell. The girl copied her, and she raised her hand to find that the reflection did the same. She must have been imagining things.

Slowly, Jacey raised her hand to the mirror. She pressed her hand against the cold material. The thing was, her hand didn't stop at the mirror. It kept moving through, as if the mirror was nothing but pure air. Her arm fell all the way through, until the force yanked her entire body after her hand.

She didn't manage to catch a last glimpse of her world. Jacey shut her eyes tight, and for what wasn't the first time in her life, she wished to die.

Chapter 11:

Everybody Knows This is Nowhere

I feel something.
No, not an emotion.
Not something silly like that.
I feel like I am not alone.
And I am not talking about her, the one who keeps repeating 'sister.'
Is someone else stuck in this world?
My eyes creak open, and I glance around, my vision more than fuzzy.
I can't tell the difference between the real hell and the imagined hell that exists here.
There's a spider in the distance.
Damn it.
I look away from the beast.
My eyes light up for the first time in a while.
Someone is here.
Someone new.
My heart leaps with joy.
They're heart probably will stop beating soon.
I watch her stand, ready to see her become like everyone else.
My heart deflates slightly. She'll become a reflection, and I'll have nothing left to do.
No one else to talk to.
It's so goddamn depressing.
She looks scared.
She should be.

My so-called sister watches her pain with pleasure.

It's one of the only emotions we want to feel, but it is scarce.

I almost want to cry out to her.

To stop her from becoming one of them.

But what can I do?

I'm in the grey area.

I am not dead, sadly.

But I am not alive either.

Her hair.

Wait.

I recognize that color.

It's a color.

It's red.

I feel something alive inside of me.

Slowly, the will to fade away fades away.

I can't believe it.

For one moment in my life, I don't want to die.

I don't want to fade away.

She lifts her hand.

It's about to happen.

I can't bear to watch.

She was the one who made me feel alive for a moment.

I will never forget that.

She will end up forgetting that, for she will no longer be anyone.

She'll forget her name.

She'll forget her age.

She'll forget her life.

And as the girl who is now her changes, she will change too.
Until she fades away.
Until they both die.
That's how the story goes.
That's how it always has gone.
I was lucky.
I think.
Maybe it would have been better if I hadn't crossed over.
Maybe I should have become one of them.
I almost did.
But she stopped me.
I felt alive.
I remembered my name.
I remembered my age.
I remembered my life.
When I saw her, I was alive.
I was real.
Now, even with her around, I feel so dead.
I wish I could stay like that.
This is so depressing.
I can't believe I wish to be dead.
Maybe it is because I have found no other reason to live.
Maybe that is what I need.
She won't be like me.
I hope.
Poor soul.
If she ends up like me, she will end up wanting nothing more than to fade away.
But she will never fade away.
Maybe she can teach me how to live.

I'm being ridiculous.
She's not going to live.
She's going to turn into a reflection.
I've seen it a million times.
Well, not really.
In however long I have been here, I have seen
it twice.
That's enough times.
It's horrible really.
To watch life fade away.
Unless its mine.
She keeps frowning at the live girl.
I don't know why.
She has red hair.
It's the color of love.
I wish every single moment of my life felt like
this.
Maybe it's not my life that is like this.
It's my death.
I think I am classified as a dying man.
Because there is no hope.
I don't even know where the other guy is.
Or if he is gone.
It doesn't matter.
I'm not his reflection.
That's worse than a life.
Being a reflection of life is worse than
anything.
But she is about to discover that for herself.
And I got to be her audience.
Why was it taking so damn long?
I never understood this.
She seemed to be arguing.

As I looked at her, a name popped into my
mind.

Cyril.
Sparks flashed in my eyes.
Cyril.
Cyril.
Cyril.
I couldn't believe it.
Oh my goodness.
I say the name over and over again.
And I smile slightly.
It feels good to say my name again.

Chapter 12:

A Pyromaniac's Guide to Lighting Things on Fire

It sounded like gunshots, as if someone was trying to kill her.

It also sounded like a bomb going off, as if war was about to break out.

It also sounded like a building collapsing, as if she was going to be crushed in the aftermath.

However, it was neither a gunshot, nor a bomb, nor a building collapsing. It was thunder, followed by a streak of lightning.

In Callie's opinion, it might as well have been either of the former options, for the thunder made her wince every time it sounded.

She was sitting outside, for it was that time of day, and she sat alone. The dark sky looked incredibly ominous, especially above the small psychiatric hospital. The thunderous clouds shook the entire sky, and Callie wondered if pieces of the sky would fall on her, crushing her with the weight of the Earth.

Someone came up behind her, and she flinched at the sound of footsteps, turning to look at the person. However, a smile popped up on her face at the sight of said person.

"Hey," she said with a bright smile, cringing again as the thunder echoed inside her skull.

Justin laughed softly. "Hey, Cat. What's the matter?"

"It's just the thunder," she murmured, glaring at the sky, as if that would stop the echoes.

He sat by her, crossing his legs. "Are you afraid of thunder?"

She nodded slowly.

"Hey, it's okay. I'm afraid of drowning. That's why I can't swim."

Callie paused to smile at him. "The lightning is pretty, though."

"It sure is," Justin agreed, his eyes softening as he glanced out at the horizon.

She poked his cheek. "What's the matter with you?"

He paused. "Tension always builds up inside of me. I release it through fire. And, it's been so long..."

Callie reached up, running her hand through his hair.

"Sorry. It's just...hard..."

She frowned and asked quietly, "Why are you apologizing?"

Justin smiled at this and shrugged.

"Ready for our one-on-one meetings?"

He nodded vigorously. "They might permit me to leave."

"Cool. That's good," Callie gave him a smile, her own eyes dark.

He tapped her on the nose. "I'm not leaving without you."

Callie smiled brightly at him, looking up at the sky. "You kn—"

She was cut off by thunder, and she jumped suddenly, clutching his shoulder. Justin laughed softly.

"It's okay," he coaxed. "I promise."

The nurse's heels made squishy sounds amongst the ground as she walked over to the two of them.

"Callie and Justin, you need to come inside so we can conduct the one-on-one appointments," she said, offering a hand to Callie.

Callie didn't accept her hand, standing by herself. She eyed the nurse, for it was the same one who always forced her to swallow her pills in front of her.

"I'll see you after, okay?"

Justin looked at her after he said that, eyes a bit sad. She nodded, and they squeezed hands before parting to enter opposite conference rooms.

The conference rooms had an entrance on the outside in case they needed to give the patient space. Inside the room was a table firmly nailed to the floor and pillows as a seat for the patient. They didn't trust them with a chair. The walls were a light green, which supposedly calmed people, and soothed them. It was quite plain, and it was meant to be that way. Calming the patients was of the upmost priority.

The nurse stood outside the door, letting Callie walk inside and sit on a pillow seat across the table from the conductor.

"How are you today, Miss Wells?" he asked, raising an eyebrow at her. His bushy eyebrow reminded her of a fuzzy caterpillar. She shook the mental image from her mind as she looked at him.

"I'm fine," Callie said. And it was the honest answer.

"I'm Doctor Pirrow, the psychiatrist who works here. I just want to check up with you and make sure everything is going okay."

She stared at him with a deadpan look. "Everything's going okay."

"Mind if I ask you a few questions?"

Callie didn't respond, waiting for him to ask the questions he was going to ask regardless of her answer.

"So, when was the last time you heard the voice or voices?"

"A week ago."

"When was the last time you took all three pills as requested?"

"Three days ago."

"How many pills did you take today?"

"One."

"Why?"

"Because the pills taste weird and they make my brain slower and fuzzier."

The doctor scribbled on his clipboard. She figured honesty was the best policy here, where they could discover your every lie.

"And when was the last time you had your menstrual period?"

"Eight days ago."

"Did you have any cramps?"

"Yes. Just one on the second to last day."

"How have you been feeling mentally lately?"

"A lot better."

"Have you gotten enough social stimulation?"

"Yes."

"It says here you hang around Justin a lot."

"And?"

"Why?"

"Because we're friends."

"Have you ever talked about the voice with him?"

Callie didn't falter as she chose to lie for the first time this meeting. "No."

"Does he know?"

"Not to my knowledge."

"Have you two ever discussed fire?"

She cursed herself mentally as she lied yet again. "No."

"Do you know his condition?"

"Yes. They told us what it was."

"So why do you hang around him?"

"He's a nice guy. He always tries to cheer me up."

The doctor tapped his pen on his clipboard. "Callie, do you feel romantically inclined towards Justin?"

She paused, looking at him curiously. "Why does that matter?"

"It's important to your condition and your ability to be released."

Callie hoped the right answer was not the wrong answer. "Maybe."

"I think it would be good for you to experience a relationship. It would allow us to assess your interactions with others, especially with people you care about."

"Is that all for today?"

The doctor raised an eyebrow. "Yes."

She stood up, walking out of the room as fast as she could.

The doctor looked at the nurse. "Those two are going to end up loving each other or killing each other. I can't decide which of those is going to happen yet."

She smiled and joked, "Wanna make a bet?"

He laughed softly. "Call in the next student."

Justin was sitting in a tree when Callie came outside, and she didn't spot him immediately. As she walked under the tree, something landed on her. She touched the leaf on her hair, looking up with a small laugh. Justin climbed down, smiling crookedly.

"What's got you in such a good mood?" she asked, placing the leaf on his head.

Justin kept grinning. "They revoked the rule."

"What rule?"

"The one that says I can't do this…" Justin murmured, kissing her cheek.

Callie's eyes widened. "Really? I mean, they told me that a relationship would be a good idea, but I never thought they meant it…"

"Well, Cat, I have something to ask you…"

She smiled widely, leaning against the tree. "Yes?"

"Would you like to do me the honor of being my girlfriend despite this fucked-up hell we now call home?"

Callie laughed. "I'd be honored, Justin."

He breathed a small sigh of relief as the whistle blew, signaling for them to go inside.

"Let's go," she said, tugging on his arm. He followed her, his mind reeling.

But just before they could cross the threshold, something took a hold of Justin. He pulled out the small item from his pocket, clicking it and tossing it behind him.

He walked away from the tree as the flames slowly crept up it.

Callie turned back and gasped, and Justin forced himself not to look back.

He forced himself to look straight.

"Justin?"

He turned, and saw Callie, who was standing there, not gasping.

"You were dreaming again."

He looked back at the tree, which was not on fire, and sighed slightly.

"Come on."

Justin couldn't bear all this tension that was building up inside of him.

"Let's go," he agreed. He led her inside, and partway down the hallway before he stopped. Justin looked at her.

"What's wrong?"

"I have so much tension, Cat..." He placed his hands on her waist, pushing her against the wall gently. "The doctor said there were two ways to relieve it."

"And what were those two ways?" Callie asked in a hushed voice.

Justin placed his forehead against hers. "I could go back to my old ways..." he said. "Or I could kiss you."

Her eyes widened.

"And I gave him back the match he gave me. I had to do it."

Callie looked up at him, touching his cheek silently.

"Because I've set a lot of things on fire in my life. I have watched a lot of things burn, and you're not one I ever want to see burn."

She murmured, "You gave up the match for me?"

"I'm here to stay, for as long as you'll let me."

Callie paused. ""Every time I hear one of those songs--those stupid and overplayed songs on the radio that I know you hate--every time I hear one, I think of you. I hear your voice telling me how they're repetitive trash that's not worth listening to. I hear you telling me to turn that crap off before your ears start bleeding. I used to like that kind of music, and now I only turn it on so I can hear your voice inside my head. If that's not love, tell me what is."

Justin smiled. "This." He brought his lips to Callie's, smiling into it.

And it felt like fire.

Chapter 13:

Flights of Dark Imaginings

Jacey opened her eyes and let out an ear-splitting scream.

The hell that surrounded her made her want to curl up in a ball and will the nightmares away. She couldn't believe where she was, or why she was here. What the hell ahd happened?

Around her, there was one apple tree. The ground looked like a desert without sand. The ground was cracked, split into pieces as far as the eye could see. In the distance, she could see a silhouette. The sky was lit slightly, but it was covered with a dark grey clouds cover. Jacey wasn't sure if she was having a dream or not now.

In front of her was someone who looked a hell of a lot like her. She had red hair, a red shirt on, and jeans, as well as a braid down her back. But there was just a rectangle randomly in front of her that contained the image of this girl. It looked like the bathroom at the memorial within this mirror, and it made Jacey miss Connor and Lakewood and he familiar room.

The girl waved at Jacey tauntingly, laughing. What she had thought was her reflection was now acting like she had a mind of her own.

"Hey, girl," she teased, looking at Jacey. "I'm Randall."

Jacey's eyes widened. "What the hell..." she muttered, reaching up to reach across to touch the girl. Her hand came in contact with a flat surface, and she pressed her hand against it, brow furrowing.

"It's the mirror that you're feeling." Randall crossed her arms, looking bored.

"What the hell?" Jacey repeated, banging on the mirror. Her breathing quickened.

Randall chuckled softly. "You're not Jacey anymore. Let's just say that."

"Then who am I?"

"You're my reflection. Nothing more. And nothing less."

Jacey banged on the mirror, looking through the rectangle at the world beyond, the world that used to be hers. "I'm not your reflection."

"You will be soon. It's only a matter of minutes. And even if you manage to escape, you'll give in eventually."

"Give in to what?"

Randall smirked. "You'll give in the power of that hell. Eventually, you'll come to see what exactly your mind is made of. That hell is made for reflections. You'll end up giving in to my will, becoming my reflection. You won't be dead, but you won't be alive."

"You're fucking crazy."

"Look around, Jacey!" Randall said, looking at the girl with exasperation.

Jacey didn't want to look back at the hell she was now in.

"See?"

She looked at Randall, eyes dark as she glared at her.

"As I grow up, you'll change to look like me. You're nothing more than a reflection of what you could have been."

Jacey snarled, "Stay the fuck away from my life."

"You don't have a life anymore."

"Why did this even happen?"

Randall rolled her eyes, acting bored. "Every single person is anchored to one mirror. It could be anywhere in the world. In that mirror, the reflection is not bound to its usual duties. If it has the willpower, it will break free. Should the person touch the mirror, the reflection can pull them through, and switch sides."

Jacey was silent, eyes wide because of shock.

"Yours just happened to be here."

"I will get back."

"You can't. I'm the only one who can hear you. And destroying me is impossible for the likes of you."

"The likes of me?"

Randall sighed. "Think of it as you have to find yourself to destroy yourself. If you try and kill me, you'll die, too. Because you're my reflection."

"I'll find a way out."

"Good luck. The spirits will eat you alive if you wander from the mirror. It's better to just give in."

Jacey banged the mirror, and Randall flinched slightly.

"I could always shatter the mirror."

Jacey's eyes widened. "This one? What would that do?"

"It might prevent you from ever crossing back through. But, I was always a kind person. So, I'll leave it up to show you what you can never have."

She cussed mentally, glaring at Randall. "You bitch."

"You are what I am, dear."

Randall moved to run a hand through her hair, and Jacey's arm broke out in pain. She cried out as her arm tried to force itself upwards, despite her attempts to make it stay down.

"It's happening already. It's time to face facts. You're not strong enough."

Jacey screamed as Randall smiled, for her face tried to curl itself into a smile. Her muscles felt like they were being torn off her face.

"Goodbye, Jacey. But don't worry. You won't be needing that name anymore." Randall waved, causing Jacey to feel like her fingers were snapping off.

As Randall walked away, Jacey felt her body go limp. She fell to the ground, eyes wide as she stared up at the black-lit sky. There was no way she was going to get out of this alive. The pain was too great for Jacey, and she simply couldn't deal with it. Her eyes glanced upward, and her mind drifted to Connor. Would Randall really take over her own life? Or would she start a new one, abandoning Jacey's life altogether?

She would never know. There were so many words left unsaid between her and Connor, her and Lakewood, her and her dad.

She was almost eighteen, too. Jacey was going to turn eighteen on—

Jacey couldn't remember. Her birthday was—

The month and day alluded her, and she slowly forgot the year.

Nineteen something.

It could have been anything.

Jacey cried out because of the frustration, unable to remember her own birthday.

It was almost silent in the hell as she lay there, chest heaving. The sky didn't move, and the tree didn't rustle because there was no wind. And there were no footsteps, for it seemed as if she was completely alone. The air was sour, like that one orange in every bundle that just wasn't as sweet as the rest.

She glanced around unwillingly, not wanting to come to terms with this hell. Besides the basic features she had glimpsed beforehand, this hell was quite barren. From where she sat, there were no other people visible. But it was not like she should have expected people. After all, those who are in hell don't tend to mingle.

Slowly, Jacey managed to stand, taking careful steps away from the mirror. It was as if she was walking against a force, for every once in a while, she would slid back a few inches.

"Hello?" Jacey said quietly, looking out. She headed toward the only sign of life she could find, which was an apple tree. It stood, in black and white, looming over her like the devil's shadow. Each red apple had faded to a dark grey that resembled the souls of those that lingered here.

Her hand curved around the smooth apple, and she pressed her lips against it.

Pulling back, she glanced at the lip stain that she had left. The dark red color stood out from the grey skin of the apple. Jacey didn't want to try eating it. She didn't want to risk it. Those apples were grey, after all, and no sane person eats fruit that isn't a color of the rainbow.

She knelt by the tree, running her hand along the tree's root. Was there water beneath? Was it possible that the tree was growing because there was life beneath the cracked ground? The more likely possibility was that it was actually a tree that had learned to survive without water. Somehow, this hell tree that had spawned here had managed to grow like it was living in nutritious soil.

The air was stiff and cold as Jacey knelt there. It was as if winter had settled in, but the air was dead. There was no breeze, and there was no wind. It made the tree look so forceful, as it loomed over her, watching her every move.

Something moved above her, creeping along one of the branches. It stared down at her, its eyes wide as it studied her.

Jacey paused, glancing upward. She felt like eyes were burning holes in her skull, trying to get her attention. She gasped slightly when she saw the black and white eyes peering at her. They mixed in between the grey leaves, and they only blinked once or twice.

"Who are you?" she whispered, as if a loud voice would break the stiffness of the air, or the stillness of the sky.

There was a soft murmur as it replied, "Who are *you*?"

Jacey paused, not breaking away from the only sign of life. "I don't know," she admitted quietly.

"Don't know," it repeated in a mutter. Its voice was as scratchy as sandpaper, but it somehow had this warmth to it that drew her to it. It made her want to curl up in its voice and rock herself to sleep.

"Where are we?"

It looked down at her, as if startled. "We..." it began, trailing off sadly.

"How do I get home?" It wasn't a question directed at it, or even anyone for that matter. She said it as she stared straight ahead, at the bark of the tree. It slowly began to peel off, and she could faintly hear a sound like nails on a chalkboard.

It coughed. "I...home..."

Jacey twisted the words around, entangling them with her thoughts. "You're home?" she asked, to clarify.

It nodded, its eyes bobbing up and down. The leaves still didn't move.

"I want to go to my home," Jacey told it, feeling a bit ashamed that she sounded so pathetic.

It almost seemed to look sympathetic. "Go home," it repeated, its voice warm.

"I can't. I'm a reflection now. I can never get back," she murmured, staring down at the ground.

There was a fragile sound, and a leaf slowly floated down. When it landed, she tried to pick it up, and found that it was too heavy to do so. It simply wouldn't even budge, or roll.

"Reflection," it muttered with hatred poisoning its very voice.

"I don't blame her. This place is hell. She was doing what she needed to." The words sounded foreign in Jacey's mouth. It was as if she respected Randall.

It shook what must have been the head covered by shadows. "Her hell."

"It's my hell, now, anyways. I'm stuck. No way out."

It sighed in frustration, looking down at her as if she was too far away. "My way out," it struggled to say, urging her with its voice.

"Do you know a way out?"

It bobbed its head up and down.

"Randall said something about finding myself. And destroying myself. Is that even possible?"

It paused. "Find self...possible...destroy self..."

Jacey sighed in frustration. "How come you can only use my words? Are you an echo?"

"You echo," it snapped, its eyes turning into daggers that glared.

"I meant," Jacey corrected herself, "is that what you represent? Or did you used to be alive?"

Its gaze softened considerably. "Alive," it whispered.

"What happened? How come you are here, not on the other side of the mirror?"

"Other side of mirror," it murmured, sadly, looking away into the distance.

Jacey paused. "Why are you not a reflection? How come you didn't turn, like she said? It makes no sense."

"No reflection," it said simply, its gaze shining.

"Is your other half...gone?"

It simply looked away wistfully, as if it couldn't decide whether or not a good or a bad thing had occurred.

"Can I make my other half go away?"

It nodded.

"How? Can I shatter the mirror? Will that destroy her? Do you know?"

It shook its head frantically, as if she had suggested that the entire world should explode. "Shatter destroy you!"

"So the mirror cannot shatter, or I will be destroyed? Then how do I destroy her? How can I stop my reflection?"

It paused for a moment, looking down at her. It was as if it knew the words, but couldn't spit them out. "Destroy reflection stop mirror..."

"What?" She shook her head, covering her face with her hands. "I don't understand any of this. You are not making any sense."

"You make sense!" it shouted happily, bobbing.

Jacey paused, looking up. "I have to make sense? What do you mean? Like, understand?"

"You understand you!"

Her eyes widened considerably. "I have to find myself. I have to figure out who I am and then I can destroy her!"

"Figure out! Destroy her!" it chanted, looking down at her fondly.

She smiled, and then it cracked. "You know, that's a lot easier to say than it is to do."

"Do," it encouraged, frowning slightly.

Jacey paused for a moment. "Did you know that broken promises and good intentions are really nothing more than just that...broken promises?"

"Good intentions..."

She shook her head. "I have good intentions. But I can't keep my promises. I can't keep myself in one piece."

"One piece." It looked confused.

"They say character is who you are in the dark. Is it really my fault that all the scandalous stuff happens at night?"

It paused, peering down at her with sympathy. "You in the dark," it pointed out.

"I don't have light. That's why I can't find myself."

"Find light," it said simply, as if that solved all of her problems.

She chuckled weakly. "I used to think I knew my light. That memorial in Manhattan was my light. Until he died."

There was no answer from it.

"I keep telling myself he didn't really leave me. But, it felt like the one person who cared had abandoned me."

"Didn't abandon," it insisted. "One cared. Didn't leave."

Jacey looked up at it. "You think he still cares?"

"Still cares," it repeated with upmost surety, looking at her with the saddest eyes she had ever seen.

Slowly, she leaned against the tree. "I hope you're right, echo."

It nodded slowly, settling down into a branch as it closed its eyes.

Jacey felt something fall from it, fall from the tree, and land on her cheek.

But, she couldn't tell the difference between her tears, and the ones that fell from it, above.

Chapter 14:

Taught to Fear the Dark

Nobody has to be taught to fear the dark.

Connor didn't fear the dark.

But he didn't like it either.

The memorial had been cast into the dark as the sun moved behind a building. It had been quite a while since Jacey had entered the restroom. He checked his watch, and then looked up, biting his lip. No one else had gone in, after all.

There was a loud creak of metal as the door swung open. He saw a girl with red hair walk out, and his heart soared with absolute relief.

"Jay!" he called out, and she turned at the yelling.

"Hello?" she said, tentative, before the image of his face and the sound of his voice clicked and she smiled. "Oh! Hey!"

Before Connor could crack some joke that would make her roll her eyes, a pair of hand jutted out from behind the building, grabbing her wrists.

Connor swore that his heart nearly stopped as the car door slammed shut behind her, and skidded away with a squeal of the tires. He jammed his hand into his pocket, swearing as he inputted his pass code incorrectly.

"9-1-1," he muttered as he punched each key, pressing the phone to his ear as urgently as he had three months ago, when she had passed out at the party.

"9-1-1, what's your emergency?"

Connor stumbled over his words, tripping on every consonant and syllable. "My friend. Got into a random car, and the car sped away."

"Sir, what's your emergency? Has someone been taken?"

"Yes!" he sputtered. "I'm in Manhattan, at the memorial for the World Trade Center. They drove away in a black car, license plate 7HGT902."

The operator paused before asking, tone calm, "Sir, just calm down. We're sending the police now. Who was taken?"

"My friend. Jacey Adams. She lives in Long Island."

"Okay. Do you need me to stay on the line?"

Connor ran a hand through his hair. "No." He clicked the line, hyperventilating, and his vision tinging with red.

What the hall had happened? He remembered Jacey simply getting into the car as if nothing had happened. It was as if she was some other girl, who had gone off to live her life.

The sound of sirens both relieved and worried Connor. There was always the imminent likelihood that they were too late. The police rushed out of their cars, glancing at the worried teeneager curiously.

"Are you the one who dialed 911?" one burly cop asked.

Connor nodded.

"Which way did the car go?" a thin woman asked, hand on her gun.

Connor pointed down the street. "That way. 7HGT902."

Three police people headed to their cars briskly, clicking ont heir sirens. Connor sat down against the memorial, staring at the cracks in the ground. Tragedy had occurred here fifteen years ago, and now tragedy was happening again. Except this time, only one person was gone.

"When did you last see her?" the woman asked, squatting next to him.

"She went into the restroom twenty minutes ago."

The cop nodded, scribbling on her pad. She brushed her black curls out of her eyes, taking a deep breath. "What was her name?"

"Jacey Will Adams."

"Address?"

"4192 Offshore Boulevard, Long Island, New York."

She nodded, looking up at him through her heavily-makeup layered eyes. "We're goingt o find her. We are going to put out an AMBER alert so that we can identify the car and find the perpetrator."

Connor sighed, looking off into the distance. "I sure hope so."

"My team will do our best. Do you have the phone number of her parent? We will need to call him. Can you work with Detective Neer on the information regarding the AMBER alert?" She gestured to a man leaning against a small tree, who almost seemed to be skinnier than the tree itself.

He nodded. "Yeah." His voice was weak and exhausted, as if he had sprinted many miles. However, he hadn't done anything except worry.

Detective Reed reminded Connor of the one person on the police team who was considered the geek. He had large, round glasses that didn't quite fit on his nose. His hair was slicked to the side, and his trench coat didn't quite fit him. Reed looked to be in his late twenties, which wasn't surprising to Connor. His dad worked for the Long Island police force, and there were a lot fo young recruits.

"What's your name?" Reed asked him, adjusting the neck of his coat.

"Connor Tarrentine. I'm a friend of...her," he trailed off, shrugging sadly.

Reed nodded, pulling out his notepad. "Can you reiterate to me everything you remember? About the car? Her? The person who took her?"

Connor thought for a moment, trying to recall every single detail that he possibly could. He wanted Jacey to be found, and quite frankly, he needed her to be found. "The car was a black Mercedes. It had tinted windows, and a California license plate. The license plate was 7HGT902. And the car had a scratch on the passenger door. It was a thin scratch, but it was quite unique and quite obvious. And also the car had a broken taillight."

"That's pretty descriptive. You got a good memory, kid."

"I have an eidetic memory, sir."

Reed looked thoughtful, as if he was praising Connor. "Did you see the driver?"

"Only for a split-second. He was clean-shaven. And had green eyes. Probably in his 30s or 40s. That's all I can tell you."

The detective scribbled down the information. "That's impressive. How does it work?"

"I just close my eyes," Connor murmured. He shut his eyes, looking at the blackness. He tried to remember the car, and the memory popped in front of him, and he could examine every detail of the picture.

Reed smiled slightly, touching one of the strands of hair on his head. "I'm going to go give this to my boss, who's on the phone with the FBI, okay? We're going to need you to call your parents and come down with us to the station, since you're our only witness."

Connor glanced at the police cars, shuddering slightly. "Okay. Let me call my dad."

The scene seemed so relaxed, with the detective calmly talking to him, and Connor answering so casually. But his mind refused to let him forget that Jacey's life was in danger.

"Connor? Why are you calling me at work?"

"Dad, I need to go to the Manhattan Police Station. I was witness to a crime, and they need me there."

The dad inhaled sharply. "What crime?"

"A kidnapping." He couldn't bear to say that it was Jacey. The truth hurt his throat, and made his heart want to explode into tiny fragments.

"Okay. Well, call me if you need a ride home. I'm in the area."

"I brought my car, though."

"I'll tow it home."

Connor sighed. "Okay."

The line clicked dead, and he trudged over to where the detectives were huddled. Jacey's fate was on the line. This was, as the saying went, a matter of life and death. If Jacey wasn't found, then...

"Ready, Connor?" Detective Reed asked, placing his hand on the boy's shoulder. Connor was grateful for the interruption of his train of thought. His eyes were rimmed with tears.

Reed led Connor to a car that didn't look much like any other car. As he opened the passenger side door, he noticed the gadgets and scanners that littered the inside. This was a detective's car.

"Are you really just a cop?"

The man sighed, chuckling weakly. "No, not really."

"But you're a detective, right?"

"Exactly."

"Are you going to find her?"

Reed paused, looking down at Connor, who seemed as vulnerable as a five-year old given the circumstances. "I'm going to try."

"What if you don't?"

"I have some good people working with me, Connor. I guarantee that we will try our hardest." Connor noted the promises that extended only to the work that they would do. There were no promises made about her coming home, for that was not necessarily plausible yet.

"Who works with you?"

Reed pulled out of the parking space, flashing his lights so that he could move around the traffic. "The FBI. There's a woman you should meet. She deals with most of the kidnappings that occur."

Connor fidgeted with the piercing on the tip of his right ear. "What's her job?"

"She works with the Behavioral Science Unit of the FBI. They deal with the psychology of the victims and the perpetrators more than anything else. She is quite the clever woman."

The younger boy nodded slowly. "What's her name?"

"Violet Jo. Of course, we refer to her as Agent Jo."

Connor glanced up at Reed, and then back down.

"She's a magnificent agent. It's quite impressive. She has solved almost all of the abduction cases that have come to her unit. I mean, she's one of those people we all either wish to be or wish to be with."

Despite the worry twisting Connor's heart into knots, he couldn't help but exhale a little bit, as if trying to laugh.

"What?" Reed's cheeks were tinged pink, his knuckles white as he gripped the steering wheel.

Connor shrugged, glancing ahead of them at the station hat was coming up. Who knows how long he would end up being here for. But, hopefully, he would come home with Jacey.

"How do you know her?"

The teenager glanced up, understand the question, but not wanting to answer. The thought of Jacey made his body shake a little bit out of fear.

"I know it's hard."

"You see this kind of thing every day," Connor muttered bitterly.

Reed placed his hand on Connor's shoulder as they slid into a parking space. "My brother was abducted when he was eleven."

"Your brother?" Connor's eyes widened as he thought of his own three brothers, and the grief his parents and two sisters would feel as well.

The detective nodded. "I see this kind of thing every day because I want to0 know that I am working against the evil that caused that abduction. It tore my family into pieces. I never understood how much it hurt until it happened. Now, I fight the evil that kidnapped my brother. There is onylg ood int his world if we choose to be good."

"Your brother must be proud," the adolescent said, his face somber.

"That's what my parents said when I told them I was going to be a detective."

"When did you decide that?"

Reed sighed. "The day I watched my brother's body lowered into the ground."

Connor inhaled sharply. He didn't know what words could come out that would console the detective.

"Whether or not we find this girl, I need you to not forget this. Because there are people in this world who simply don't have the morals that you and I do. No matter what, you need to understand that we are the only thing styanding in between the innocent and the evil."

The teen nodded, looking at Reed with wide eyes.

"What?"

"It's just that...you're so brave."

"Me? Brave? I'm scared to pull a trigger, Connor."

Connor shrugged that off. "That doesn't matter. You are brave enough to stand up to your past experiences and your troubles."

"You think that's brave?" The childlike gaze of happiness that Reed directed at Connor made Connor smile slightly.

"Of course. Not many people can do what you and Agent Jo do."

Reed smiled back. "Thanks. Now let's go find that girl of yours, shall we?"

Connor got out of the car quickly, and Reed glanced over to the police station. "We're in luck. The BSU and FBI were still here after their case ended yesterday."

A woman turned around, her ponytail whipping behind her. Her long black hair was carefully tied back, and she had on an FBI shirt, as well as black pants. Judging by the smile on Agent Reed's face, this was Agent Jo.

She looked intimidating, but feminine. Her eyes were dusted with blue eyes shadow, and she had on lipstick. Moreover, Agent Jo looked like the kind of girl who could be shooting you in the head the first hour, and be dancing at a club the next.

"Vi, it's good to see you," Reed said with a small smile, holding out his hand as they shook hands.

Agent Jo smiled warmly at Reed before glancing down at Connor. "And who are you?"

"Connor Tarrentine. I was the witness."

"Come inside. We need to issue the AMBER alert immediately, and we need the description of the victim." Jo then turned on her heel, clicking away into the police building. She paused at the top of the stairs. "Either of you coming?"

Reed quickly followed her, hands in the deep trench coat pockets. Connor was a bit reluctant to enter the building, but did so for Jacey. This was the same station where he had met her that night so many years ago. She was troubled. But that didn't stop him from caring or loving her.

"Come sit," Jo called, sitting down at a makeshift desk she had assembled in the conference room immediately to the left. It was a plain, simple room, that could have been used for interrogation. The walls were white, and the table was nailed to the floor.

"What's going on?"

"We need you to tell us. Everything."

"Again?"

Jo flipped open her notebook, glancing at Reed. "Yes. Starting with her."

"How is this going to help? She might be fucking dying right now!"

The agents acted calm, as if they were used to this. Reed cleared his throat. "The faster you tell us, the better a chance we have. Connor, screaming at us is not going to fix the situation."

He sat down on the edge of his seat, gripping the armrests. "What do you want to know?"

AMBER Alert:

Manhattan :: New York

Black Mercedes. License Plate 7HGT902. Scratch on passenger door.

Caucasian male. Green eyes. Black hair.

Missing: 17 year-old Girl.
Jacey. Red hair.
5'5". Hazel eyes.

Chapter 15:

A Dream's Whisper

Her hair was red.

That was all I could focus on as I wandered amongst the sour air particles.

I needed to remember that color.

If I didn't remember, then I knew I would not manage to live.

I assumed I was somewhere in between.

I'm not dead.

But I'm not alive.

And I feel like she might make the difference between the two.

Maybe.

But why would one person matter so much?

She tells me that I should ignore the girl with the red hair.

I look at her, silently.

Her hair is almost white.

Her eyes are grey.

Her small, childish smile wasn't even bright.

In fact, in blended in with the darkness.

Seven, she tells me.

She is seven.

How does she remember her age?

I don't even remember the years.

Time doesn't really matter.

I glance away from her.

The girl with red hair.

Does she have a name?

Probably.

The better question is, does she remember her name?

Does she understand what's going on?

Can she remember her old life?

Red.

I can't stop looking at the colors that are sparking from her.

It's like....fireworks.

I whisper that word.

The girl who calls herself my sister looks at me.

She asks me how I can remember such a thing.

It's such a happy thing, as well.

I ask her why the girl with red hair is so bright.

She shrugs, face pinching in a glare.

I ask again.

She exhales loudly.

I lose myself for a moment thinking about her breathing.

Why is she breathing?

Sometimes I forget I am.

My gaze falls on the girl again.

I'm going to call her Red.

It will be the one thing I remember.

I will make sure I will hold on to that.

Red is sitting against a tree, eyes closed.

I think she was talking to someone.

But who would be here?

A spirit?

I touch my cheek, staring into the distance with the apple tree.

Sister clears her throat slightly.
I don't know if she likes Red.
It's like she wants me to forget Red.
But I can't.
Why would I?
It's a whisper that makes me want to live.
The word itself gives me a small spark of
hope.
Sister glances at the girl.
I ask her why she hates Red.
She sighs again.
It's not hatred, she murmurs.
Then what is it?
Sister pauses.
Jealousy.
I don't understand the word.
It sounds like an emotion.
Like love.
Like happiness.
I glance at her, confused.
Sister nods, trailing off.
She doesn't want to talk about it, she says.
I'm not really listening anymore, though.
Because I am too focused on the colors ahead
of me.
How can such a beautiful thing exist here?
How have the colors not been sucked from
her yet?
I almost don't want to question it.
If I question it, maybe I'll ruin it.
It's like magic.
I can't believe my eyes.
In such a barren hell, I appreciate her.

Sister rolls her eyes at me.
Be careful, she warns me.
Why?
Sister looks at me, seriously.
Because people leave.
And caring is never good.
I frown.
She keeps trying to refer to something.
Something that happened.
She says it's the reason why I am here.
But why would I be here?
How is there a logical reasoning behind that?
I wish I could remember.
Maybe if I found my way in, I could find my way out.
Something inside me causes me to glance at sister.
She wouldn't be able to go.
I'm sure of it.
Part of me wants to shake in fear at the thought of leaving her.
Maybe she belongs here, I lie to myself.
Who would belong here?
Not even the devil could live here.
I paused, looking at sister.
Is she dead?
I say the words out loud, and she freezes.
All I can do is stare at her.
And wonder.
She looks at me with a sad glance.
I want her to respond.
But I am scared for the answer.

I don't know if I really want to know.
Maybe I just want surety.
Surety would be nice.
I don't know anything anymore.
I don't know my name.
My age.
My height.
My hair color.
My eye color.
My birthday.
My hometown.
My parents.
My old life.
Nothing.

Every time I start to remember, the memory gets yanked away from me.

I want nothing more than to actually be able to say that I know something.

For a moment, my gaze wanders.
And it lands on Red again.
I do know something for sure.
Her hair is red.
But, what if that is my imagination?
I try to destroy the thought.
If it is my imagination, then I...
I trail off, inhaling sharply as if the thought hurt me.

My mind wants to squeeze itself shut and never wake up.

The pain of thinking it was just a figment of my imagination is too much.

Sister looks at me.
She will be gone soon, she says.

I shake my head.
No one gets out of here.
She argues that Red isn't meant to be here.
Was I meant to be here?
Or was I meant to do other things?
I don't even know what lies on the other side.
On the other side of the mirror is life, she says.

I glance at her.
Life.
But this isn't death.
Not yet, she says.
I run a hand through my hair, wishing I could understand.
Words form on my lips, and tumble out quietly.
I want Red to hear.
But there is a difference between her hearing and her wanting to listen.
Sister pauses before saying that this is so close to death.
This side is closer to death that the other side.
I have placed myself at risk.
I stare at Red.
I want to approach her.
I want to drown out Sister's words.
She says that there is the light places.
The living places.
I ask her what this place is.
Even though I am scared to know the answer.
She pauses, staring out at the apple tree.

She murmurs, it's hard.

Because all that is here is darkness and death.

I nod.

Slowly, words manage to form from my mouth.

There's no escape, I say.

No escape from the dark and dying places.

Chapter 16

The Invention of a Dance

Callie glanced in the mirror, looking at her reflection.

"You look magnificent," her roommate giggled, handing the guard the curling iron. The guard made sure there were no other dangerous items before slipping out of the room.

"Really? You think so?" Callie touched the corner of her lips, smiling slightly at the girl staring back at her.

Carina nodded happily, smiling. "Yeah."

"You look amazing, too," Callie said, glancing at the girl behind her.

Her roommate smiled shyly, looking around the room. "I don't know why they even have this dance." But Carina smiled at the mirror proudly nevertheless.

"I don't know. I guess it gives us a chance to have a real experience as a teenager, you know?"

"I guess."

"And you're going with Cody," Callie nudged Carina, laughing softly.

With the black and white thinking Carina had, Callie was careful on how she worded things. But Carina smiled with intense joy. "It's so kind of him to take me to the dance!" She twirled around, brushing her hands against the ruffles on her light blue, short dress.

Callie smiled, glancing at herself in the mirror. Her strapless red dress hung to a little above her knees, and was bedazzled with jewels below the top of the dress. Her red heels matched the color of her dress, and as did her eye shadow. Her hair, which had been done by Callie under careful watch of the guard, was curled and pinned back. She felt elegant, and she felt beautiful.

"Can we go now?"

Callie hoped Cody would be ready, and wouldn't be late. She murmured a quick prayer before nodding.

Carina bounded out the door, her flats sliding on the floor as she moved down the hallway. Callie glided down after her, nervously messing with a strand of her curly hair as she headed toward the meeting place.

"Carina!" It was a soft, but deep voice that echoed slightly down the hallway. The boy in Callie's small group, Cody, looked incredibly well-groomed. He looked a bit uncomfortable at the sight of all the people walking around, but he calmed at the sight of Carina.

"Cody!" Carina wrapped her arms around his neck, hugging him. She pulled back slightly. "Sorry," she giggled softly.

Cody looked pained for a moment before he gently wrapped his arms around her waist in return. "S'okay. You look gorgeous, by the way." He smiled, and it was the first time Callie had seen him with a genuine smile.

Callie left the two alone, waving goodbye to Carina. She clicked around the dates and the groups of friends, looking for Justin. She smiled slightly at some of the people from small group, before sitting down on the bottom of the staircase, glancing around with a sigh.

All the couples, and the single people, looked incredibly happy. She figured it was just him running late. After all, Justin wouldn't ditch her. He never had.

But what if this time he had ditched you?

Callie inhaled sharply, unsure if that was her own thought, or the voice. She didn't want to know the answer. She leaned her head against the windowsill of where she was sitting, sighing slightly as her eyes shut so she didn't have to watch everyone.

She opened her eyes suddenly as someone placed a hand on her shoulder. The room was empty when her eyes shot open, and it was cast in almost complete darkness.

"Callie?" someone murmured, and she turned to look at the all-too familiar face.

She didn't say a word, eyes watering slightly as she glanced at the clock, and then back at Justin. He was wearing jeans, and a loose t-shirt, and it looked as if he hadn't even remembered.

"I didn't forget," he swore, looking at her. In the silence, he took a deep breath. "You look beautiful, you know."

Callie bit her lip, looking down. She wanted an explanation, but she didn't want to hear the wrong one.

"They held me back. I couldn't leave until now. They didn't want me near you tonight. I don't know why," Justin sighed, frowning.

She looked up at him. "Really?"

"Callie, I would never lie to you." Justin stretched out his left arm to show her the gauze wrapped around from where they had drawn blood.

It took less than a moment, in Callie's mind, for her to wrap her arms around his neck, pressing close to him. He exhaled as he held her tightly, arms wrapped around her waist.

"I'm sorry," he murmured, lips brushing the top of her head as he spoke. They were like that for a while before he pulled back, standing up.

"Are you leaving?" she asked, her voice a little too quick, and it filled with worry.

Justin chuckled weakly, shaking his head. He extended his hand for her. "May I have this dance?"

Callie's eyes widened, and she reached out her hand, gently sliding her hand into his. She stood up, following him as he walked backward to the center of the room. There was no music, but that didn't really matter.

Justin watched as she placed her arms on each of his shoulders, so her hand connected behind his neck. He tentatively placed his hands on her waist, giving her a small smile.

"This is nice," Callie murmured as they swayed, looking at him with her eyes still wet from earlier, when he had first appeared.

Justin was silent for a moment. "They told me something."

Callie looked at him, pausing for a bit before continuing her swaying. "What?"

"I'm going to be discharged."

She inhaled sharply before biting back the immediate response that flew to her lips. "That's good. I'm happy for you."

"I made a deal with them."

Callie tilted her head, frowning slightly. "What deal? Don't tell me that you're staying!"

He shook his head. "If a legal guardian discharges you, then you may leave, given your condition. I talked to your mom when they had me there. She signed the papers and faxed them over."

"She's taking me back?"

Justin paused. "Not exactly, Cat. They're legally discharging you to someone of age eighteen or older that they trust."

Her heart sank slightly, but she tried to hold onto to that glimmer of hope. "Who?"

He smiled at her, tucking a loose curl behind her ear. "Me."

"Wait, really? They're letting us leave?"

"If we come back every month for the tests, then yes."

She tightened her arms, pressing as close to him as possible. "I can't believe it!" Her eyes watered slightly as she pressed her forehead against his neck.

"We get to be together, and get out of this hell," Justin laughed weakly, holding her tight.

It was silent for a long moment as Callie tried to overcome her tears of joy. "What happens now?"

Justin pulled back slightly, wiping away one of her tears. "My parents left me an apartment as part of the deal that I disassociate myself from my younger siblings. We can stay there. This place put in some safety measures on the apartment so it's been deemed safe."

"We're...living...together?"

He inhaled slightly. That was something that was touchy for the both of them, and was a very big step. "We can make this work, I think. Stay in different rooms, or whatever. I just want to be able to keep my promise of never leaving your side."

Callie looked around at the white walls, and dreary atmosphere. "Anything to get away from this hell," she murmured, looking at him and bringing her lips to brush against his cheek.

Justin touched his forehead to hers, slowly bringing his mouth closer to hers.

"Thanks for showing up," she said, her voice filling with quiet gratitude.

"I'm sorry I couldn't make this a night to remember," he replied, sighing.

Callie looked down at their feet as they swayed. "Trust me, it is." Her mind was still reeling from the idea of staying and living with him, but she figured it was worth it. Her mind wasn't really focused on the logic of it, as much as she was focusing on the fact that she would get to be in a caring environment.

"It's really late. We should probably go, so we can pack up, okay?"

"When do we leave?"

"Either tomorrow or the day after that. Depends on whenever we finish packing, and everything."

Callie nodded slowly, smiling softly at him. "I really appreciate this, Justin."

Justin smiled. "Anything for Cat." He bent suddenly, sliding one arm under her legs, and one arm on her back. She squealed as he picked her up, bridal style.

"Don't drop me!" she said seriously before breaking out in a fit of giggles.

He held her close. "Of course not," he laughed.

Callie smiled, leaning against him. She listened to the steady beat of his heart as he walked through the halls, tracing the familiar path back to her bedroom.

When they reached the door, Justin slowly let Callie slide down, giving her a bright smile.

"See you tomorrow?"

Justin nodded. "Definitely. Night, Cat." He paused before turning away, taking a step down the hallway.

Callie turned her back at his retreating figure, sighing.

"Cat, wait!" Justin called out. She turned on her heel, just in time, for he crashed his lips against his as if his life depended on it. Her back hit the wall, and she placed her hands on his shoulder, grateful for the heels that added to her height. She pulled him closer, if possible, eyes fluttering closed.

Justin eagerly kept his lips there, feeling the tension he had built up in his body spill out into the kiss.

He couldn't get over the fact that it was just like fire.

She pulled back, needing to catch her breath. Her cheeks were flushed as she looked at him, chuckling softly.

"I think that qualifies as a good night," he joked, running a hand through his hair.

Callie nodded.

"You know, Cat—"

Before he could say the words that had been on his mind for at least a month, a bloodcurdling scream echoed from behind Callie.

Justin rushed inside the room, letting out a cry at the figure that was lying on the ground. He tried to block Callie from seeing as nurses and doctors sprinted in, but a glimpse was all she needed for the memory to be permanently instilled in her mind.

Carina's body was outstretched on her bed; the white sheets were soaked with more blood than Callie thought could hold. Her arms were covered in crimson, and there were deep gashes. Her legs were cut as well, and it was impossible to tell the cut flesh from the flesh that had been spared. Her face was the only clean skin on her body. Her neck was resting in a pool of the blood. A shard of what could have been glass protruded from the base of her neck.

Callie couldn't help but scream. She stumbled backward, her back hitting the wall in the hallway. The nurses glanced at her, but were more focused on the girl who was losing more and more blood by the moment. Justin knelt by her, holding her close.

Carina had been diagnosed with borderline personality disorder. She thought of the world as in black and white. Small acts of kindness filled her with intense joy, while acts of pain, or perceived acts of leaving, caused intense depression. She had attempted suicide twice before coming here, and the medicine had seemed to be working. She was kind most of the time. It was just that she was wary of people.

Some people started filling the hallway, glancing at the room filled with nurses and doctors.

"What's going on?" Cody rushed down the hall in sweat pants and a tank top, eyes wide with worry.

The nurse held him back, brushing him off. He shoved her aside, and immediately two doctors went to constrain Cody as the nurse landed on her leg with a sickening crack.

The crack brought a fire to the boy's eyes as he fruitlessly fought the doctors' strong grip. Cody's sadomasochism was something that made him quite dangerous, especially given that the one person he cared about was 'under siege.'

That could be you, the voice taunted, and Callie screamed at the pain that exploded from that voice.

She curled into the warm body next to her, willing for her vision to go away. For a moment, all she could think of was ending it.

What scared her was that that moment
lasted for a lot longer than she thought it would

Chapter 17

Footsteps of Those to Come

Jacey pretended that the colors of her old life still existed. The purple of the sky, the deep blue of the ocean, the greenness of the trees. And of course, the dark crimson of all that blood that seemed to rain down everywhere.

She was shivering slightly as she took shelter in a smooth, curved dent in the trunk of the apple tree. The apple that she had held a while ago was lying on its side in the blood rain. The drips of what she imagined to be crimson streaked the grey apple, but didn't disrupt the color of the lipstick. But she didn't have to imagine the bright red that came with the lipstick.

A drop landed on her arm, staining that part of her skin with that imaginary shade of maroon. She cried out slightly. In her mind, it wasn't water. Water represented life. It had to be blood. There was no other explanation.

Blood was the one thing that Jacey couldn't deal with. Paper cuts, even despite their small size, produced so much blood before clotting that Jacey feared getting a paper cut.

Hemophobia. That was what they called her fear. But, in Jacey's opinion, it sounded much too calm for the effect blood had on her.

"Why the hell is it raining blood?" she frowned to herself.

"Raining?" it asked. The familiar pair of eyes bobbed above her. She glanced upward, almost taking comfort in the wide, hazel, eyes. At least, they looked hazel to her. But she could have been imagining the wrong color.

"Do you not see it?" Jacey asked. "I hate blood. I have a fear of it."

It glanced at the landscape. "Not see it. You see blood."

"Yes, I see blood. But how come you can't see it?"

It thought for a moment, unable to echo the needed words. "You see it. I can't."

"Of course. My fear, my problems."

"Fear!" it repeated loudly, bobbing its eyes.

Jacey frowned slightly. "Is that why I see it? Because I'm afraid."

"See because afraid."

Her eyes widened slightly in realization.

"You see your fears here?"

It nodded.

"What do you see?"

It paused, eyes looking sad as it glanced at Jacey. "You," it murmured.

She couldn't quite hear the word, and decided to ignore the question. Jacey glanced out at the horizon, sighing slightly at the barren wasteland. Her eyes flicked over an odd shape, and she continued scanning before her jaw dropped.

Jacey reexamined the strange shape, and made out a human figure.

"Is that another person?"

It almost smiled. "Another person," it agreed.

She stood; looking at the general features she could make out of what looked to be a boy. What made her panic inside was the fact that he was looking directly at her.

"Should I talk to him?" she mused, thinking.

It nodded, smiling with its eyes. "Talk to him!"

Jacey looked at the boy, and tilted her head. He did the same, his gaze never leaving her. She slowly pointed to him, and then gestured for him to walk over. He didn't move.

The blood rain quieted, and she took a step forward, and he did the same. She sighed, looking down at the ground. Slowly, she knelt back by the tree.

"I just want him to come over," she murmured.

It paused. "Come over," it agreed.

"Will he?"

There was no response.

The uncomfortable silence that followed that caused Jacey to feel more alone than ever. She looked up, and sighed when her eyes didn't meet its. After a moment, she glanced out. What she expected to see was the empty land and the blood rain. What she didn't expect was the boy to be walking towards her.

He trudged along slowly. "He's actually coming?"

"Coming," it suddenly said, smiling down at her.

Jacey watched the boy come into focus as the blood rain stopped. He didn't looked dead, but he didn't quite look alive. His hair was hidden under a beanie, but the strands that poked out could have been imagined to be white-blonde. His eyes were a bright grey, and Jacey let her mind fill his eyes with a startling blue. He was quite tall, and his skin was pale. His clothes hung loosely off his figure, and he had his hands jammed deep in his pockets.

"You're alive," she murmured. He stared at her, almost shyly. Jacey looked at his eyes, wondering what was running through that mind of his.

"Are you a reflection?" Jacey asked, running a hand through her hair. He shook his head.

She nodded. "How long have you been here?" He shrugged, mouth closed tightly.

The air filled with solitude and silence once again. Jacey frowned, and let her eyes run up and down the boy again. He could have been a senior at her school, easily. He looked modern, but a bit older than her. She noticed the piercing on the tip of his right ear, like Connor.

"What's your name?"

His eyes sparked with recognition. Yet, not words came out. Jacey leaned against the tree, trying to figure out what was going on with this boy.

"Can you talk?" He paused before nodding. "Will you?"

The boy thought for a long moment, eyes flickering from the apple to Jacey. Then, he shrugged, sitting down a few feet from her.

"Have you seen anyone else alive?"

He shook his head, gesturing to her and then the tree.

"Well, besides me. The tree? It's alive?"

"Me!" it protested.

Jacey made an 'o' with her mouth as she realized what he meant. "You mean the echo?"

"Echo," it said with disgust, and she glanced apologetically up at it.

He nodded, his face expressing the smallest hint of a smile as one of the corners of his mouth turned up.

"It's quite a funny little personality," Jacey agreed.

It mused, "Personality."

"Do you like that name?"

"Name," it agreed.

There was a silence that followed. Jacey brushed her hair over her shoulder, noticing the way the boy watched her. His gaze was almost wistful.

In a way, this boy faded in with the black and the white. But when she imagined the colors on him, he stood out like a star. His eyes shined, and his hair was mussed on top of his head beneath his beanie. She wondered how someone so silent could be so loud at the exact same time.

"Why did you come over here, if you're not going to talk?" It sounded a bit rude, but the boy didn't seem to take any offense.

He shrugged, and then gestured to her and the tree.

"The personality?"

He nodded.

"And me?"

He shrugged, but then looked at her in such a manner that made her feel like he was inspecting her. He couldn't seem to look away. She couldn't blame him. She couldn't stop looking at him because it felt so nice to see the warm face of someone alive.

"What do you think of your reflection?" Jacey asked quietly.

The boy made a face, shaking his head.

"Did he pull you over on purpose?"

He nodded, eyes filling with what resembled guilt.

"Why would they do such a horrible thing?"

After a moment, the boy shook his head, and Jacey assumed he just didn't know how to respond.

"Do you want to go back?"

He looked at Jacey for a long moment, and pointed to her, raising his shoulders like he was asking a question.

"Yeah. I do."

He nodded, pointing to himself before looking out at the distance.

"Do you miss everyone?"

There was confusion in his eyes as he raised an eyebrow.

"From your life?"

He looked at the ground sadly, running his hand along the hard ground. He shrugged, but it wasn't as if he didn't care about the answer. It was more like he simply couldn't find the words, or the memories to answer.

"Have you started to forget things?"

The boy nodded instantaneously, looking at her curiously.

"I hate it," she swore.

He nodded in agreement, touching his forehead.

"What do you miss most?"

His mouth opened slightly, and a small word slipped out from his mouth. "Red."

Chapter 18:

Seven Ways to Skin Your Soul

Connor didn't know why he was making this harder on himself.

Over the past hours, days, or perhaps minutes, he had put himself through what could only be described as hell and back again. There was no way any sane person would have done any of what he had done.

So, it was good thing that he wasn't sane.

Detective Reed and Agent Jo constantly called him, or answer his numerous calls, to update him on the case, and any new developments that had occurred.

The car had been spotted an hour away from Manhattan, to the north, at about six at night. That was about nine hours ago, as of now. His phone was by him as he sat by the window of his apartment.

The last thing he had told Jacey was that he didn't love her. His best friend was now somewhere far from him, and he would never be able to tell her that it was all a lie. But he had to do it. If he hadn't told her, he would have ruined their entire friendship as well. The fact that he liked Lakewood was something that he knew Jacey would have a problem with, and he didn't want to risk either of the friendships he had with the two.

His feelings felt all jumbled up inside. His brain was a mix of alphabet letters from that soup he used to eat as a kid. The letters could spell words to explain something, but instead, they simply spelled gibberish.

Connor had never considered the fact that he was bisexual before last year. When he had met, Lakewood, a lot began to change. Growing up in a family with five other siblings, Connor was used to being ignored. He wasn't focused on the attention. And while Jacey did pay attention to him, there were times where Lakewood went the extra mile to help him. Whether it was asking Connor what he would like for dinner, or offering to take him with the family on their trip to California, or giving him a ride somewhere, Lakewood always seemed to do the kind thing.

It wasn't that Jacey was someone who he didn't want to be with. In fact, he really did love her. More than anything, he wanted to be that special part of her life. But, he never really expressed that. It became this overall idea of being a mere possibility. Jacey slowly became a friend who he loved and cared for. Nothing more, and nothing less.

Lakewood was another case. He was someone who Connor had gotten to bond with over the six years he had known Jacey. He became someone Connor enjoyed seeing, and he always felt his heart skip a beat around Lakewood. Yes, he had felt this automatic romantic inclination toward Lakewood for only two years. However, he felt like Lakewood was someone he wanted to spend a lifetime with, or at least a significant part of his lifetime with.

He was certainly twitterpated with Lakewood. That word perfectly described everything Connor felt toward Lakewood. More than anything, he wanted to be able to say something to Lakewood.

Connor knew Lakewood was homosexual. Jacey didn't know, and their dad didn't know. However, Connor had seen Lakewood with one of the guys from NYU. It was one of those things where he didn't need to promise twice about not saying anything. Lakewood didn't seem particularly embarrassed either. He was simply worried that his own family would judge him, or that they would intrude in his life.

Of course, Connor had never considered coming out. The stories of bullying and harassment frightened him. There were so many people who were scared of change, and they were scared of a change to the status quo. Even now, four years after gay marriage was legalized, people still judged. Especially in New York. His dad wasn't unsupportive of gay rights, it was just that they didn't really care. Even still, Connor didn't want to risk it. He had heard too many stories about gay children being cast out of their homes.

It wasn't that Connor had simply decided to be bisexual. He never woke up one day and decided that he was going to be that way. He woke up one day and realized he liked a guy. It was just like how other people woke up and realize they liked someone of the opposite gender. The difference in gender didn't make a difference, in Connor's opinion. It was something he accepted.

However, it is hard to accept something when all your friends and parents do is talk about growing up, and him marrying the perfect girl. That happily ever after image was something Connor knew he didn't want. Yes, he could like a girl, and he did right now, but he was leaning more toward gay than straight. Lakewood was someone who exemplified what exactly he wanted in a partner.

But the fear of what people would say made Connor want to hide. He didn't want to express all of this to someone, and have the world judge him. He had heard the horrible stories of bullying when students came out as lesbian, gay, bi, or transgender. It was something that seemed impossible to change in the status quo.

Through and through, Connor felt more alone than ever. His mind was a jumble of fears and thoughts of Lakewood, and worries about Jacey. With Jacey gone, he was experiencing this emptiness that he had never expected to occur. It was something that was incredibly cold, to Connor, and made his insides freeze over with that painful ice.

Words couldn't describe the look on Lakewood's face when they told him what had happened when he got to the Manhattan police station. He made a guttural sound, and hit the wall with his right hand. His hand had caused a hole to develop in the plaster. The police tried to calm him down, but there was no way to calm down someone who was in that much grief. Eventually, he collapsed into a chair, buried his head in his lap, and cried.

Those tears were something that felt like a stab to the heart to Connor. Agent Jo had glanced at Lakewood with pity. She saw this kind of thing every day, and it was obvious that she knew exactly how the family of victims would act. Detective Reed had stood by Jo, staring at Lakewood with an expression of recognition. It was almost like Reed saw some of his old self in Lakewood.

When Jacey's dad got to the station, Connor had stood by Lakewood as Richard Adams slammed a door shut so hard the frame shook. He sat in his car, banging the steering wheel occasionally. It was a loss everyone felt. Connor couldn't get the image of Jacey being grabbed out of his head.

More than anything, Connor wanted to hear the ring of his cell phone so that Agent Jo could tell him that they caught the perpetrator, and that Jacey was coming home. He wanted to hear the sigh of relief in her voice, and the way her voice increased a half of an octave when she smiled. He wanted her to smile because Jacey was safe. But he was also scared that his phone would ring and Agent Jo would say they were too late. That they had found Jacey, but her body was coming home still. That her body would never move again because they were too late.

It was early in the morning, and all that Connor could hear out of the window was the sound of glasses clinking and the sound of rough laughter from those that roamed the alleys. He was sitting in the outstretched windowsill seat, back against one side, and his left leg outstretched so that it touched the other wall. He rested his arm on his right leg, which was bent and propped up.

The sights of Long Island from his window made it look like any other city at first. But there was a familiarity to it that made Connor feel more at peace, especially in such a hard situation. His phone was in his pocket. As much as he wanted to pull himself away from the world, his phone was the one connection he needed to have because Jacey was one of the prominent people on his mind.

Connor lived close enough to Jacey to be able to see her apartment building just a few blocks away. It seemed empty now, with barely any lights on in the windows. It seemed abandoned in the early hours of the morning.

He glanced at the second to last floor, which was the seventh one, where the Adams' lived. A light was on, and Connor thought that looked like Jacey's apartment. He imagined Lakewood sitting on the couch, unable to hold it together. After the surgery, this was something that came as a huge blow to the family. People had started leaving flowers. In Connor's opinion, flowers reminded him of a funeral.

After a moment, he slid his phone out of his pocket, glancing at the screen. What he wanted to do more than anything was call Lakewood and be able to be there for him, especially given the situation. He saw his fingers dial the familiar number, and suddenly, the phone was by his ear.

"Connor? Thank God you called."

There was a soft pause as Connor felt himself smile sadly, looking at the apartment. "How are you doing?"

"Shitty. I can't get any sleep, and I keep waiting for Agent Jo or someone to call me and tell me what the hell is going on."

"I know what you mean. But you really should get some sleep, Lakewood."

Lakewood sighed audibly. "I've tried. Just because I am twenty three does not mean that I can't have nightmares."

"I know what you mean," Connor repeated. "I haven't been able to get any sleep either."

"Maybe we could stay on the phone? Keep each other company?"

Connor nodded, and then murmured, "Yeah. Of course."

"Dad left at midnight. It's so empty here."

There was another silence. "Why don't I grab some food and come over?" Connor wasn't sure if Lakewood wanted him there, but he figured it was worth a shot.

"Yeah. I'd like that. Thanks, Connor."

"Don't worry about it. I think that nobody should be alone right now."

Lakewood paused. "Yeah. I'll see you in a bit."

"Definitely."

"Thanks, Connor. It—it means the world to me."

Connor just smiled sadly as the line clicked dead. He slid out of his seat by the window, running a hand through his hair. He grabbed his keys from his desk, yanked on a grey beanie, and slid on flip-flops. He was wearing ratty jeans and a loose University of Southern California tank top, but he didn't really care.

After leaving a note for his parents by their door, he turned to leave.

"Where are you going, Connor?"

He turned on his heel, glancing down at five year-old Annie.

"I'm going to visit a friend who's sad."

Annie tugged on the end of her pink nightie. "I want to come."

"It's really early in the morning," Connor murmured. "I'll be home later."

She glanced up at him, frowning.

"Come on, Annie, let's get you back to bed."

Annie reached up, and Connor picked her up. She slid her arms around his neck, holding on tightly. He slowly walked in to the girls' room, glancing at Brooke to make sure she was still sleeping. The ten year-old was still very much asleep, and Connor took the chance to tuck Annie in. He pulled the sheet up to her chin, kissing the top of her head.

"Good night, Annie. I'll see you later, okay?"

She nodded sleepily, curling up with her plush cat.

"Okay. Love you."

"Love you, too," she mumbled back, eyes fluttering closed. Connor glanced at his sisters with a small smile before slipping out of the room. He carefully walked to the door, managing not to wake anyone else.

As Connor stepped outside, he shivered slightly. The air was cold, and pricked Connor's skin with small drizzles of rain. He trudged to his car, sliding into the driver's seat, and rubbing his hands, blowing hot air on them.

He clicked the radio off, not wanting to be subjected to the moody songs that always were played this early in the morning. The road was relatively quiet, except for the one or two commuters who woke up this early to go to work.

There was an open-late drive thru, and Connor pulled in. He stopped his car by the menu, waiting for an employee's voice to come through the intercom-like thing by the menu.

"Hello, what would you like to order?" someone's lazy voice echoed from the intercom.

Connor glanced at the menu once more. "Two cheeseburgers, and a large fry."

"Would you like a drink with that?"

"Yeah. Two lemonades."

There was a silence. "Will that be all for you today?"

"Uh, add a side of onion rings to that."

"Okay. Your total will be eleven dollars and thirty-two cents at the first window."

Connor sighed, driving up to where a man was leaning out of the window, his hand outstretched. He placed the twenty dollar bill in the man's hand.

The cashier, whose nametag read Lee, was leaning against the wall, running a hand over the hair that didn't exist on his head.

"Here's your change. Drive up to the second window for your food."

Connor did as Lee said, and was greeted with a bag of food, and two cups. He placed the cups in the cup holders, and the bag on the seat next to him. With a nod of his head, he drove the extra block to the Adams' apartment.

Once he had parked, grabbed the bag of food, and the cups, Connor slowly got out of his car, shutting the door with his leg. He walked up to the front door, using his teeth to hold the bag as he opened the door. After the struggle, he managed to get inside. The desk where someone usually sat, like the doorman, was empty. Connor pressed the elevator button, and immediately was let in.

The elevator ride was too long, and was too full of awkward music for Connor, he was grateful when the doors slid open, revealing the familiar apartment door. He knocked quietly with the heel of his foot.

Lakewood opened the door, and smiled immediately when he was Connor. He, too, was wearing ratty jeans, as well as a NYU hoodie.

"Here, let me help," Lakewood offered, taking the cups to that Connor could come in with not as heavy of a load.

"Thanks," Connor murmured, placing the bag on the counter. He pulled it open, and Lakewood placed two paper plates by Connor.

Connor placed one burger on the plate, and the other burger on the other plate. He split the large fry between the two of them.

"It is pretty quiet here," Connor said suddenly, handing Lakewood his plate. Lakewood sighed, and nodded slowly.

"Thanks for coming over. It really does mean a lot."

Connor shrugged, trudging over to the couch and sitting down by one of the armrests. "Don't mention it."

There was a silence as Lakewood took some small bites from his burger.

"Here, let's turn on the television," Connor suggested, and Lakewood nodded, grateful.

As the television turned on, the news popped up. The lady, who looked all too perky for someone doing the four o'clock in the morning news, adjusted her papers, and began to recount the news.

"In other news, a Long Island girl was taken when visiting the World Trade Center memorial yesterday, at around five in the afternoon. An AMBER alert was sent out, and the police and FBI are asking anyone with any information to come forward. The suspect was driving a black Mercedes, with a scratch on the passenger side door. He is a Caucasian male, with green eyes. The victim is Jacey Adams, who has red hair, and hazel eyes. The anonymous tip hotline is on the bottom of this screen. Please call if you have any information."

Connor shook himself out of his reverie, changing the channel as soon as possible. He glanced at Lakewood, who was staring at the screen with such sad eyes that Connor felt his heart twist.

"I'm sorry," Connor murmured, although he didn't know if he was apologizing for not changing the channel soon, or for what had happened to Jacey, or for another reason altogether.

Lakewood placed his plate on the glass table, placing his head in his lap. "Agent Jo said that, in America, the average time it takes after the initial kidnapping for the kidnapper to kill his or her victim is three hours."

Connor was silent, biting his lip.

"It's been ten hours," Lakewood cried out, sighing. His heart twisted, biting his lip.

It took only a few moments for Connor to move by Lakewood, handing him a tissue. Lakewood took it, sitting up.

"I just can't believe that this is actually happening!" Lakewood cried out, sounding like a wounded puppy. Connor looked at the man next to him. He was twenty-three, and still looked as vulnerable as a child. His eyes were red-rimmed and full of tears that leaked from his eyes. In Connor's opinion, there was nothing more heartbreaking than the way Lakewood reacted to all of this.

"I know," Connor fought back his emotions as his lip quivered slightly. "I can't forget what I watched, and it kills me every single time I think about it."

Lakewood looked at Connor, biting his lip. "What was she wearing?" he whispered.

Connor looked at Lakewood, who was trying to form some final image of what his sister had looked like. "She was wearing her old acid-wash jeans, and a red tank top. She had on those black ratty sneakers. Her hair was pulled back in a ponytail. And she was wearing just a little bit of makeup."

"What makeup?" Lakewood's whisper cracked as he looked at Connor, looking beyond broken.

Connor closed his eyes, trying to remember. "Red eye shadow, and a thin line of eyeliner. Some mascara, and a light lip gloss." The image of Jacey before she was taken came too easily to his mind. But he didn't want to forget that. Because, even despite the attempted optimism, he knew there was a chance that that was going to his last memory of her.

"Was she wearing the necklace?"

His eyes still closed, Connor nodded. "The one with the brown necklace chain, and the key. Yeah, she was."

Lakewood buried his face in his hands. "I gave that to her when she turned ten. I told her that she needed to keep the key to her heart safe. I told her to only give it to the right person."

Connor opened his eyes, feeling a bit ashamed of the lie he had told her.

"You loved her, didn't you?"

Connor's heart skipped a beat.

"I saw the way you too interacted," Lakewood whispered wistfully. "It was like watching two people who loved each other more than anything. I couldn't believe my eyes."

"I wasn't right for her," Connor said, his voice shaking slightly. Despite his love for her, he knew that for a face. He was not the one who was man to be with her.

Lakewood looked at Connor, tilting his head. "How do you know?"

"I don't deserve her."

"You treated her like a queen. She deserved to be loved. Thank you for loving her."

Connor looked away. "She doesn't know that."

"I think she does. She told me that first year you guys were friends that she had a good feeling. She always knew."

He bowed his head, not meeting Lakewood's eyes.

"I know what you told her."

Connor froze, jaw set.

"I doubt that she believes it, Connor."

"She should. It's better for the both of us."

Lakewood sighed, placing his hand on Connor's knee. "You know, they say if you love someone, to let them go. If they come back, then it was always meant to be."

"I didn't *let* her go," Connor said, shaking slightly. "I watched her be taken."

The pain that flashed in Lakewood's eyes made Connor want to curl up and hide from the world. "She'll come back. I know she will."

"What if she doesn't?" He hadn't meant to say it out loud, but it has slipped out.

Lakewood tightened his grip absentmindedly on Connor's knee. "Don't say that. Please. I can't think about that possibility."

"It kills me, Lakewood. I feel like I could have done something."

"You couldn't have. Don't blame yourself."

"I watched it fucking happen!"

"It's not your fault, Connor," Lakewood said firmly.

Connor bit his lip, looking out the window. "I'm sorry, anyway."

"We're all sorry..."

As Connor turned to look at Lakewood, he tried to ignore the thudding of his heart. "She'll come back."

Lakewood squeezed Connor's knee one final time before letting his arm drop and rest by his side. "She will."

It was silent for a moment as they looked at each other.

"You love her a lot," Lakewood murmured suddenly. "My dream is to find someone one day who is like you. Someone who can love me like that."

Connor smiled weakly at Lakewood, wishing that he could tell Lakewood that his dream had already come true.

Chapter 19:

Splintered Reality

There's a thin veil between this world and the next.

And I was curious to see what lies on the other side.

The problem with seeing the other world…

Is that it sees you, too.

And now, I was in it.

It sees me all the time.

And it steals my memory.

Her voice brings words flooding back to my memory.

Music.

Smile.

Laugh.

Bright.

Light.

I don't know why I approached her, to be honest.

Something inside me felt like I had to listen to her beckoning me.

More than anything, I wanted to see her up close.

To see Red.

She asked me all these questions.

I wanted to tell her my name.

Cyril.

After all, she is the reason why I remember it.

I don't think she known that she is still full of color.

She asked me what I missed most.

"Red."

I said the word aloud.

She looks at me, mouth agape.

It's as if she didn't believe that I actually could talk.

I look at her, not prompting any more conversation.

I watch her as she touches her hair, slowly running her fingers through it.

I want to tell her so many things.

But my heart twists every time I try to make sound.

I think my brain is fighting my heart.

She pauses, looking at the thing in the tree.

The it.

The personality.

I want nothing more than to tell her who exactly the personality is.

She knows the personality.

I remember what the personality told me about her life.

I remember the words, and let them flow through my mind again and again.

I never want to forget anything about her.

But I can't talk.

I can't let her think I'm here to stay.

Because she can get out.

I can't.

Sister is standing next to me as I think this.

But Red doesn't even seem to notice sister.

She seems to only notice me.

This entire time, we've been sitting in silence.

Until Red tilts her head and looks at me with those colorful eyes.

She tells me, "I keep wondering what your name is."

I shrug slightly, as if it doesn't matter.

Why does she care?

She understands my body language.

"Because you're a person," she says.

I make a strange scoffing sound.

I don't really believe her.

"You...fascinate me," Red murmurs.

My eyes widen.

I look at her.

"I mean it, you know," she tells me.

I shake my head and shrug, asking why with my shrug.

"I don't really know why," she admits.

I don't look away.

"But it's true," Red says before looking away.

I pause, hearing the sincerity in her voice.

My mind has a war with my heart.

The following passing moments are the small battles that take place.

My heart wins.

"Cyril."

She looks at me like her heart has stopped.

Then, Red smiles.

I point at her.

"What?" she asks.

I point at her again.

"Oh, you want to know my name?" she smiles slightly.

I nod, sending her the smallest of smiles.

"Jacey," she tells me.

I say the word over and over again in my mind.

Jacey.

Jacey.

Jacey.

She pauses, looking at me softly.

"I'm glad I met you, Cy," she tells me.

Cy.

Jacey has given me a nick name.

Sister bits her lip, but all I do is smile like an idiot.

I nod, giving her the smallest of smiles again.

"Are you a shy person?" Jacey asks me.

I shake my head.

"So, you're extroverted?"

I shake my head.

"But you said you're not shy. So you're not an introvert."

I frown.

It speaks up for me. "Not shy. Introvert."

I watch as she glances up.

"He's introverted? But..." she trails off.

I nod at her, running my hand over the ground.

"You should talk more. I like the sound of your voice," she says.

I look up at her.

I watch as she closes her eyes, leaning against the apple tree.

My mind isn't really focusing as I slip off my jacket.

I watch my hands drape the jacket over her as she starts to fall asleep.

I don't close my eyes.

I simply look at her.

Jacey.

Jacey.

Jacey.

After a moment, I find myself smiling.

Sister rolls her eyes.

But I don't care.

Because, right now, colors are all that matter.

Right now, all I can see is her.

It's magical.

Magic.

I like the way the word sounds.

Like fireworks.

I like fireworks.

She moves slightly in her sleep.

I'm glad she has my jacket.

It'll protect her.

From the dark and dying places.

I prop myself up using my hands, leaning back.

"Jacey," I murmur.

I'm not trying to get her attention.

It's just that the word flows like music.

And, now, all I can do is smile.

"Jacey," I whisper.

And I smile.

This is hell, but it is also my new reality.

It is splintered.

And it is screwed up beyond imagining.

But, slowly, she's healing the splinters.
Slowly, my reality is becoming more and more real.
And less and less like hell.
And she is becoming my own reality.

Chapter 19:

Bridges Left Burning

Callie was sitting in the office, waiting for the paperwork to finish being signed.

Her parents were about ten feet away from her. Of course, they were in the room next to her, but she could hear their voices drift through the walls. Here, in the waiting office, she was simply waiting to be discharged. What made her smile was the fact that she wasn't going home. She was going with Justin.

There was a knock on the door, and one of the nurses entered. "They said you could have a visitor," she murmured, and Callie nodded slowly. Who could be here that would want to see her?

The person that walked into the room brought immediate tears to Callie's eyes. She slowly stood up, looking at the face that looked so much like her own. Her mouth opened and shut, but no words formed. Callie couldn't stop looking into the eyes of her twin. Her heart twisted with every passing second.

Trent's arms wrapped around her, and he pulled her close to him. She slowly pressed against him.

"I'm sorry," he murmured. "For everything. This shouldn't have happened to you."

Callie breathed in the familiar scent, which was almost like evergreen. "You came," she managed to whisper.

"They said you weren't coming home with us," Trent's voice shook. "They said that they didn't want you there."

She knew exactly who 'they' was. After a moment of silence, Callie pulled back. "I'm being discharged, and I found another place to live."

"With who?"

"One of the people here. His name is Justin."

"Is he a doctor?"

Callie shook her head.

"He's a patient?"

She nodded.

"Why, Callie?"

Callie looked up at her twin. He's the only one besides you that accepts me. He doesn't care about the voices, or anything that has to do with whatever condition I have. All he cares about is me."

"What was he diagnosed with?"

"Pyromania."

Trent cringed slightly, and Callie bit her lip. He sighed. "I'm not going to say I disapprove. You know that, Callie Cat. I would never disapprove of something that makes you happy. If he makes you happy, and he cares, and he's willing to help you, then I can't disapprove."

"He's a good guy, Trent. I swear."

Her twin smiled weakly. "Maybe I can come over for dinner sometime," he joked.

Callie laughed, and then her expression darkened. "If they even let you."

"I don't know what's going on with them, Callie. I really don't. Dad is succumbing to everything mom says. Dad wants you home, but Mom somehow convinced him that you're a danger to Cameron."

"How is Cameron?" she asked, the image of her little eight year-old brother drifting across her mind.

"He's doing okay. He asks about you a lot."

Callie glanced at the wall. "Is he here today?"

"No, they left him at one of his friend's houses. They didn't want him to see you."

She bit her lip. "Why?"

"Well, first of all, they think you're a danger to him. And they also don't want Cameron to see you because then he'll bug mom about seeing you for the next eternity."

"Remember that box in my closet? The gift-wrapped one?"

Trent paused and then nodded.

"Give that to him when mom isn't watching. Please, Trent?"

"Okay, Callie Cat. I will. I promise."

Callie smiled sadly. "I'm going to miss you, Trent. I have missed you."

Trent ran a hand through his hair. "I'm going to miss you too, sis."

"How about we meet back up on the fourth of July?"

He couldn't help but smile. "The day we turn eighteen. Yeah, I'd like that."

Callie smiled at him. "Stay strong, Trent."

"I can't without you," he whispered.

Quietly, she pecked his cheek, like she used to do when they were kids. He would run away screaming, and she would laugh. Now, all her twin could do was smile.

"I'll see you on July fourth," he vowed. "By that old ice cream parlor down the street."

Callie nodded, fighting back tears. "Of course."

There was only silence as Trent began to walk to the door.

"Goodbye," she whispered, watching the door close.

The nurse caught the door before it closed. "Come on, Miss Wells. It's time to leave."

"Everything is signed?"

"Yes. Justin was discharged about an hour ago. He should be waiting for you at the apartment."

Callie stood up, slinging her purse over her shoulder, and grasping the handle of her large suitcase. She denied the nurse's offer to help, stepping out of the door. The air of the mental hospital was cold, and stale. As Callie walked to the exit, which was just down the hall, she glanced into the window of the room next to her. Her eyes met her mother's eyes, and there was a silent moment before Callie broke the glance. She caught the heart-breaking gaze of her father, but didn't say a word. She simply kept walking.

When she got to the exit, she stopped short. That door had been the one thing holding her back for so long. For many months, she had looked at this door, hoping she would one day walk out of it.

Now that she could walk out of it, she felt like she was leaving something behind.

"Is everything alright, Miss Wells?"

Callie paused and shook her head, pushing the door open. The cold, morning breeze hit Callie, and she breathed in, smiling slightly. The cars flew past her on the street just ahead, and it felt so normal.

"This way," the nurse said, leading her to one of the company vehicles. Callie followed, and when she arrived by the side of the car, she let the nurse put her suitcase in the back. She kept her purse with her, and slid into the backseat.

As the door shut, she could see the looming building through the tinted window. She touched one finger to the glass, closing her eyes. The car revved, and she slowly buckled her seatbelt, getting ready to drive away from this place once and for all.

She dug a hand in her purse, looking for nothing in particular. Her hand came across a small paper that had been folded multiple times. Slowly, Callie retracted her hand, and unfolded the paper.

Her heart stopped slightly as she saw the familiar writing. Callie's eyes locked onto the paper as she read the words of her father.

Dearest Callie,

I hope you understand that I miss you. And I hope you know that that is indeed true. More than anything, I wish you were back at home. I miss your laugh, and your smile, and the way you played guitar. I miss everything about you. You are my only daughter, and I can't forget you. No matter what your mother does or says, I'm here for you. I always have been and I always will be. I know that you're going out there to start a life in the real world. I know that this boy you are to be staying with is quite kind, and I am happy that you have found someone like that. I hope he treats you like a queen, because you deserve it, my dear. More than anything, I wish for you to come home. Please don't think ill of me, or turn to hate me. Callie, I wish you were here more than anyone. I know that your mother is strict, and that she is scared. You must understand that I have to listen to her fears. While I do not believe they are valid, I do believe that she known what she is doing is good for her. Callie, I miss you. You were the light in my life and I don't know how to get on without you. This may sound strange, but please do not give up on playing guitar. I love the way you play and I believe that you could go far. It is something that sheds light in everyone's life and I know that you have more potential than you think. Ignore what the doctors say about your condition. You have the ability to do so much and I love you. Please, remember that loving someone can get you so far. I have no doubt in my mind that you are going to grow up and become a successful woman. And also, please don't forget about me. I still want to be there for every important moment in your life. I never want to be neglected from your life. I still want to be the one who hears the news first. I want to be the one who you can call when you are sad, and I want to be able to be the one who gives you away and walks you down the aisle. I love you, Callie. I can't stop writing that because I want that to be burned into your mind. Trent and I talk about you so often. He's a good kid, too. Please don't let either of us slip out from your life. Every day, I think about what you might be doing. I think about what you could be doing if you ere home. I imagine that you would be playing guitar for us on the couch as we all laugh and clap along. That is what I think about. I want to be able to see you, my dear. I want to be the one who sees you and hugs you and says sorry for all the horrible things you have gone through. I really hope you do know that I care. I wish I could stand up to your mother, but you know how hard that is for me. I know that I care about you, and that will always be true. Remember how we used to collect quarters? I have continued to collect them and I have even found that old 1950 one that we have been looking for forever. I also started a collection of foreign coins. It's our collection. It represents us, and the amazing relationship we have built up. I am one bridge I don't want you to burn. Please hold onto me, Callie. Please try to understand that I am going to do everything I can to make sure you come back home. I hope I can meet this boy one day, and we can talk like old times. It shouldn't be this way, and I know that. I know that for an absolute fact. Every day I tell Cameron about you, and the amazing things you have done. I tell him about how you can play guitar. I tell him about how you can write, and sing. He says that you must have a pretty voice since you're so pretty. I agree with him. Never let anyone else tell you otherwise. I have enclosed a list of my favorite quotations for you. I want you to be able to read them and feel the way I do about them. Some of them are a bit childish, and others are quite inspirational. I trust that you still have that old journal I gave you. Maybe tape this page inside there. That way, whenever you feel like giving up, you can read these. When you read them, you can think of me and I hope that will give you strength. You're a strong girl, my dear. You have the power to do almost anything. You can set your mind to be the best, and I know that you can do it. You can do anything if you set your mind to it, honestly. I believe in you. I know that your dream was to grow up and become a marine biologist. I know how much you love the ocean. As soon as I can, I plan to take you to the Great Barrier Reef. I want you to be able to achieve your dream and be motivated. And yes, I do mean to actually carry through with this. I want you to know that I will one day take you to these places. I hope that you can be homeschooled, like they said. Trust me, kids of your age are cruel. They are mean, and they are vicious. Don't listen to the horrible things they say. I know that you are better than them, for you do not pick on someone for who they are. Everyone is an individual, and they all deserve a chance to be them. Do me a favor, my dear, and try to find a way to write me back. I want to see your writing, and know that you still care for me. If you do not believe anything I have written, or said, then I hope I can one day change that. You deserve to be loved, and cared for. I plan to show you that, and to prove that to you. When you wake up in the morning, know that you are loved. And when you go to sleep at night, know that you are loved. Never forget that. Some people forget it, and that is why they end up losing themselves. They choose to give up their only life. I know that it is hard for you. But I know that it would hurt all of us if you gave up. You have such a wonderful life ahead of you, my dear. I can't wait to see the wonderful flower you grow up to be. You're a lovely blossom, and I am here to watch you grow. Maybe one day, when we meet back up, I will simply compare you to a rose. Because no flower could possibly end up being as wonderful as you. Despite everything you have gone through, you manage to push through. I write this long letter because I never want to sign it. I want to pour out everything. Yet, to everything there must be a conclusion. Everything has an ending, and as will this letter. My dear Callie, I love you. I care about you. I am your dad, and I am someone you can always turn to. Don't hesitate to call, or write back. I miss your voice, and I miss you so much.

    Love forever, Dad.

Callie ignored the tears, pulling out the attached quotations.

    Callie, here are my favorite quotations. I hope you cherish them forever.

> 愛   'It is during our darkest moments that me must focus to see the light.'
> ~Aristotle Onassis

- 愛 'Nothing is impossible. The word itself says 'I'm possible!'' ~Audrey Hepburn
- 愛 'Try to be like the turtle—at ease in your own shell.' ~Bob Copeland
- 愛 'Sometimes the questions are complicated, but the answers are simple.' ~Dr. Seuss
- 愛 'What we achieve inwardly will change outer reality.' ~Plutarch
- 愛 'Believe you can and you're already halfway there.' ~Theodore Roosevelt
- 愛 'We can't help everyone, but everyone can help someone.' ~Ronald Reagan
- 愛 'Someone's sitting in the shade today because someone planted a tree a long time ago.' ~Warren Buffet
- 愛 'It is never too late to be who you might have been.' ~George Eliot
- 愛 'There are two ways of spreading light: to be the candle or to be the mirror that reflects it.' ~Edith Wharton
- 愛 'You've got to dance like there's nobody watching, love like you'll never be hurt, sing like there's nobody listening, and live like it's heaven on earth.' ~William Purkey

愛 'Sometimes people are beautiful. Not in looks. Not in what they say. Just in what they are.' ~Markus Zusak

愛 'Things change. And friends leave. Life doesn't stop for anybody.' ~Steven Chbosky

愛 'The one you love and the one who loves you are never, ever the same person.' ~Chuck Palahniuk

愛 'The only way out of the labyrinth of suffering is to forgive.' ~John Green

愛 'Some infinities are bigger than other infinities.' ~John Green

愛 'Where there is love, there is life.' ~Mahatma Ghandi

愛 'Of all sad words in tongue or pen, the saddest are 'it might have been.'' ~John Whittier

愛 'Get busy living or get busy dying.' ~Stephen King

愛 'The flower that blooms in adversity is the rarest and most beautiful flower of all.' ~Walt Disney Company

愛 'Do I not destroy my enemies when I make them my friends?' ~Abraham Lincoln

愛 'Don't say you don't have enough time. You have exactly the same number of hours per day that were given to Helen Keller, Pasteur, Michelangelo, Mother Theresa, Leonardo da Vinci, Thomas

Jefferson, and Albert Einstein.' ~H. Jackson Brown Jr.

愛 'The unhappiest people in this world are those that care the most about what other people think.' ~C. Joybell C.

愛 'Monsters are real, and ghosts are real, too. They live inside us, and sometimes, they win.' ~Stephen King

愛 'In the name of God, stop a moment, cease your work, and look around you.' ~Leo Tolstoy

愛 'Why are you trying so hard to fit in, when you were born to stand out?' ~Oliver James

After a moment, Callie saw a tear drop onto the paper. She touched her hand to the Mandarin Chinese character for love, and smiled sadly.

Callie wiped her eyes, trying to stop the fresh flow of tears that started to come. Her dad had always been sappy, and a little bit cliché. But this was too much for Callie. She felt like her dad really did care. And the quotations just made her day so much better. She couldn't believe that she had gotten the chance to actually read such a letter. It made her feel like she was special, and as if she could do anything.

The car lurched to a stop, and Callie glanced outside, wiping her eyes. It was time to start a new life, as her dad said. She tucked everything back in her purse, stepping out of the car. The driver handed her a key with the apartment number, and placed her suitcase on the curb. Before Callie could even think about worrying, the driver sped away.

Callie slowly walked to the entrance. She pulled her suitcase behind her, glancing around at the décor. It was so wonderful. The carpet was a magnificent area rug, and the desk was made of a beautiful wood. She walked up to the silver elevators, pressing the up button.

The elevator slid open, and Callie entered. The number on the key was nine hundred and seven. She pressed the nine, the second highest floor, and leaned against one side of the elevator. She was excited to be able to start a new life, especially since it was with someone who cared.

When the doors slid open, Callie smiled. The hallway was so cozy, and decorated with this dark green paint. She walked past a few doors, and couldn't stop her racing heart as she reached number nine hundred and seven.

Rather than knock, Callie placed the key in the lock, turning it. The door clicked, and slowly, Callie opened the door.

The room she entered, which she assumed was the living room, looked so normal. She shut the door behind her quietly, placing her suitcase by the door. Callie tucked the key in her pocket, glancing around.

The walls were painted a dark blue, which she took to be royal blue. The ceilings, which reached about nine feet, had crown molding along the edges. The living room had a few pieces of black furniture, which all pointed toward a television in the front. There was a bookcase surrounding the television, and Callie smiled at that.

She walked into the open doorway to her left, which led her to the kitchen. It was a simple kitchen with a refrigerator, a dishwasher, cabinets, and a sink. She assumed that all the typical kitchen items, such as a microwave, an oven, and a stove, had been removed for safety reasons.

Callie walked out of the kitchen, and she heard the sound of footsteps. Justin sauntered into the room, wearing normal clothes. He looked up, and when he saw her, his face lit up like lights on a Christmas tree.

"Cat!" he exclaimed, quickly approaching her and wrapping his arms around her. She laughed, and hugged him back, smiling.

"Justin, this place is absolutely wonderful!"

He grinned sheepishly. "You like it?"

"I love it," she promised, smiling widely.

He pulled her close again. "I was waiting and waiting and waiting. I'm so glad you're here."

"We're finally away from them. We can live our own lives."

Justin pulled her to the couch so they could sit. "I never dreamed my homecoming would be as wonderful as this."

Callie sat by him, placing a gentle hand on his knee. "I never thought I would have a homecoming, so this is wonderful."

He grinned, ruffling his hair. "Took you long enough to get here," he joked.

"Paper-signing took way too long," she sighed. Callie pecked his cheek, and he smiled.

"Usually, they would glare at you for that. But now, we can just be us. There's no people who are watching to make sure we don't put anyone in danger."

Callie smiled. "Because I trust you."

"And I trust you," Justine murmured, tapping her on the nose.

She smiled widely, cheeks tinged red. "I don't care about the voices. Not here, and not now."

"It's not even like I need fire," Justin said after a moment. "I feel this tension, and this build-up is just too much. Fire was the only way to release it."

"Is that the only way to get rid of our tension?"

Justin ran over what the doctors had said in his mind. "Anything that releases stress. But it has to be on such a high level."

Callie touched her forehead to his, pressing her lips against his before pulling back an inch. When she talked, her lips brushed his. "Releasing stress like that?"

Justin felt his tense body push close to her. "Oh, Callie, I need you," he whispered. "That is exactly why I need you."

She smiled, and their lips brushed against his, so lightly he could have imagined it. "I need you, too."

He couldn't quite take it anymore, and he pressed his lips to hers, needing her. Callie was caught by surprise, and fell backward, her head landing on the arm rest. Justin paused, breathing heavily. He was perched above her, with a leg and arm on either side. She looked up at him, her chest rising and falling rapidly.

"Sorry," he murmured. He tried to bottle up the stress again, so he didn't lose control again.

"If it helps you, don't be sorry," Callie murmured.

Justin looked down at her, eyes wide.

"But maybe the couch isn't the place to be romantic," she commented, rubbing the back of her head.

He chuckled softly, picking her up like a bride. "Sorry, Cat."

She shrugged, pressing close to him as he walked into a room with dark purple paint. She gazed at the bookshelves, and the large bed that stood in the center of all the magnificent books. Justin carefully laid her down, smiling.

Callie noted him still standing, and she tilted her head, confused.

"I don't want to lose control, Cat. I don't know if I can stop myself."

"I trust you, Justin."

He sat on the bed and looked at her. Slowly, Callie sat as well. "I've never tried to release tension before like that."

Callie wasn't quite sure what was happening. "We're fine, though."

"You have to tell me when I lose it. When I go too far."

Her eyes widened with realization.

"I don't know why you're even letting me suggest this."

Callie paused. "Because I love you."

Justin didn't reply. He pressed his lips to hers with such passion that there need not be a reply from him.

The moments that followed that were tucked away into Callie's memories. She didn't want anyone else to know how happy he made her, and how they could be so happy. She didn't want anyone to taint those memories.

Eventually, Callie placed a hand on his chest, and slowly pulled away. Her chest was rising and falling quickly, and he was breathing harder than before. She adjusted her shirt, laying down next to him.

"Told you you'd be fine," Callie whispered. "Nothing bad happened."

"An innocent kiss," Justin agreed.
Technically, it was just that. It was just that, for the two of them, such an act meant a lot.

Callie ran a hand through his hair, and he chuckled, pulling him to her.

He murmured into her ear, wrapping his arms around her waist, "There are approximately one million, thirteen thousand, nine-hundred and thirteen words in the English language but I could never string any of them together to explain how incredible I think you are."

Chapter 21:

The Other Side of Time

Jacey's eyes slowly opened as she awoke from her short moments of peaceful sleep. When she was greeted with the same hellish sight, she panicked for a moment. Her eyes then glanced up, at the apple tree, and she sighed. Everything was still here. The air was now colder, and she looked down to see a jacket draped over her. Her eyes flickered up, meeting Cyril's eyes.

"Is this yours?" she asked, making sure she wasn't imagining things, which was extremely likely here.

He nodded, sending her a small smile.

Jacey looked at him, in his loose t-shirt and jeans. "Aren't you cold?"

Cyril shrugged, and he leaned backward, looking at her.

"Do you sleep? At all?"

He raised his hand, making a 'sort of' gesture.

"How come?"

Cyril shrugged, yet again. Jacey chuckled slightly. No one knew anything about this place, that was for sure. It was a mystery that couldn't be unfolded.

"Time doesn't really exist here, huh?"

He chuckled and nodded. For some reason, he seemed so *normal.* As if he was a normal kid, going to her school. Except for the fact that he rarely talked. And that he was stuck here.

"Do you want your jacket back?" she asked.

After a moment, Cyril shook his head, a small smile playing on his face.

Jacey sighed slightly. "You're really nice, you know."

His eyes widened, and he pointed to himself, as if to make sure she was indeed talking to him, and not someone else.

She laughed softly, eyes sparking, like fireworks. "Yes, you. It's not there's anybody else I could be talking to."

"Anybody!" it spoke suddenly, and Jacey laughed as the personality glared.

Cyril laughed softly as well, and Jacey thought to herself about what a soft laugh he had. It was gentle, and sounded like a deep version of a wind chime.

She picked up the grey apple, looking at the stain from her lips, which still remained. Slowly, she sighed, gripping the apple tightly. Cyril reached over, taking the apple from her hand. He was careful not to touch her, but the heat radiated from his hand as he took the apple.

Jacey watched as he sat back again, and glanced at her hand, which was now cold. Cyril looked at the apple, turning it over and over in his hand. She watched as he looked at the lip stain, pressing a finger against it.

"Red," he whispered, looking at the apple like his livelihood was hidden inside it.

She tightened her ponytail, looking at Cyril curiously.

"Cy, do you remember any colors?"

He looked at her sadly, and she pitied him for a moment. Cyril shook his head, his head falling.

"Do you remember rainbows?"

At the sound of the last word, he looked up at her. The word sounded so familiar, but all that came into his mind was a streak of red.

"Close your eyes," she told him, smiling slightly.

Cyril did as she instructed, trusting her.

"Okay. Remember red? Well, a rainbow starts with the color red. Then, there's a line of orange beneath it. Orange is the color of surprise. It's vibrant, and it's like red. It's the color of astonishment, and the color of absolute shock. Then there's yellow. Yellow is like a bright light. It's the color of a halo, and of brightness. Then there's green. It's the color of life. It's a subtle color that seeps into every tree, and every bush. Then there's blue. It's the color of peace. It colors the sky with its serenity. Then there's the last color. It's purple. Purple is the color of passion. It's like red and blue together. It's love, and it's calm. It is what you see when you feel passionate for something. All those lines curve, and that's a rainbow. It appears in the sky, which is—"

"Blue," Cyril finished. His eyes remained closed as he kept the rainbow there. He was afraid that if he opened his eyes, the magic would be ruined. He never wanted to forget the lovely colors.

Slowly, when he was sure the memory had been stored away forever, he opened his eyes.

When he looked at her, he was struck with colors of such great vibrancy that he inhaled sharply.

Her hair was a sharper, but calmer shade of red at the same time. It filled him with this fire that ran through the veins he didn't know still worked. Her eyes were a mix of blue and green and what he remembered to be brown. They shined, like how yellow did. They were bright. Around her was something that resembled an aura, like she was glowing. Cyril stared at her, in absolute awe of the display of colors.

Jacey noticed him staring at her, and looked at him curiously. "Everything okay?"

He nodded, smiling softly. "Yeah."

She smiled at the sound of his voice. "How come you don't talk much."

"Thinking."

It was like she was conversing with a little kid who was learning to speak, and was learning his colors. Cyril had been stuck in this place so long that he had lost touch with everything that had to do with life.

"Why don't you say what you think?" she asked, tilting her head.

He made a face, like he was surprised that people did that, and then he shrugged.

Jacey nodded, slipping on his jacket as the air became colder. Slowly, the temperature was lowering, and she couldn't do anything for either of them.

Cyril opened his mouth, as if he wanted to say something, and then shut it, shaking his head.

"Go ahead. Trust me, you can tell me anything," she said, sending him a friendly smile.

He paused, looking over at the personality, so that he didn't meet her eyes. "You're full of color."

Her eyes widened as she looked at him. "No, I'm not…"

Cyril shook his head, protesting her protest. "You are," he said firmly.

Jacey looked down at herself. What had once been black and white to her, like everything else, flashed with color. For a moment, she was bright, and she felt like herself.

"Told you," he murmured, smiling softly as he looked at her.

"You're really fascinating," Jacey murmured, shaking her head in utter confusion. "I never know what to expect from you."

His eyes widened, and he smiled slightly. "Really?"

She nodded, grateful she could hear his voice. She tried to egg on the conversation, encouraging him to keep talking. "Of course."

"You, too."

Jacey chuckled at this, and shook her head. "I wish I was special or fascinating. I'm really not. I don't really know who I am, anyway."

"You're colorful."

She paused, looking at him. "That's a start."

"You're nice."

She smiled at him, unable to fathom words for the compliments from this strange boy.

Cyril adjusted his beanie, looking out at the horizon. He paused, looking at Jacey with a strange mix of awe and wonder. He seemed to find something about her incredible, and she simply didn't understand what.

"We're going to get out of here, right?"

He paused, the awe and wonder slipping from his expression. Cyril shrugged, looking a bit sour.

"How long have you been here?"

Cyril opened his mouth to answer, and then paused, biting his lip in frustration. After a moment, he shrugged, face contorting with anger and utter frustration.

"I promise we'll get out of here."

"All for one, and one for all," he muttered.

Jacey paused. "Why are you so bitter?"

Cyril shrugged helplessly. "I'm not dead, and I'm not alive."

"Don't you want to be alive?"

He looked at her, and wanted more than anything to say yes. Instead, no answer came out.

"Look, I'm scared too. But that doesn't mean I can be bitter about it."

Cyril tilted his head. "Scared of what?"

She hung her head for a moment, fighting back the lump in her throat. "I'm scared to love. And you're scared to live. You know, that's pretty much the same thing."

"Love," Cyril mused, murmuring the word.

Jacey looked up at him, nodding. "Yeah. Love."

"My sister always said that red is the color of love."

She touched her hair absentmindedly. "It is. Wait, your sister? What is she like?"

Cyril hadn't even realized the word 'sister' has slipped out. "She's young. Seven, I think she said."

"Is she on the other side?"

It took a moment for him to shake his head.

"She's here?"

He slowly nodded, pointing to the empty space next to him.

Jacey's heart twisted with realization. He was imagining that his sister was still with him. She looked at him, sighing sadly.

"What?"

She didn't have the heart to say anything, of course. "Nothing, Cy."

He nodded after a moment, looking off into the distance.

"Do you remember love?" she asked.

Cyril paused, and then shook his head.

"I think I do. Sometimes I feel like I could remember what it felt. But every day here, however long that is, makes me lose the memory more and more."

He looked at her. "Who did you love?"

Jacey ran a hand down the tree. "He was a friend of mine. But, you know, there are people in this world who don't love us back. It wasn't meant to be between us."

"Why wouldn't he love you?"

She chuckled softly. "I'm a mess."

"I don't think so."

"That's because you don't what I've done in my life. You don't know the real me, Cy."

Cyril looked at her, eyes gentle. "Then tell me."

"Why?"

"Because I want to know."

Jacey was surprised not only at the amount of sentences he had been uttering, but also at the sincerity that filled his tone.

"You're not unlovable. The real you is great."

"No, it's not."

"Then prove me wrong. Tell me so you can prove yourself right."

Jacey looked at Cyril, whose voice was full of so much determination that it made her eyes widen slightly. "Where do I start?"

"Anywhere."

She looked at him. In most situations, she would feel awkward, and out of place. But now, all she felt was worry. What if she managed to prove him wrong? The look he gave her, which was full of care, and determination, made her heart skip a beat.

There was a small silence as she took six deep breaths.

"I'm Jacey Will Adams. My mother gave me my first name, and my father named me Will because that was his father's name. I was born in the United States, while my parents were visiting my Uncle Leroy. My parents originally lived in England. During that same trip, they got a divorce."

As the word spilled out of her mouth, Cyril seemed to burst with color. She felt emotion pouring from her words, and her veins pumped blood with new perseverance to live. Cyril nodded, encouraging her to go on.

"I moved back to England, and grew up there with my father. My mother went off and married some French boy. Every summer, I would go to the United States and spend it with my Uncle Leroy, and his wife, Katherine. The summer where I turned five was the last summer I spent with my Uncle. A month after I had returned to England, we received word that he had been working in the World Trade Center when a terrorist crashed a plane into it."

Cyril's eyes filled with sympathy, which was something he never remembered feeling. He nodded slowly, absorbing every single word that came out of her **mouth.**

"He fell into a coma, you see. His mind didn't work right. But he wasn't brain dead. My aunt reluctantly had him placed on hospice. A nurse came home with them, and spent every moment by his bedside. Slowly, his vital became worse and worse. She kept him on the ventilator. The thing is that she kept telling us he wouldn't recover. And we wouldn't believe her. Believing meant giving up hope. I didn't want to admit that my uncle was dying."

The look on Cyril's face made more words tumble out, despite the fact that the was almost in tears.

"My dad and I moved back to the United States. My brother, too, but he didn't really play an important part in Uncle's death. When I was nine, I went to visit him again. They slowly turned off the oxygen, and I watched my Uncle die."

Cyril ignored the tightness of his throat, and the way his eyes felt wet.

"My Uncle always used to tell me that I could find someone who would love me. Someone who would stay by me, like my aunt did for him. He always said that I could find love. But, even my uncle can be wrong, I discovered. When I was ten, my brother gave me this key necklace. He told me that I couldn't give the key to my heart to anyone who didn't deserve me. I wear this every fucking day, imagining that someone will arrive who will take the key."

There was a silence as Cyril blinked back what he would never admit to be tears.

"I go through school, and people think of me as a slut. I make out with guys, and I don't dress like I should. I got drunk at a party once, and almost got taken advantage of. I play volleyball, and guys watch because they like to see me in short shorts. No one respects me. No one gives a damn. I've given up on what people think of me. My own mother fucking left me."

Cyril pauses, and tentatively tilts his head.

"I don't think I'm lovable. I'm beyond saving. I simply cannot be saved. I am past the point of being able to return, Cy. If anyone said they could love me, I would laugh. It's not possible."

He paused, looking at her. "And?"

"Do you expect me to go on about how much of a bitch I am?" Jacey asked, wiping her eyes.

Cyril shook his head. "No. I'm asking you, how does that matter?"

"It's my life! I fucking screwed it up!"

He shook his head again.

"Stop shaking your head. Don't try and lie to me and tell me all of that's okay."

"We all have ups and downs in our lives. I know it. When you talk, you helped me remember my own life. It's pretty fucked up, too. I'm not who I am, if that makes sense. But I know that maybe, if I find a reason to live, I can be myself. If you find a reason to love, maybe you can find yourself, too."

Jacey looked at him, her eyes brimming with salty tears. "Love has given up on me, Cy."

"Don't say that. It's not true."

"How do you know that?"

"Because I can see the real you poking through. I know that you have made mistakes, but that doesn't mean that you are a mistake. One mistake doesn't mean the person is a mistake. We're humans. We make errors. I've made errors, and you've made errors. It's okay. Because there will always be something that encourages us to keep going."

Jacey realized that was the most words she had ever heard him speak. "Then how did you keep going? How *do* you keep going?"

"I didn't turn into a reflection because I had my sister. She helped me keep a small part of myself. Without her, I would have immediately given up. It would have been impossible for me to keep going."

"But I don't have anyone!"

Cyril ran a hand over the ground. "You have to find them."

"You think I can?"

"I know you can."

There was a small silence. It was fragile, as if the wrong word could shatter everything they held dear. "How do you know?"

He had the words, but he couldn't utter them. No, he couldn't because then she would know what he was hiding, and then he would ruin everything for sure. So he just shrugged helplessly. "I just know, Jacey. I just know."

"I wish I knew, too..."

Cyril looked up at her, eyes full of sympathy. "I promise you that you will find someone who cares. Someone who can and will love you."

Jacey wished she could protest, but the certainty in his voice was almost overwhelming.

"Shit happens in life. And it's hard to get over it, but we eventually have to. Your uncle would want you to trust people. He would want you to find someone that could make you happy. I know he would. And don't ask me why or how I know. It's one of those things that I just know."

"But...I'm broken."

Cyril chuckled weakly. "We're all broken, Jacey."

She quirked a sad smile at what seemed like a nick name.

"We're a lot like glass, you know."

"How?"

"You see, glass is breakable. We are, too. Glass is sometimes clear, or obscure, or cracked. When you hold it up to the light, you see the good, and you see the bad. When we find our light, they see the good and the bad. But they call us a work of art anyway because they care. Sometimes, we have to take our own risks. Even if it means possibly breaking. Because even breaking is worth the risk."

"The risk of what?"

"Loving."

"Why are you wasting so many beautiful words on me?"

Cyril paused. "I haven't talked in a while. You gave me a reason to talk. You gave me a reason to say words, and to do what everyone else does."

Jacey smiled slightly, eyes still wet. "It's only because I'm alive."

He shrugged. "I didn't think I was alive. And if I was alive, I told myself I didn't want to be alive. Being alive meant being hurt. I didn't want to be hurt. When you arrived here, I felt like there might be a reason to live. I really can't explain it. It was like…electricity."

"Electricity?"

"It was like something sparked inside me. I simply knew that there was a reason to live. I began to remember my life, and details about myself. Every time I look at you, I remember something new."

Jacey's eyes widened. "It's the same thing with me. When I look at you, I find myself not slipping away. I think that giving up may not be the best, and I slowly stop myself from thinking like that. I don't understand it, but I am grateful for it. More than anything, I want to always remember the feeling that I shouldn't give up. I haven't felt like that for a while. I don't really want there to be an explanation for that, though. It ruins the magic."

"The magic," Cyril repeated, agreeing. He tilted his head. "I didn't think I could make anyone feel alive when I feel so dead."

"You make me never want to die. I don't know why. The contrast between this hell and you is so great. I look around, and I am overcome with depression. But when I look at you, I feel alive. I feel this happiness inside me soar. I wish that I could identify what exactly it is. Because it is happiness, but there's another name for it."

"I know what you mean," Cyril agreed. "It's a strong emotion. But I have never felt it before, so I can't identify it either."

Jacey sighed slightly, looking up. "It's like you were meant to be here."

"Meant to?"

"Not as in you were meant to be sent to hell. I mean, I think you were supposed to be here. Because you saved me. You came here, and you saved a life. You saved me from the dark and dying places."

Cyril tilted his head. "I thought you were the one that saved me."

"We saved each other," she murmured, looking around slowly and quietly,"

He chuckled weakly, nodding. "I've never had a legitimate friend, you know."

"Really?"

"People liked me for my soccer skills, or for other reasons."

Jacey extended her index finger. "I promise to be the first then."

"I thought it was pinky promise," he laughed.

She shrugged, just realizing that as well. "It'll be how we promise."

Cyril hooked his index finger on hers, and smiled slightly. "I promise that love has not given up on you."

"I promise to be the first friend you've had, and to give you a reason to live."

The two looked at each other, reluctantly retracting their fingers from each others'.

"I've had a lot of people promise me things, and they had such good intentions. I doubted them immediately. I never really wanted to trust them. But, when you tell me this, I don't want to doubt you, even though that is my first instinct. I want to believe the sincerity in your voice, and I want every word you say to be true."

"Then it's your lucky day," Cyril grinned. "Because what you want is now a reality."

Chapter 22:

Breathe in the Darkness

Connor slowly opened his eyes. He squinted, unable to see anything in the darkness that surrounded him. He sat up, rubbing his eyes, trying to have his vision adjust to the pitch-blackness.

"What time is it?" someone murmured, and Connor jumped. He glanced at the small digital clock to his left, the only light he could see.

"Nine o'clock at night," Connor mumbled. He paused before jerking, sitting up straight. "Fuck!"

Lakewood opened one eye, and then the other, sitting up. "Check the phones."

Connor glanced at his phone, and noted the three missed calls. Grateful there was a voicemail, he opened it, cursing himself for sleeping.

"Connor, this is Agent Jo. You should come down to the police station when you get a chance. There's been some developments in the case."

That was all there was to the voicemail. He almost dropped the phone, catching it before anything bad happened, such as the phone splintering.

"Did you get the message from Agent Jo, too?" Lakewood called from across the house.

"Yeah. Let's go. I'll drive."

Lakewood stumbled out in flip-flops, eyes wide. "Yeah."

Connor cursed himself and his stupidity for falling asleep the entire way down the steps, and the entire way to the car.

"Come on," Lakewood mumbled to himself, murmuring a short prayer after that.

The doors flew open as the two boys clambered in. The car revved as Connor twisted the key. Seatbelts were merely an afterthought as the car drove off.

It was completely silent the entire drive to Manhattan. Both were too worried to even voice what they were thinking.

When the station came into view, Connor yanked the key out, and they both jumped out of the car. Lakewood walked quickly ahead of Connor, turning and entering the station. They both walked into the conference room, met by the eyes of Reed and Jo.

"Where have you two been?" Agent Jo asked, placing her hand on the desk with a loud slap.

Connor rubbed the back of his neck. "Never mind that. What's going on?"

"We found the car."

Lakewood paused. "Well? Who was in it?"

Agent Jo looked at Detective Reed. "We're doing lab tests, so we're not quite sure."

"Lab tests for what?" Connor asked warily, raising an eyebrow.

"Ashes."

Lakewood hit the desk, bowing his head. "When do the lab results come back?" His voice sounded pained.

"They should be in within the hour."

Connor bit his lip. "It might not be her, right?"

"It might not," Reed agreed. "But please don't deny the likelihood of it being her."

Lakewood sank into a chair, and Agent Jo paused, looking at the boy. There was silence in the room for a few moments as Connor and Lakewood digested the information.

"What happened exactly?" Connor croaked, voice sounding tired and dead.

Reed touched Jo's arm, saying he would explain. "About nine hours ago, we discovered the car abandoned on the side of the freeway. We assume that the perpetrator ditched the car since many tips were coming in on its location."

"So no one saw him?"

"We assume he got picked up from someone on the freeway. We got one tip about it being a grey truck, but we can't verify anything. We also can't send out any more reports or ask for more tips when there is the likelihood that this case is mostly over."

Lakewood inhaled sharply, gripping the edge of the table.

"It is not guaranteed, though. That is something you must remember. We don't know what cards we have been dealt, sir. It could be anyone. Or it could be her."

Connor glanced sideways. He didn't really want to think about it.

The door slowly opened, and a man walked in, carrying a stapled stack of papers. "Jo, the lab results came in about a minute ago."

Connor and Lakewood both looked at the paper that held the truth about whether or now Jacey was ash or not.

"What did it say?"

"The ashes belong to a girl," the guys said, reading the front page, and Connor felt his heart twist. "Some girl named Sally Yearling."

Connor's eyes widened as Lakewood exhaled loudly. Yes, he was happy that it wasn't Jacey. But it was possible that the nice girl from the drugstore might be the one who was now in ashes.

"Is there a picture on the report?" Connor asked.

The officer nodded, flipping to the third page. The old photo of Sally made Connor's heart skip a beat. He sat down in a chair, placing his head in his hands. The fact that someone so lovable and so happy could die so easily made Connor want to scream. Why did people get taken away from life so quickly?

"Well, we'll set up a new AMBER alert, if we can, since the car has been found. I would assume this means Jacey is still alive, so we are going to continue the investigation with that thought in mind."

Lakewood nodded, sounding relieved as he asked, "What was the tip about the grey truck?"

"Someone called in a while ago," Agent Jo told them. "It was that a man and a girl were seen getting into a grey car near the area where the black car was left. It could be Jacey and the man who took her. We're going to assume that, since that is the best lead we have."

Connor nodded. "Okay."

Detective Reed glanced at the pair. "Do us a favor and try to increase the volume of your ringtone so we can give you timely updates."

Lakewood glanced down sheepishly. "Yeah. Sorry about that." His heart felt lighter. A minute ago, he was sure he was going to hear the worst news he had ever heard. But, he had been spared.

A phone vibrated, and Lakewood's eyes widened. "I'll be back. I should take this." He slid out of his chair, pressing the phone to his ear.

"What's going on, Lakewood?" Richard's voice was tight and strained.

"They found the car on the side of the freeway. There were ashes inside, but they belong to a different girl. Someone called in an anonymous tip saying they saw a man and a girl getting into a grey car near where the black one was left, so it is possible that was Jacey and the man who took her."

Richard was breathing heavily and audibly. Lakewood held the phone slightly away from his ear. "Anything else?" his dad asked.

"No. Where are you?"

"A hotel in Manhattan."

Lakewood frowned and paused. He dreaded the answer, but he asked the question anyway. "Why?"

"I left last night and...I went to a bar."

"You?" Disbelief filled Lakewood's voice.

"I basically had drunk myself into a stupor. So, I crashed at a hotel."

Lakewood shook his head. "Why? You never drink."

"I couldn't stop thinking! I needed to forget about it for a moment, and get away from my myriad of nightmares."

"Your daughter has been kidnapped! You can't fucking drink that away."

Richard sighed. "I didn't know what else to do."

"Try and help. You could have aided the investigation, or called, or tried to get updates."

"I didn't want to know…"

Lakewood groaned in frustration. "Dad, don't bail on her now. You told her after her surgery that you would try and change. She's gone for now, but that does not give you an excuse to break your promise to her. You have no right to go and escape your life through alcohol.

Richard sounded pathetic as he replied, "Why not?"

"Cause then you are no better than Mum!"

The shock Richard felt filled the silence. They both knew the disappointment Mum had caused, and the havoc she had wrecked. She had simply up and abandoned them. But, Lakewood needed to get his point across. He needed his dad to understand that this was not the way to deal with any problem.

"Dad?" Lakewood's voice was firm but quiet as he made sure his father was still on the line.

"I'm sorry. I don't know what I was thinking, Lakewood."

"Come home, dad. At least get some sleep to get rid of your hangover. Then you can come down to the station and help out?"

Lakewood's dad was almost like a small child. He broke promises, and acted completely irrationally. It was hard, but sometimes, they managed to have a good family dynamic.

"Okay?" Lakewood asked.

Richard sighed. "Okay."

"Call me when you wake up, okay?"

"Okay. Bye, Lakewood. And...sorry."

"Just stop apologizing, dad. Please. Jay and I have heard too many apologies."

Lakewood hung up the phone, shoving it into his pocket. He leaned on the railing, bowing his head slightly. The air was calm, and the cold breeze kept him awake. When he shut his eyes, all he could see was Jacey. She had so much potential, and he didn't understand why she constantly threw that away.

But, even with Jacey and how complicated she could be, Lakewood confused himself. He wasn't sure exactly what was going on in his mind one hundred percent of the time, and that could be quite risky. As Lakewood had discovered, it led to things like your best friend's sister seeing you with a guy.

Lakewood wanted to crush that memory. He hated how the status quo made him feel ashamed that he was gay. It was something that made him want to hide from the world so he was never judged. And now, Connor knew. Apparently, given the lack of rumors, Connor had kept the secret, and he was okay with it, which was something Lakewood appreciated.

Lakewood just wanted to be able to tell his dad. He wanted his dad to understand him, as impossible as that sounded for their family. It was one of those things where they simply had a complicated relationship. His dad had minored in psychology, and Lakewood often doubted this because of the lack of social skills his father had.

Perhaps it was because of the fact that a kid in his college had been beaten, stripped, and tied to the flagpole for being gay. Although that type of hate crime was rare, it made Lakewood fear any form of telling anyone, even his sister.

"You okay?"

Lakewood jumped, turning to glance at Connor. "Oh. Yeah. Just thinking."

Connor leaned on the railing, standing next to Lakewood. "About what?"

"Life," the older boy chuckled weakly.

Connor laughed slightly. "I've been doing that a lot lately, too."

There was a silence before Lakewood asked, "Do you ever feel like people would hate you if they knew your deepest secret?"

"Yes," Connor said quickly. He sighed, and then nodded. "Too often."

"Why? You have that whole group of friends and everything."

"Some people have this image of me. I feel like my secret taints the way they see me, even if I don't think it's a bad thing."

Lakewood nodded slowly.

"Do you ever feel like that?"

"Yeah. All too often," Lakewood sighed. "Every fucking day is a new struggle."

Connor thought he knew what Lakewood was talking about, but he remained silent.

"I hate it."

The younger boy's voice was gentle, and kind. "Have you ever considered coming out?"

"Yes," Lakewood answered. "And no. That kid was who was tied to the flagpole was one of my old friends. The one who was in the news?"

Connor nodded slowly. He remembered that. It had been a hate crime at NYU against those who were LGBT.

"I can't tell anyone. No one can know."

"I know."

Lakewood paused. "But you're trustworthy and..." He trailed off.

"There are other people out there who need to learn to accept you. I accepted you, did I not? It has nothing to do with me being trustworthy, Lakewood."

"But what if they don't accept me?"

"Then it's there loss."

The older boy frowned. "Do you know what's it like? To care about someone and fear telling that person because society may judge you to hell?"

Connor knew that the answer was yes. And, rather than lie, he murmured, "Yes."

Lakewood looked taken aback. "Really?"

"Yeah."

There was a silence before Lakewood asked, "What did you do?"

"I didn't do anything. I regret that."

"Really?"

"Regretting something is one of the worst things that has even happened in my life, to be honest."

Lakewood nodded slowly. "I guess you're right. Regrets do suck."

Connor nodded as well, looking at Lakewood. "At least tell your dad."

"I know I should. It's just hard. What if he throws me out?"

"Your dad wouldn't do that. You know him. Come on, Lakewood. I think you'll be glad you did it."

Lakewood sighed. "It sucks because I know you're right."

Connor grinned. "Exactly. Come on, let's go see what we can do for the investigation."

"Hold up...what's you secret?"

There was only silence from the younger boy.

"Come on, Connor."

Connor cleared his throat. "I'm scared to tell people that I like someone."

"Who? Oh, Jacey?"

He shook his head. "If only it was that easy."

CHAPTER 23:

CROOKED HALO

Callie finished zipping up her jeans and walked out of her closet. Her hair was wet, and fell down her back, leaving wet stains on the back of her loose shirt. She walked through their apartment, heading to the kitchen.

"Hungry?" Justin asked, turning around from where he was by the sink.

She raised an eyebrow, smiling. "You cooked?"

"I tried," Justin corrected her, laughing softly. "I made fruit salad."

Callie grinned at him, kissing his cheek. "Sounds great. Thanks."

He slid the bowl in front of her as she sat down. "How'd you sleep?"

"Good, of course." She took a bite of some yellow melon, smiling at the amazing taste. "Canary melon? Nice touch."

Justin sat down across from her, shrugging. "I tried."

She took a bite of watermelon, and set her fork down, chewing slowly.

"You okay?"

"Yeah. Just, not incredibly hungry. It's really good, though."

Justin cast her a worried gaze, running a hand through his hair. "Everything okay?" he repeated.

Callie nodded. "You know how hard it is."

"I know, Cat. I'm sorry."

She paused, taking a bite of honeydew, and giving him a small smile.

Justin smiled, plucking an orange slice from her bowl. He placed the entire thing in his mouth, and after a moment of concentration, he smiled at her. The peel covered his teeth. Callie laughed, sticking her tongue out at him playfully.

"How handsome," she teased. He raised a brow.

"I know you're ticklish," Justin warned.

Callie shrieked, running from the chair. Justin followed suit, managing to grab her by the waist. She curled up, sliding to the floor, and he pinned her to the carpet. One hand held each arm, and he straddled her so she couldn't kick.

"No fair," she pouted. "But you can't tickle me anyways. You're using both your hands!"

Justin nodded at this realization. "I can't tickle you," he agreed.

"Then let me up!" she laughed and tried to get up, failing miserably.

He leaned in, brushing his lips against hers. "Still want to get up?" he teased.

Callie thought for a moment, and then nodded.

Justin mock-pouted as he let her up. When she sat up, Callie tackled him, straddling him so that he couldn't sit up.

"Ha!" she declared victoriously.

Justin gripped her waist, pulling her close and then trying to pin her down again.

"Hey!" she giggled, fighting. The two ended up facing each other, lying on their sides. Callie brushed the wet hair out of her face, laughing softly.

"You're quite strong," Justin commented, chuckling. "I'm impressed."

She smiled proudly. "I got used to this. Trent always tried to tickle me. I always managed to just barely evade him."

"Well, then, I still am impressed."

Callie rolled her eyes, propping herself up with one elbow. "You made me tired and sweaty. I just took a shower!"

"Oops," Justin grinned guiltily. "My bad."

She laughed. "What do you want to do today? I mean, I don't have to figure out schooling until next week."

He grinned mischievously. "Indeed, there is the imminent question of what we should do. What would you like to do?"

"Shower," Callie giggled, and then shook her head. "I don't know. Did you have something in mind?"

Justin shrugged. "Did I have something in mind? I can't remember if I did or not, actually."

"Oh, stop it, you," Callie teased, pushing his shoulder.

"Stop what?" he feigned innocence, and then broke out in laughter.

Callie looked at him.

"Okay. So I was considering going miniature-golfing, and watching a movie. Typical cliché dates."

She smiled widely. "That sounds really fun."

"Really?"

"Yeah!"

"I'm glad you like the ideas," Justin said, propping himself up on his elbow as well.

"Why wouldn't I? I don't usually go on dates at all, to be honest. On the weekends, I usually stay home or go out and do something with Trent."

Justin grinned. "Well, that's all about to change, Miss Wells."

Callie smiled. "I can't wait. Just let me dry my hair."

"Of course," he chuckled.

When all was said and done, Callie came out, hair tied up in a ponytail.

"Oh, Cat, you got a voicemail," Justin called from the couch, gesturing to the phone that was on their bedside table.

Callie frowned slightly, taking the phone. She sat on her bed, and pressed the phone to her ear once she had dialed.

"Hey, Callie, it's Connor. I assume you remember me. I know you were Jacey's friend, and I wanted you to know that, uhm, Jacey is gone. She was kidnapped two days ago. I just figured you deserved to know. If you have any questions, you can call me. Sorry."

Callie's lip quivered, and the phone went crashing to the floor.

"Cat, is everything okay?" Justin called.

When she was unable to respond, he quickly got up, and peered into the room. His footsteps got louder as he padded over to her, wrapping an arm around her.

"What happened, Cat?" He looked down at her, eyes filling with concern.

She buried her head in his chest, and let out a cry of agony. Justin was surprised at first, but then wrapped his other arm around her, gently rubbing her back.

"Cat, everything's okay," he coaxed.

Callie sniffed and cried in mental agony. "No, it's not!"

Justin used one hand to cup her chin, bringing her eyes to meet his. "Cat, what's going on? I can't help unless I know..."

She gripped his shirt with one hand, trying to stay steady. "Remember that friend I told you about? Jacey?" In between each of her words, she took a small, quick breath.

"Yes," Justin murmured.

"Her friend called to let me know that she was...she was..."

Justin gently rubbed her back. "She was what?"

"Kidnapped!" Callie wailed, pressing her face into his shirt again, as if trying to get away from the world.

"Wait, she was kidnapped?" Justin murmured, eyes reflecting the shock and horror that he was feeling.

Callie nodded, shutting her eyes tightly, as if that allowed her to escape from reality.

Justin sighed, holding her closely.

She pulled back, wiping her eyes. "I need to help."

"What can you do? Cat, it's best if you leave this to the police."

Callie shook her head. "No. The police didn't do anything for me, and they can't do anything for her."

"There's a difference between what they can do for you and what they can do for her."

She frowned, sniffling. "What do you mean?"

"A kidnapping and an illness are different."

"I'm not ill."

Justin shrugged. "I'm ill. I know that."

"I'm not ill."

"Cat, it's okay."

She looked at him, jaw set defensively.

"Cat, it doesn't make a difference to me whether or not you are ill."

Callie didn't say a word. She simply glared at him, eyes narrowed.

"Cat, come on."

"What?" she sniffled and then went back to glaring.

Justin ran a hand through his hair. "Why are you mad?"

"I'm just frustrated. I need to go out there."

"You'll just put yourself in danger."

Callie frowned again. "And?"

"I'm not going to let you get hurt, Cat. I refuse to watch you put yourself in danger."

"I put myself in danger by choosing to live with you."

The air grew cold as she said that, and the look in Justin's eyes turned from worry to something completely new altogether. It looked like hurt and utter pain. As Callie looked at him, she glanced down guiltily.

"I didn't mean it like that," she murmured.

Justin's arms retracted from her. "There was no other way you could mean that."

Callie bit her lip, and glanced down, and then back up at him. "Justin, you know I didn't mean that."

He sighed, eyes still looking pained. "I wish I could believe you."

"Why can't you?"

"Because no one says something like that and doesn't mean it."

Callie reached over to touch his hand, and he slowly pulled it away. It looked like the very action caused him an immense amount of pain.

"I'm trying so hard for you, Callie."

She winced at the sound of her first name instead of her middle name, like he usually called her. "I know. I really appreciate it."

"I guess I understand why your parents sent you away now."

Callie bit her lip and she tasted a drop of blood. "What?" her voice came out as a cracked whisper.

"You don't understand what people do for you. You build them up, and tear them down."

"Justin, no, please..." The words he uttered made her feel worthless, and pathetic. She shook her head, eyes brimming with tears.

Justin glanced away. "I thought this would work. I thought you cared about me like I cared about you." His eyes glinted with tears, but he tried his best to ignore them.

"I do care. Justin, I really do. I swear," she murmured, voice unwillingly cracking at the end.

"I can't tell what the truth is and what it isn't with you anymore. I really wish we could have just had our happily ever after. But you seem to be fighting against it."

Callie shook her head. "I'm not fighting against it, Justin."

He stood up. "I don't know what you're fucking doing here."

"Justin, don't do this. Please."

"I can't believe you," he said, voice tinged with hurt and disgust.

"I care! Don't you dare question that," Callie's voice was slowly rising as she looked at him.

Justin turned to look at her. "Really? You do? I trusted you to be able to be there for me, Callie!" His voice rose at the end, until he was almost yelling.

"If I didn't care, I wouldn't have moved in!"

"Oh, but it was a danger to move in with me," he rolled his eyes, voice dripping with sarcasm.

Callie balled her fists. "I moved in because I cared about you enough! Don't twist my words."

"That was exactly what you said!" Justin yelled, heart twisting as she cringed at his loud voice.

"I could have gone anywhere! I could be back with my family instead of here!"

"Your family didn't want you! This was the only place you could go!"

Callie opened her mouth to yell back, but no words could form because the pain was simply too great. She shut her eyes, walking past him.

"Where do you think you're going?" he called, frustrated beyond belief.

"Do you even fucking care?" she snapped, turning on her heel. Tears were streaming down Callie's face, and Justin wished he could stop them. But this had snowballed into something bigger than either of them.

Justin sighed, slamming his hand on a wall. "Yes! Yes, I care! I have always cared, Callie."

"Do you hear yourself? You say these cruel words to me, about my family not wanting me and me being ill, and you expect me to believe you!"

"Those don't matter! Everything that's wrong with you is something that makes you wonderful."

Callie shook her head, biting her lip. "You don't understand." Her voice grew quiet, and Justin stepped forward.

"Then make me understand!" He took her hand, and placed it directly over her heart. "My heart beats for you, Callie. Make me understand!"

She looked down, unable to meet his eyes as she felt his heart beat. "I'm broken. I'm the toy the kid falls in love with at the store, and then discards later because I'm useless."

"I hate it when you say that," Justin frowned, letting her hand fall.

"Why? Because the truth hurts? You said it yourself, Justin. My family doesn't want me."

Justin shook his head. "Don't let that hurt you, Callie."

"Why not?"

"Because, yes, your family is supposed to love you. They're the ones who are supposed to nurture you, and watch you grow up, and shower you with love."

Callie bit her lip. "And?"

"Maybe you don't need your family for that love and support."

She tilted her head at him. "I don't think you understand. I have watched people leave me every single day of my life. People who were scared, or people like my mother who were ashamed. The voices tell me that I'm worthless, and every single time I believe them. They tell me I should be giving up, and I can't help but nod my head and try to give up. I don't want to give up, but they're right. I'm worthless."

"What makes you think you're worthless?" Justin asked, voice gentle despite the pain that still glimmered in his eyes.

"I can't do anything. I tear apart my family, and I'm not there for my friends when they need me. I tear apart relationships, and I'm screwed up. I'm so broken and worthless that my parents sent me to mental hospital. I'm so worthless that they discharged me, but refused to take me back. If I had worth, they would have taken me back!"

"Maybe they didn't deserve someone as wonderful as you with them," Justin suggested.

Callie bit her lip. "I just wanted my mother to tell me she loved me. I wanted to know that someone loved me. Every day, my mother weighed me and gave me medicine. She never really cared or loved me."

"That's all you wanted?" he asked, tilting his head to the side.

She nodded. "Of course."

"I love you."

Callie inhaled sharply, taking a step back. She opened her mouth to say something, and when words failed her, she ran out of the door, tears beginning to fall. The door slammed shut, and Justin stared after it, wondering how the right words could feel so wrong.

CHAPTER 24:

THE REST IS SILENCE

She smiles at me.

I like her smile.

It's something that simply makes her colors grow more vibrant.

I didn't plan on talking.

And now she has me spilling out paragraphs.

But that's okay.

It's worth it.

"I wonder what you were like on the other side," *she tells me.*

"Why is that important?"

Jacey shrugs. "I don't know if it is. It's just what floated into my mind."

"What else floats through your mind?"

I watch as she thinks.

The look on her face is almost embarrassment.

Another emotion.

I smile proudly.

I almost feel normal around her.

Like I could say anything.

Usually, I just thought what I wanted to say.

But I never said it.

She had this strange effect on me.

But that was okay.

Because it left me with a light feeling.

"Things about you," *she finally answers.*

Now it's my turn to feel embarrassed.

But I smiled widely despite myself.

I can't help it.

Her hair gleams red in the nonexistent sunlight.

"Me? Why would you think about me?"

I smile to myself, propping one leg up.

I feel so at ease.

It's the first time I have felt like I belonged here.

Maybe she was right.

Maybe we were meant to be here.

To fix each other.

I never had thought of myself as broken.

Especially now that I'm around her.

I'm healing.

"Why wouldn't I?" *she shrugs.*

"I'm not that interesting."

A small smile slips onto my face.

I'm developing my old personality.

I feel more like myself than ever.

She tries to avoid my gaze.

I can tell.

But she doesn't manage it.

"What's that?"

I look at her outstretched hand, which is pointing at me.

My eyes trace her hand to the small sliver of a red band around my neck.

My heart stops.

Memories come flooding back to fast.

I want to shut my eyes.

I want the memories to stop.

It's my old life.

But I don't want to remember it.

I see the flash of a gun.
I touch my shoulder.
It burns with more pain than I have ever felt.
I glance at Sister.
I hear myself cry out her name in the memory.
Christabelle.
Chrissie.
Chrissie.
But, I can't do anything about it now.
I slowly try and calm my breathing.
My eyes flicker to hers.
She's perched on her heels, as if ready to run to me and help me.
"It's a memory. And old scar."
No, it's not my literal scar.
No one can see that.
It's the scar that tore through my old life.
It's unbearable.
"You can tell me."
Her whisper shatters the fragile wall of secrets I have built up.
I watch the secrets come tumbling down.
Part of me wants to collect as many as possible.
And run.
But I can't run from her.
It's wrong.
And I would regret it.
I just know I would regret it.
There's no other way to explain it.
"I can?"
I don't know why I question her.

I guess no one has wanted to hear my secrets.

They left me alone.

And, now, I realize that I am tired of feeling so alone behind my wall of secrets.

Jacey nods, and at that nod, I exhale.

It feels nice to breathe freely, I note.

"It's what happened before I came over."

She looks at me, intently listening.

I see her glance, and I have no choice but to continue.

I want to continue.

It's an urge I cannot deny.

"I played soccer in my old life."

"And, I ended up winning this state tournament."

"My parents took me out for dinner."

"With sister."

"Right before dessert, we were interrupted."

"He entered with a gun."

"We couldn't do anything about it."

"All we could do was scream."

"Chrissie was hit by a bullet."

"I watched her die."

"I watched my sister die."

"And then I ran."

"But he followed me."

"I was in the bathroom."

"Just as I leaned against the mirror, he shot me."

"All I can remember is pain."

"And all I could hear was my sister's screams."

"It replayed in my mind."

"I can't forget it."

"It's my fault."

"It's all my fault."

I look away.

I hope she didn't see the tears.

Sister, Chrissie, looks down at me.

It's a mix of pain and pride.

Jacey is silent.

I hope she understands.

I need her to.

Slowly, her hand reaches out.

I should pull back.

But I don't.

I let her hand touch mine.

She looks at me.

She doesn't have to say a word.

Her look says it all.

I glance at her hand.

It covers mine.

Like a puzzle piece.

We both fit each other.

I don't voice that thought.

There are some things that can't be said.

I glance at her.

Jacey's eyes flicker to meet mine.

I want to say something.

But it will shatter the silence.

It will shatter the magic.

I look at her hand.

It feels warm.

Heat radiates off of it.
I feel something rise inside of me.
I want to scream it to the world.
But I don't.
Because I know that this is something special.
This is a moment I will never forget.
The corner of my lips curve upward.
It's more than a smile.
It holds so much more than that.
My heart is beating loudly.
I don't think I've ever felt more alive.
I don't think I've ever wanted to be alive more than right now.
Sister fades into the background.
I don't need her.
Not here.
Not now.
I need Jacey.
I meet her eyes once again.
And, despite the lack of words, she understands.
She understands all of me.

May
2016

Chapter 25:

Search for the Beginning

If Connor said that he loved Jacey, it would be a lie, but saying that he didn't would also be telling a lie. To be honest, he had no idea what he felt towards Jacey.

Yes, she was still on his mind despite the fact that she had been missing for three months. 'Presumed dead' is what the authorities said. But Connor didn't want to presume anything. He wanted to have some hope. Hope was the only thing that was keeping him in one piece as opposed to shattering him into a million shards of hopelessness.

He sat on the roof of Jacey's apartment building, staring out at Long Island like they used to do. It hurt, but he felt as if he deserved it. It was his penance for not being able to rescue her. Not that it was actually his fault. But since the police had failed, he, in turn, had failed as well.

It nearly killed him to see how Richard had ended up. Since they had told him Jacey was presumed dead, he had spiraled into a void that Connor wasn't sure if he could recover from. He ended up at more bars than he had ever been to before the incident, and he often was drunk at home. No one could stop him from constantly jumping into his drunken reverie. Richard rarely went to work. In fact, he simply was given a leave of absence.

Lakewood was still in college, and that was pretty much all he did nowadays. Coming out was no longer important. Everyone was too upset over the mystery behind Jacey's presumed death. He didn't really go out anymore. College and home became his new world. He seemed unable to heal. Usually, they encourage people to move on. But there was simply no closure. The lack of closure made it impossible for anyone to forget, forgive, and move on.

Even Connor had slowly shrunk away from his old life. He still hung around his old group of misfit friends, but things were a bit different. He was more distant from them. They didn't know him like Jacey did, and they couldn't really tell between the old Connor and who he was now, given that he had tried to put a façade up. His grades were relatively stable, given that he studied in his free time.

He glanced up at the first star he saw, closing his eyes.

"Starlight, star bright, first star I see tonight, I wish I may, I wish I might, have the wish I wish tonight."

Connor's voice was nothing more than a whisper as he wished.

"I wish that—"

He wanted to wish that he would see Jacey again. But part of him felt selfish for wishing such a thing.

"I wish that Jacey would find the love that she so rightfully deserves."

With all of his heart, he knew that the love he felt for her was not worthy of her. She deserved someone who only cared for her. Since he cared for both her and Lakewood, it was too risky.

He sighed, glancing up at the star, which seemed to be gleaming brightly. It was one of those things where magic seemed to be real. Connor glanced down, at the city. He tried to bite back the idea of jumping off.

No, Connor was not suicidal. But something about the situation made him feel incredibly guilty.

A cell phone rang, interrupting the fragility of the silence.

"Hello?"

"Connor, its Detective Reed."

There was a silence. "Does this have to do with the case?"

"It has everything to do with the case."

"What happened?"

Reed exhaled audibly. "You better come down here, Connor."

"Why?"

"Just come down."

Connor hung up, breathing heavily.

He ended up driving to Manhattan without telling Lakewood. The fear of what might be waiting for him was too great.

When Connor pulled into the police station, Reed was waiting for him.

"I need you to do us favor."

He nodded slowly.

"I need you to identify the man who took her."

Connor inhaled sharply. "Like in a lineup? Why? What happened?"

"We need you to identify him. Can you do that for us?"

Despite his questions not being answered, he nodded.

Reed led him, with shaking legs, to a room in the back with a one-way glass. The cement walls reminded Connor of when he had come here to watch Jacey get taken home by her father for getting drunk.

Seven men stood next to each other. Each held a white sign with a number.

"Which one is it, Connor?" Reed murmured.

Connor glanced at each of the men, scanning their figures intently.

Number one had slicked hair with these dull green eyes that matched the glare that captivated his entire face. Number two had spiked hair was what were obviously green color contacts. Number three had too many laugh lines. Number four...

Number four had the mussed hair. His eyes were piercing, with so signs of sanity or emotion locked behind them. And his skin was the same pale tan. Connor closed his eyes, looking at his memory. He couldn't tell the difference between number four and the guy from his memory.

His eyes flew open as he realized they weren't different people.

"Number four."

Reed smiled, as if the world and life itself made complete sense. "Good."

"Why?"

"Connor, I think it would make your night significantly better to go see Agent Jo in the conference room."

Connor quirked a brow, and his feet slowly led him to the conference room. He slowly opened the door, and his hear skipped at least three beats.

Agent Jo was sitting next to a girl with red hair, who was happily sipping water from a bottle. They both turned their heads at the sound of the door opening.

"Connor!" she cried out, running up to him. She launched her arms around his neck, and crashed her lips against his.

He stumbled backwards slightly, kissing her back. It was surprise, and happiness, and shock, and something else he couldn't quite identify. His arms wrapped around her, and he smiled. Something seemed different, but he didn't care. No. What mattered was that he was there with her, and they were together.

As he relaxed and kissed her back, Randall smirked against his lips.

Chapter 26:

Illusive Disillusioning

"Good," Callie encouraged, smiling slightly at Justin. "You're doing a great job."

He gripped the handle of the pan so tightly his knuckles grew white. She watched him carefully, eyes flickering to the fire extinguisher on the counter. His face was concentrated as he adjusted his grip on the pan.

"Now flip it with the spatula," she instructed, handing him the spatula.

Justin took the spatula, trying to ignore the heat that was coming from the fire beneath the pan. His self-control was at the max that it had ever been at. He carefully pushed the spatula under the layers of tortilla and cheese, flipping it. As it rested. It sizzle.

"Now turn off the stove."

After a moment, Justin quickly spun the dial so that the flame turned off immediately. He was breathing heavily, and his mind hurt. He had never tried something like that before.

"Good!" Callie took the pan, sliding the quesadilla onto a plate. "You did great."

Justin wrapped his arms around her quickly, trying to forget the image of the flame. His grip was tight, but Callie had been used to it. It was dangerous, what she was doing. But she thought it might be able to help him in the long run, given that she was also quite tired of cold food.

"You did great," she repeated in a murmur. Slowly, she moved backward, smiling up at him. His face had lines of tension, which she knew would have to be released later. But Callie wouldn't let him do that with fire. No, that was something that couldn't be done.

"Let's eat," he suggested. She smiled, taking the knife and sliding it quickly across the quesadilla in four fluid motions. He got another plate out, eyes constantly flickering toward the stove. Callie moved four triangles onto his plate, and took her own portion to the living room so she could eat there.

"Can you grab me a soda?" she called out as she sat down, smiling slightly.

Justin chuckled, grabbing one from the fridge. He leaned in through the doorway, tossing it to her. Callie barely caught it.

"Hey!" she cried indignantly before laughing.

"You know you love me," he teased, collapsing onto the couch next to her.

It was silent for a moment as she smiled, clicking on the television. Of course, Callie avoided the news. She changed the channel to an old movie, looking at the screen with a smile.

"Another old movie?" Justin stuck his tongue out at her, clicking the remote so that the channel changed to a sci-fi movie.

Callie rolled her eyes. She would never win this battle, and that was something that she would eventually have to accept. After all, he was stronger, as he had proved on multiple occasions of attempted tickling assaults.

"See, this is quality television," he said with a laugh, smiling at her and winking.

"Sure," she said, closing her eyes.

Happy, Callie?

She shivered, and Justin glanced over. "You okay, Cat?"

"Yeah," Callie lied, and he paused before going back to his movie.

I want to get out of here.

This was a new voice. A female voice. And as much as Callie hated to admit it, it sounded oddly familiar. Like a recurring voice in a dream. Or a voice in a nightmare.

"I'm going to go to the restroom," Callie murmured, and Justin nodded as she got up, trying to act casual as she walked into her bedroom, and shut the door. She locked the door behind her.

Callie sat on the bed. "Who are you?"

Who are you?

"Why are you in my head?"

You're the one talking in my mind!

She paused, breathing out. "I need to know your name." It gave her a feeling of surety, to know exactly who was in her mind.

I think its Jacey.

Callie inhaled sharply. "Jacey? Jacey Will Adams?"

Yeah...why?

"It's Callie."

Wait, Callie? Why the hell are you in my mind?

But Callie was too busy putting all the pieces together to reply. It all made sense. Leroy, one of the nicer voices, was Jacey's uncle. He had once been beyond the mirror, and he had returned. That was what he told her. Raymond, the meaner voice, was someone who had gotten trapped. He had told Callie that someone had forced him beyond the mirror. She had always thought that beyond the mirror was more of a nightmare than a reality.

"Jacey, are you beyond a mirror?"

Wait, yeah. How did you know?

She wasn't kidnapped. It must have been her reflection. Her entire life she had known about the mirrors and what had lain beyond. But now, she realized this was something was real. Callie had been afraid to look at the mirror because she might fall through. The voices in her mind were people trapped on the other side. She wasn't actually ill at all.

"I've known about this. I thought this was a nightmare, not a reality. Wait, what's your reflection's name?"

Randall. Why? Have you seen her?

"She was kidnapped, Jacey. Someone thought you were her. It makes sense, for you two do look exactly alike."

Holy crap. Callie, how do I get out of here?

Callie racked her memories. "You need to go back to your mirror. You have three options. The first is to kill someone, and then use their mirror."

Yeah, that's not happening.

"The second is to pull your reflection back through."

Okay, that's more plausible.

"The last is to stab your mirror. If you have found yourself, then it will destroy your reflection. If not, then it will destroy you and you will die."

What if I cannot get back?

Callie paused. "I believe in you. You can find yourself. I know you can."

"Callie, what's going on?"

There was silence in her mind. Apparently, Jacey couldn't hear Justin.

"I'm fine," she called back.

Justin paused, clicking the lock with the small tool. He peered in.

"What?" Callie asked.

I didn't say anything.

"No, not you," she murmured.

Justin looked at her with extreme concern. He paused, running a hand through his hair. It looked as if he wanted to say something. After a moment, he leaned against the door frame.

"What?" Callie repeated.

I said I didn't say anything.

"I'm not talking to you!"

Justin bit his lip. "Callie, did the voices come back?"

"Justin, it's not schizophrenia. It's something completely different. There are people beyond the mirror who are talking to me."

He looked at her, and tried to hide the pity in his gaze. "Cat, what are you talking about?"

"People are beyond the mirror. They are our reflections."

Justin inhaled sharply, eyes widening in realization. "You know about that?" he whispered.

Callie frowned. "Justin, do you understand?"

He sat down next to her, biting his lip. "Of course I do."

"How?"

Justin didn't look at her. He couldn't let her see the shattered pride in his eyes. "I didn't want to tell you, Cat."

"Tell me what?" She touched his hand, trying to have him look at her. "You can tell me anything, Justin. I told you that three months ago. It's still true."

"I was a reflection, Cat."

Her eyes widened, and she inhaled quickly. She remembered the hell and what it had been like according to the voices of those beyond the mirror.

"I forced the person on this side to be my reflection. I pulled him through."

Callie touched his leg, eyes filling with sympathy.

"I'm not evil, I swear."

"I know you're not," she said immediately.

Justin shook his head. "He was a bad person. He went to jail so often and I hated reflecting that evil. I wanted that to change, Cat. That was all I wanted."

"You did a good thing," she tried to console him.

"He deserved a life. I took Raymond Thompson's life away from him. He had a family. He had friends. He had love."

Callie frowned. "Raymond?"

"Yeah. Raymond."

"That's the name of the evil voice. The voice that constantly threatens me and tells me to give up."

Justin slowly looked at her. "He is the one who has been torturing you?"

"Yeah. He said his name all the time because he wanted to give me a name to remember when I thought of fear. I hated his name. It was tainted with pain and hurt."

"I can't believe that. My reflection is now the one who is haunting you."

Callie ran a hand through her hair. "You shouldn't have been afraid to tell me. It doesn't change how I feel or who you are."

"But I pulled him to the other side! Isn't that evil?"

She shook her head. "We all make mistakes in life."

"I'm sorry he has been torturing you. Was that who you were talking to?"

Callie shook her head. "Jacey's beyond the mirror. It's her reflection that was kidnapped."

His eyes widened. "How is she going to get out?"

"She only has three options. I don't know if she will be able to, to be honest."

Justin squeezed her leg. "How come?"

"It's difficult."

"There's nothing we can do?"

Callie sighed. "I would go beyond the mirror, but I would have to find the one mirror that I am linked to."

"And it's too dangerous," Justin said, raising an eyebrow.

"What am I going to do?"

"Well, you can talk to her right?"

"Yeah."

"Can you talk her through it?"

"She has to find herself."

"That's hard," Justin agreed.

Callie buried her face in her hands. "I don't know what to do anymore. It's so weird. Why can I hear them?"

"I don't know," Justin murmured, desperately wishing the answer would come to him.

She closed her eyes, thinking about everything. Literally everything. Part of her was happy that she didn't actually have something such as schizophrenia. But part of Callie was upset because this made everything so much more confusing than before. And it wasn't likely anyone would believe her, either.

"Maybe I should go beyond the mirror," he suggested after a moment. "I know that place better than anyone."

Callie's eyes widened, and fear spilled into them. "No. You can't put yourself at risk like that."

"It's for your friend, Cat. I'm willing to do it."

She shook her head and repeated adamantly, "No. You told me three months ago that you wouldn't let me put myself in danger. Now, I'm telling you the same thing."

"Cat, there's no other way. I have to go back."

"How will you come back here?" Callie asked, her lip quivering slightly.

Justin ran a hand through his hair. "I'll think of something."

"That's not good enough."

"Why not?"

Callie shook her head, biting her lip. "I can't hesitate anymore. I lost you once and I am *not* going to lose you again."

Justin flinched at the painful memory after their fight in February.

"Justin, please stay."

"I have to go back. It's my penance for coming to this side. Let me make things right. Cat, please."

His words echoed in her mind. She shut her eyes tightly, trying to focus. Callie's mind was a blur of thoughts and worries. She couldn't help the images of Justin dying from floating through her mind.

I will destroy you, eventually, Raymond chimed in.

Something sparked inside of Callie.

"Promise me something."

Justin looked at her, eyes wide. "Anything."

"Promise me that you will come back."

Chapter 27:

Tomorrow Isn't Coming

Jacey glanced up at the apple tree, eyes scanning for any signs of live fruit. Just like every day before this one, she found none.

There weren't really 'days' here. After all, time was nothing. It simply did not exist. She counted days passing as a full time of her being awake, and then sleeping. When she awoke, it was a new day. But, when the supposed 'morning' care around when she awoke, there was no morning sunshine to greet her. She never got the chance to simply look at the sun and think about what a great day it had been.

Her eyes flickered over to Cyril, who was drawing something in the dirt. Despite the fact that he often acted like a five year-old, he was someone she enjoyed being around. He was very enthusiastic, and it gave her this lightness she hadn't felt in a while. Cyril was the most colorful being or thing that existed here.

"Where are we?" she murmured for the millionth time, and it was more of a rhetorical question than anything.

"Somewhere," Cyril answered, continuing his dirt drawing.

Jacey rolled her eyes. "Why, thank you, Mr. Specific. Your attention to detail astounds me."

"I was rather eloquent, wasn't I?" he commented, glancing up to send her a crooked smile. She let out a small chuckle.

After a short silence, Jacey said, "They say when life gives you lemons, you should make lemonade. I feel like we got rotten lemons."

"They say that, but it's not true. When life gives you lemons, make lemonade. Delicious atomic powered world conquering lemonade."

Jacey laughed again, and the sweet sound kissed the cold air. She could have sworn it warmed for a moment. "You think you're so funny," she drawled, teasing him.

"It's a science, really. I would explain it to you, but I'm fresh out of crayons."

"You're such a twit."

"A twit is defined as a pregnant goldfish. I am neither pregnant, nor a fish. I am, however, gold."

She stared at him, slightly dumbfounded.

"I know I am simply too brilliant for words, but you should close your mouth before the frogs jump in."

"I thought it was supposed to be flies," Jacey pointed out.

"Your mouth is simply too big for it to be just flies."

She shook her head. "Do you have a comeback for everything?"

"No."

Jacey laughed slightly. "If I had a dollar for every time you were sarcastic or sassy, I'd get change for those dollars, put the change in a sock, and beat you with it."

"How violent. Don't you have a conscience?"

"Yes," she said indignantly. "Don't you?"

"Of course," Cyril said, rolling his eyes. "It's in a box in the back of my closet, screaming 'Let me out! You're making bad choices!'"

Jacey couldn't believe how sarcastic and absolutely sassy Cyril was, even after knowing him for however long they had been here. "In my opinion, you have absolutely no common sense or intelligence."

"I'd agree with you, but then we'd both be wrong."

Cyril watched as she laughed, shaking her head in disbelief. "Okay, I give up."

He laughed, focusing his attention on the dirt.

"Hey, Cy?"

Cyril glanced up at her silently.

"What did you want to be when you grew up?"

He thought for a moment. "God emperor of mankind."

Jacey looked at him in exasperation.

"Failing that, then an FBI agent. Or a soccer player."

She nodded, mulling that idea over in her head. "I could see that."

Cyril smiled slightly at that. "What about you?"

Jacey sighed, tugging on the ends of her shirt. "I really like photography, and that whole idea of crime. I always thought a forensics investigator would be pretty cool."

"I see you like crime as well," he commented. "Or the idea of stopping it."

Jacey chuckled and smiled. "Just now, a thought crossed my mind…"

"Must have been a lonely journey." Cyril ducked to avoid the hand she swatted at him, laughing all too loudly.

"Anyways," she muttered, biting back a laugh, "I was wondering why it was so calm here. We're in hell, and we're simply chatting it up like we were hanging out."

Cyril nodded slowly, thinking about that. "You have a good point."

"Isn't this where people turn into reflections, and they suffer in hell?"

"I guess it's because of the fact that we both seem to be almost immune to the hell around each other."

Jacey ran a hand through her hair. "Why would that be?"

Cyril didn't voice the immediate answer that floated to his lips. "I would say it's because of the fact that we are strong, so we didn't turn into the reflections. And because of that, we are colorful."

"I don't mean to question it, but it is weird," she murmured.

"I know what you mean. Trust me, I definitely know what you mean."

Jacey glanced at him silently.

Cyril noticed her eyes and quirked a brow. "What?"

"I was going to say something...but I forgot it when I looked at you."

He paused, eyes softening as he looked at her. Cyril wasn't sure if he had understood what she had meant by that, but nevertheless, he smiled slightly and opened his mouth.

"Don't you dare say something sarcastic," Jacey warned.

Cyril laughed, and the warm sound filled the air, washing away the darkness for a moment.

Jacey smiled, relaxing against the tree. She looked at Cyril again, who was still drawing. "What are you drawing?"

"Colors."

She tilted her head, confused. "What do you mean?"

"I'm drawing colors," Cyril said simply. Despite his sarcasm abilities and the way he could make anyone laugh, he was acting like a child now. There were moments where he would slip into this phase where he did things only a child would do.

"Cool."

He shrugged. "I really like the colors. The happiness they bring make me smile."

Jacey nodded slowly, smiling slightly at him.

"If you tell anyone I have emotions, I'll kill you," Cyril warned, not bothering to glance up.

She shook her head, rolling her eyes. After a moment of absolute silence, she looked at him again. "Tell me about your life."

"What?"

"I told you about my life when we first met. Tell me about yours."

Cyril paused, figuring she meant everything except for the horrible incident that caused him to cross over. "My life? Why?"

Jacey shrugged. "I want to know."

"Where do I start?"

"Start from the beginning."

He smiled softly at her, getting entangled in his memories. "Well, I was born in the United States." Cyril paused, trying to remember. "In California."

Jacey smiled, encouraging him to go on.

"My parents were very casual about their marriage, I remember. I eventually ended up with a younger sister named Christabelle, or Chrissie. And..." He trailed off, looking frustrated. "I think I had an older brother. But I can't remember."

She bit her lip. "It's okay. Keep going."

"I played soccer when I was four, and I never stopped after that. I loved the way I could forget anything when I was in soccer. My parents never really forced it one me, but they encouraged me all the way." Cyril paused, thinking. "I wasn't the brightest kid. I mean, I knew my history. That was my only good subject, to be honest. Other than that, I didn't really have any good grades, per say."

When Jacey closed her eyes, she could see a younger version of Cyril running around on a grass field. She smiled, opening her eyes again.

"I guess I was popular in school. I, uh," Cyril rubbed the back of his neck, "tended to be liked by the ladies." He seemed embarrassed at this, as if the thought bothered him. "That was pretty much who I was at school."

Jacey ignored the embarrassment. She knew what it was like to have that kind of reputation. "What about outside of school, Cy?"

"Outside of school? Besides soccer?"

She nodded.

"I really liked roller coasters. I know that's kind of odd, but it is true. On the weekends, I would teach Chrissie how to play soccer."

Jacey paused, and asked him a random question. "What did your room look like?"

Cyril thought for a moment, and then looked at her, recognition sparking in his eyes. "It had dark navy paint. My bed was a mattress on the floor, for I never cared for high beds. I had a desk, and a cabinet of drawers. That was pretty much it."

She could see that simple room design when she closed her eyes.

"Hey, Jacey, can I ask you something?" The way he said her name was soft and gentle, as if throwing it around would break it.

Jacey glanced at him, quirking a brow. "Yeah. Shoot."

"You were, uh, saying a name in your sleep," Cyril murmured, blushing ever so slightly.

She glanced at him, looking confused and surprised. "Really?"

"Yeah."

Jacey immediately thought of Connor, and she ran a hand through her hair, glancing down.

Cyril chuckled slightly. "Uhm, actually, I guess that wasn't exactly the right way to begin the premise to that question."

"Huh?" She tried to flush away her flushed cheeks.

He looked slightly uncomfortable, shifting where he was lying propped up. "I guess my question would be, what were you dreaming about when you were sleeping?"

She thought back to what she had been dreaming about, losing herself in the dream she was able to remember so well.

She glanced around. "Cy?" she called out. The hell she was in was darker. The sky was pitch black, which was incredibly eerie. She couldn't remember her own name, and it made her feel hallow inside. It was like knowing something but not being able to say it because it was on the tip of your tongue. She looked to the side, at where she thought the apple tree would be. But it wasn't there. In fact, she couldn't see an apple tree for miles. Her eyes pinched in utter fear. She glanced up, at the black sky, shivering slightly. The air was still, and she wished for a hot wisp of air to fix the cold air. She bit her lip, trying to taste something, anything. But no blood came out. She almost winced at the lack of blood that didn't come to her tongue. She glanced at the ground, which looked a dark shade of black. After what she thought was a minute passed, she tried to count. But she didn't know what to say first. She closed her eyes, wishing away this hell. She paused, glancing around. "Cy!" she called out. It was the only name she could remember. It was yelled with such desperation that it hurt her heart. When she placed her fingers on where she should have been able to feel her pulse, she felt nothing. Her heart twisted despite the lack of pulse, and she forgot how to breathe. "Cy!" she screamed, voice shaking the blackness above her. "Cy!" As she finished her last scream of fear, her breath ran out, and the world went black.

"It was..." Jacey trailed off, shaking her head.

Cyril glanced at her, his gaze almost tentative. "It was what?" His voice came out as slightly more than a whisper.

"This place is getting to me," she shrugged slightly, goose bumps forming on her arms and the back of her neck. Jacey shivered slightly, glancing around.

He paused, running a hand over his jeans, biting his lip. His stomach made a small sound. Living off apples and water was not the best diet, it turned out.

"I hate it here. The nightmares are too much..."

Cyril nodded slowly. "But why my name?" he murmured.

"It was the only one I could remember," Jacey said honestly. "I didn't know what else to say."

He sighed awkwardly in the silence, uncomfortable with the serious conversation and all that it held. "The weather's nice," he said weakly.

Jacey couldn't help but laugh slightly. She wasn't sure if she was glad that he had changed the subject, or if it pissed her off. "I hate you," she murmured.

Cyril merely smiled, and put one hand in front of him, leaning forward. Their pinkies brushed. "Yeah. I do too."

She didn't say how happy that made her. She simply tucked those words away with the rest of the hidden codes and unsaid messages between them.

They were in a strange stage, where they were the only ones who were still alive here.

"With all the tornadoes uprooting chaos and chasing me down, at least I can count on you to be my constant."

Cyril quirked a brow. "How do you know that, though? How do you know I won't let you down like I let everyone down?"

"I don't know; I believe. I believe that you won't run anymore because we're both tired of chasing storms."

He chuckled weakly. "I am tired of running." Cyril's face grew somber. "I ran from my family to save myself. I ran from my older brother. I ran from everyone."

"You need time to stop and smell the flowers. To experience life."

Cyril shrugged slightly, rubbing the back of his neck. "I think it's too late for me. I had my chance to make a difference. I had my chance to stay. But I didn't stay. I ran, and this is where I ended up."

"Maybe that was to teach you a lesson," Jacey suggested. "That it was time to stop running."

"Do you really think life would give me another chance?"

Jacey couldn't nod. She merely shrugged. "I think that you stayed alive for a reason. I think that you could have turned into a reflection, but life knew not to let you."

"I thought I was alive because I was crazy. I thought I had no place."

"I think you just have to find yourself."

Cyril sighed loudly. "Everyone ends up losing themselves every once in a while. How come I fucking get stuck here when I knew who I was!"

"Maybe," Jacey was tentative as she began, "Maybe you didn't know yourself as well as you thought."

He opened his mouth, face contorted with frustration and hurt. But then Cyril closed his mouth, glancing down.

"What?" she asked softly.

"I can't disagree with you."

Jacey sighed. "It happens to everyone, Cy. We all lose ourselves and go mad once in a while."

"This place makes the best of us go mad," Cyril said, cracking a small and weak smile.

"True," she murmured. "Very true."

He sighed. "I have one thing to be thankful for."

Jacey raised an eyebrow. "And what's that?" She expected him to crack some sarcastic joke.

"For you."

She looked at him, furrowing her brow slightly at the vagueness. "What did I do?"

"You came here," Cyril murmured simply. "Thanks for joining me in hell."

Chapter 28:

Until the End of Tomorrow

Cy.
I love the way it sounds.
It's nice to finally have a name.
Now I want a face.
A face to match what I now know is my name.

Cyril something.
I can't remember that.
But maybe I will remember it soon.
Every day more memories come back.
Red.
It's all because of her.
Jacey.
Jacey Will Adams.
She remembers her full name.
She remembers where she came from.
Because of her, I remembered where I came from.

California.
It's a sunny place.
Sun.
I miss the sun.
I miss the brightness.
Bright.
Light.
They say you go toward the light when you die.

But that is a different light.
A light of death.

The one in California is different.
Brighter.
Happier.
It shines with this vibrancy no other light can muster.

Jacey smiled when I described this to her.
She said she wanted to see this California.
I love her smile.
It has sincerity.
My reflection wasn't sincere.
She's the only one who ever has been sincere.
And probably ever will be.
I mean, we've been chasing storms.
All our life.
She knows what this is like.
Jacey and I.
Sister glances at me.
She says not to love.
I didn't expect her to say that.
My eyes widen.
I never thought about that word.
She says I look like love.
How do you look like love?
You can't.
Right?
I look at the sleeping girl.
She hasn't said my name in a while.
In a long while.
That's good, I try to tell myself.
It means that she feels safer.
She stopped having the nightmares, I assume.

What does she dream about?

Does she dream of an escape?
Does she dream of her old life?
Does she dream of her old love and her old friends?
Does she dream of her family?
Does she dream of—
I don't finish that one.
It's too big of a risk.
It's also too big of a possibility.
I don't want to know the answer.
Unless it's yes.
It's horrible.
I can't believe I am that selfish.
But, at the same time, I am human.
I get scared.
I fall in love.
I have nightmares.
I make mistakes.
Even the best of us make mistakes.
It's my natural instinct to run.
To escape.
To leave.
But Jacey has a point.
I'm tired of chasing storms.
I'm tired of the chaos that comes with leaving.
A constant.
That's what she called me.
What does that mean, though?
Does it mean she knows I can't leave the place?
Or does it mean that she knows I'm calm?
Or that I won't leave this place without her?

I think I'm reading too much into this.
But why?
I've dealt with my fair share of girls.
I know how they act.
Why they do the things they do.
Why they think the things they think.
Why they say the things they say.
But she's almost—
Different.
Different is not a bad thing, though.
I'm different.
And that is something I will never forget.
Because I think I'm different all too often.
And it is good that I think that way.
It prevents me from fading into the
background.
Like Chrissie does.
I glance over at her.
She's watching me.
But why?
I shake my head.
I have better things to do than consult the
ghost of my sister.
Do I have better things to do?
That's actually a good question.
Because, I wasn't sure what I was doing until
I saw the colors.
The colors that brightened my day.
My night.
My life.
Those types of things.
I love the red.
The blue.

The green.
The yellow.
The orange.
The purple.
The pink.
All of them.
All of the colors.
My mind sketches the colors out.
It paints a picture in my mind.
Of a rainbow.
I reply her voice in my mind.
"Remember red?"
I nod even though its merely a memory.
"Well, a rainbow starts with the color red."
"Then, there's a line of orange beneath it."
"Orange is the color of surprise."
"It's vibrant, and it's like red."
"It's the color of astonishment, and the color of absolute shock."
"Then there's yellow."
"Yellow is like a bright light."
"It's the color of a halo, and of brightness."
"Then there's green."
"It's the color of life."
"It's a subtle color that seeps into every tree, and every bush."
"Then there's blue."
"It's the color of peace."
"It colors the sky with its serenity."
"Then there's the last color."
"It's purple."
"Purple is the color of passion."
"It's like red and blue together."

"It's love, and it's calm."

"It is what you see when you feel passionate for something."

"All those lines curve, and that's a rainbow. "

"It appears in the sky, which is—"

"Blue," I murmur, just like I had before.

Her smile flashes in my mind.

I like the brightness that comes with it.

It makes me smile.

It's all I can see right now.

It's all that I care about.

But, Sister—

I can't bear to think about that.

To think about Sister.

To think about the dead.

The dead are creatures I don't know about.

I don't want to get too attached.

But the thing is, she has been keeping me alive.

She stopped me from turning into a reflection.

She gave me a reason to live.

So why do I need a new reason to live?

I bite my lip.

It tastes salty.

My hand travels toward my face.

It's wet.

Slowly, I look at the wetness that is now on my hand.

Tears, Sister tells me.

Tears.

Tears that taste like salt.

I can finally taste something again.

My heart leaps, and I smile slightly.
But the damper is still on my heart.
My smile falls.
It falls like the brightness that used to be in my eyes.
I look around.
My tears stain the wet ground.
Tomorrow.
The word floats into my mind.
It's a method of time, I realize.
Time.
I have a sense of time.
Tomorrow.
The word feels light.
But it feels like it will never come.
I glance at Jacey.
"Tomorrow," *I whisper.*
I keep my eyes on her.
We'll get out of this hell.
We're only trapped here until the end of tomorrow.
If tomorrow ever comes.

Chapter 29:

Lights in the Abyss

The air was colder than he remembered. It used to be hot, and the air would be still. Now it is cold, and it is sour. The air tastes bitter, as if it was rejected by reality, and can't get over the separation.

Justin glanced back at the glimmer of the mirror. He knew the way back, at least. If he managed to get back. He had promised Callie that he would return. Yet, despite the sincerity he had given her, there was no surety in the claim that he would indeed return.

The world around him looked whiter. He glanced at his feet, and then inhaled sharply. His brain tried to ignore the fire that was on his feet. It was fake. It wasn't real. It was nothing more than his imagination playing tricks on him. His fears were being taken over by this hell that he had been born in.

The instinct to go back to the mirror was difficult to overcome. He was born a reflection, and he was meant to be one. After all, switching sides doesn't switch your fate.

He wished it did. Justin looked at his hand, at the scratches he had etched into the palm of his hand. "J-u-s-t-i-n," he read aloud, his voice a murmur. "Justin," he said, nodding slowly. It was the only way that would ensure he remembered his name. Without it, he would fade into the background. He would become nothing more than a reflection. Pen and permanent marker washed away. He knew that. But these scars would always remain. Even this hell couldn't destroy that.

Slowly, he began to feel himself fading as he walked. He didn't remember the girl's name who he was supposed to be saving. Justin didn't remember anything Callie had told him. But he remembered Callie. He opened his other hand, glancing at the permanent scars there. "C-a-l-l-i-e," he whispered. The whisper was stolen by the wind, and tucked away in the folds of the black sky.

The ground was cracked, and it shook slightly as he walked. Justin feared that he would be swallowed by the black and the white. He had little time to spare. If Raymond found that Justin was over here, he could go back. And everything would go back to the way it should be.

Raymond was the one name he couldn't forget. It was impossible. After all, Justin was a reflection of Raymond. Whatever happened to Raymond, happened to Justin.

The one thing that kept prodding at his mind was what Callie had asked. She had asked if it was possible to simply kill Raymond off. Then, there wouldn't be the problem of Raymond returning before Justin did.

But if Raymond died, so would Justin. If Raymond died on this side of the mirror, then Justin would to. It needed to happen elsewhere. On the other side of the mirror. Justin couldn't bear the possibilities that he could die so easily. He had gone through too much to watch it all die. All because of that damned Raymond.

Raymond was a reflection of himself. It was hard for Justin to accept the fact that that was untrue. Justin was the reflection. He always would be the reflection. It is something that was hard for him to specifically focus on. He wanted to be his own person. He wanted to be his own person. He was different from Raymond.

It was all because of the fact that he tried to switch his fate. It was the fire Raymond had been in that caused all this to begin. The mirror Raymond had been looking at to see his burned flesh was when Justin decided he couldn't take the pain anymore. The arson he reflected was someone he did not want to be. He wanted to be done with everything. It was all too much, and it was ridiculous.

Justin had managed to treat his burns after he crossed over. But he never saw his reflection. He didn't have a reflection because Raymond was, to put it simply, mad. He didn't have the sanity required to maintain the role of being a reflection. Raymond had lost himself even after losing himself, even if it seemed impossible. There was no way Raymond be able to actually have the mental understanding to copy everything Justin did and how he moved and acted.

When he had been Raymond's reflection, and was on the proper side of the mirror, it had been like being the reflection of a man who had nothing inside. He was a hallow shell of a crazy man who simply could not function properly. And he didn't have a mental illness. This was simply who he had turned into. As he grew up, he was a prominent at-risk child. Teachers knew it, his parents knew it, his siblings knew it, and Justin knew it.

"Justin," he murmured again, making sure that he did not forget the name as he got lost in the memories of being a reflection. Taking a deep breath, Justin glanced at the all too familiar sight of the lone apple tree.

But now, it seemed strange. Perhaps it is because of the two strange figures that are sitting beneath the tree. Usually, there would be no one. Justin bit his lip, fearing that they were spirits. But upon closer examination, he realized with a dropped jaw that they were live humans.

The girl looked alive. She had this strange color to her. His eyes widened. The spirits told tales of the colored ones who would roam this side of the mirror, but he had doubted them. After all, who is trust here?

The boy sitting next to her had colors, too. But he was fading fast. The colors he wore flickered and dimmed. Sometimes, the colors disappeared for a moment. Justin knew that he was barely holding on. He was almost a reflection, but was holding on to some life line that he wished he knew.

Their voices drifted toward Justin, and he bit his lip again. The voices were bright, and full of life. The boy might not make it, but the girl seemed extremely strong. She seemed to be the epitome of life in this dark and dead place.

Justin assumed the girl was the one Callie wanted him to bring home safely. He cautiously crept forward, aware that he looked just like the spirits. He was black and white, which contrasted with the people in front of him. His aura was bleaker than ever, and Justin was almost fading into the background.

Slowly, he opened his mouth, worried his voice wouldn't work. "Hello?"

The girl's head snapped up immediately. She glanced at him with suspicion and wariness, and she had every right to do so. The boy, on the other hand, looked at Justin with a mix of fear and confusion. It etched across his face as he looked at Justin.

"Callie told me to come," Justin tried, his face contorting with desperation. The girl's eyes lit up in recognition.

"Wait," the boy murmured to her, and Justin watched as the girl sat back, looking at Justin with hope. She wanted to get out of this hell, and he could tell. The boy stood, slowly walking over. Justin didn't like the way the boy was approaching him, and he dug his fingernails into his palm defensively.

The boy adjusted his beanie, and then delved his hand into his pocket.

"What's your name?"

Justin opened his mouth to reply, and then found himself glancing at his hand for the answer. "Justin."

The boy couldn't tell if it was a lie or not, considering that it was carved into his hand. "Who sent you and why?"

"Callie. Callie told me to go find her friend." His voice came in short gasps.

"Who is her friend?"

Justin sighed, shaking his head. "I don't know."

The girl stood, slowly walking over. When the boy caught sight of this, his face grew worried.

"I came because Callie wanted me to help. I mean no harm. I swear," Justin raised his hands, as if he was surrendering to them. If he was honest, he would have admitted that he was incredibly terrified of dying here, and wanted to get out as soon as possible.

The girl frowned. "Why would you come? How could you help me cross over?"

"Sometimes, there have been myths of ex-reflections being able to share a mirror. So since I was once a reflection, I can share my mirror with you," Justin said, looking around nervously.

"Why do you keep looking over your shoulder?" the boy asked him, eyes narrowed. Spirits constantly tried to trick people, and it was something that the boy obviously knew a lot of.

Justin frowned. "You can trust me."

"You have barely any color," the boy pointed out.

"But that doesn't mean I'm evil," Justin pleaded. "I'm just trying to help."

The girl's eyes softened slightly. "What if he's telling the truth?" she asked the boy standing next to her.

"He can't be," the boy insisted. "I've heard stories about people who try and lure people to their deaths by insisting they can help them get home."

"But he knows about Callie," the girl insisted.

"I'm not going to watch you die because he is lying to you about all of this. We can't trust anyone here. He is an ex-reflection. He pulled the person on the other side to this side. That's a mark of evil," he argued.

Justin looked back and forth. "He was the evil one."

"No!" the boy exclaimed. "The reflections are evil. They simply can't be good."

"Maybe I am the exception," Justin pleaded. "You can't generalize like that."

The other boy shook his head. "I remember my reflection. And I have heard horrible stories."

"But what about the good stories that you don't hear?" Justin asked, eyes wide. "They may be few in number, but you can't act like they don't exist!"

"But they are so few in number, if they even do exist, that they are rare. Who says you are one of the good ones?" the boy challenged.

"Maybe your reflection wasn't evil!"

The boys tumbled backward, shaking his head furiously, losing himself in the scary and painful memories of that day so long ago.

He shoved the door open of the men's restroom, heart pounding in his ears. Cyril felt the soccer medal press against his chest, the cold medal feeling wet with the blood of his own sister. He tossed the trashcan against the door in his frantic dash, hoping that it would stall the gunman, even if it was only for a moment.

Cyril heard the footsteps get louder, and he wasn't sure if it was sweating or crying. He was extremely tired from today and from his dash to what he hoped could be a safe place. It was silent except for those footsteps that had begun to slow.

There was a loud bang, and Cyril scrambled onto the sink in fear. He was curled up on the counter, huddling, as if he could hide.

The hooded figure that resembled a shadow stormed into Cyril's view, and Cyril let out a bloodcurdling scream. There was a gunshot, and Cyril screamed once more as his shoulder exploded in extreme pain.

"Fucking kid," the gruff voice cursed, aiming the gun once more. There was barely any fear or hesitation in his eyes as he aimed the gun again.

Cyril was pressed against the mirror, waiting for death. A pair of hands grasped his shirt, and he felt himself being yanked backwards, as if he was going through the mirror.

Suddenly, he was looking through a rectangle at the gunman. He saw what looked like him on the other side, and his eyes flashed with panic. The gunman looked extremely confused, and Cyril watched himself duck. But he wasn't ducking.

The bullet came straight toward him, and he flinched, crying out at the pain in his shoulder.

The bullet made a resounding echo as it hit the rectangle, and Cyril screamed out of fear and the continued pain in his shoulder.

The image before him shattered into pieces, and suddenly he found himself not only in hell, but looking at it as well. There was no more of the other world inside the rectangle, and it was simply a barren wasteland.

Cyril glanced at his shoulder, collapsing to the ground in misery and pain. His mind was unable to comprehend the night's events, and he screamed out again.

"Cyril, it's okay," a small voice called out.

He glanced up, vision fuzzy. Someone, or something, was standing in front of him.

"It's okay," the voice assured him, and it was soft and gentle.

Cyril screamed out in pain once more, his mind and shoulder hurting more and more. He couldn't take the confusion mixed with the pain that was unlike anything he had ever experienced.

"Please, look at me," the voice begged. "I'm here for you, Cyril. I really am. I need you to look at me. You're going to be okay. You hear me? I know you'll be okay. Please, look at me."

The pained Cyril brought his eyes up slowly to meet eyes that looked all too familiar. He cried out in shock at the figure of his sister, who was standing over him.

"You're supposed to be dead," he whispered.

Christabelle Thompson shrugged softly, kneeling by him. She was nothing more than a black and white figure, and he was a bit scared by her black and white eyes. Her irises were nothing more than black, and as were her pupils.

"Help," he whimpered, holding the place where his wound was. His eyes filled with pain and immense fear. "I don't want to die."

She touched his pale, white cheek. His colors were fading, and he felt like he was dying. "You're not going to die," she promised him.

"How do you know?" Cyril asked, voice gravelly as he dug his fingernails into his palm. That was what he had told her before she had been shot. And now...well...

Christabelle sighed, her black eyes blinking fast. If he still had some sense, Cyril would have believed in the black tears that dripped down her face. But instead, he tried to pretend he was imagining things.

"Where am I?" he asked, gripping her wrists with his blood-soaked hand. The blood was a mix of crimson and black.

"The other side of the mirror. Your reflection pulled you over," Christabelle said, using her jacket to make strips for his shoulder.

Cyril winced, crying out at the pain of the bullet that was still in him. "That bastard," he whispered, breathing heavily. His eyes were fading. "He took my life away."

"No," Christabelle said, shaking her head. But Cyril was blacking out anyway. He saw her mouth move, and then everything was black.

"Evil reflections," Cyril murmured, glaring at Justin.

Justin looked at her. "What can I do to earn your trust?" He directed his question away from the boy on purpose. He was scarred from some memory, and he would never trust Justin.

The girl looked thoughtful. "Find my middle name. Callie is the only one who would know besides my dad. If you manage to find my middle name, then I can trust you. Because then I know that you really do know Callie."

"Your middle name," Justin paused. The boy obviously wasn't going to let her leave without him, and this was what he would have to do. For Callie, he reminded himself. He nodded, and turned on his heel, breaking into a sprint.

After all, Raymond was still out there.

Chapter 30:

And Then There Was One

Jacey knew that it was a waste of time to send the stranger back. She knew Callie must have sent him, even if Cyril didn't believe it. She wasn't sure why she was letting him waste time. Then again, he didn't really understand the severity of what might be going on.

She stood by the tree, rubbing her jaw at the discomfort that had been there for quite a while now. In her estimation what had to be time, it had been probably a few weeks.

Cyril was looking at Justin's retreating figure, eyes watching him nervously. Something about Justin had caused Cyril to be put on guard, and Jacey couldn't argue with instinct.

Something tightened inside of her, as if a hand was slowly squeezing her heart. She inhaled sharply, placing her hand over her heart. It wasn't as bad as it usually was, but it didn't feel good, either. Slowly, Jacey bit her lip, trying to take control of what was going on.

"Jacey, are you okay?" Cyril's voice drifted over as he turned to look at her. His face was struck with worry at the pained expression on her face.

"I'm fine," she promised, practically lying through her teeth. "It's a cramp."

He tilted his head, looking at her. "You're a really bad liar."

Despite the pain, she laughed softly, running out of breath sooner than she had expected.

"What's going on?" Cyril murmured, slowly walking over to her.

She shook her head, and then made a small noise, trying to prevent herself from crying out. Her legs shook slightly, and Cyril barely caught her as she collapsed onto her knees. He carefully laid her on her back, biting the inside of his cheek.

He touched her neck for a pulse that was too rapid. "Jacey, where does it hurt?"

"Heart," she managed to murmur. She bent over, coughing and hacking. He placed his hand on her back, wincing only slightly at the blood that spattered the ground at her last cough.

"Why would it hurt, Jacey?"

She shook her head.

"Jacey, I need to know."

"Surgery. I had—surgery. Heart surgery." Her breath was short. "This has happened a few times."

Cyril shook his head, trying to keep his eyes away from the blood. "Why didn't you tell me?"

"It's because I don't have my medicine," Jacey mumbled, closing her eyes. "It won't last for that long."

He glanced at her. "What type of medicine?"

"Blood thinner medicine."

"Jacey, that is to prevent clots. Clots after surgery can cause a heart attack."

Jacey frowned. "I have a...clot?"

He shrugged helplessly, not sure what he was doing. The sarcasm he usually threw around was gone. Cyril placed his hand over her hand that was on her heart. "You'll be okay," he tried to convince her.

It was a boldface lie, and Jacey knew it. "I need to get out of here."

"I don't want to trust that kid."

"We might have to."

Cyril shook his head slowly. He looked at Jacey as she inhaled slightly, and then exhaled quickly. Her expression became panicked as she fought for the air that wouldn't come. And he couldn't do anything except squeeze her hand and promise her things that he couldn't promise.

She closed her eyes again, and her breathing slowed. The pulse beneath his fingers stilled, and he couldn't find it. His eyes darkened and he frantically pressed his fingers against her neck in a desperation that he didn't know he had. Nothing mattered except finding the pulse of the girl dying in front of him.

Jacey's eyes flew open, and Cyril felt his own heart stop momentarily. "You scared the heck out of me!" he said, voice rising as her breathing slowed. "I thought I had lost you."

"So you admit it then," she murmured, sounding a bit breathless as she looked up at the cloudy skies that would never see the light of day.

Cyril glanced at her, confused. He followed her gaze up to the sky, and then met her eyes once again. "Admit what?"

"That you do care."

He sighed slightly. "Of course I care. But caring is such a...small word. Anyone can care."

"I beg to differ," Jacey pointed out, shivering as she glanced at the blood that was next to her. "Caring for someone who is broken is quite a task."

"We're both broken, you know," Cyril countered, glancing down at her and retracting his hand.

She nodded in agreement. "We're shattered and I don't think anything could ever possibly tape us back together."

"But I'll tell you what- I would rather slice my hands on our shards than just walk away," he murmured.

Jacey glanced up at him, her expression looking pained.

"What?" he asked, biting the inside of his cheek again.

She shook her head. "I can't," she mumbled, sitting up.

"Can't what?"

Jacey moved over, leaning against the tree.

"I can't do this."

Cyril cocked his head at her. "Can't do what?" He furrowed his brow in confusion.

"I can't do this. I can't pretend like we're so happy and we're going t leave this place and it is all going to be the same."

"What do you mean?"

She ran a hand through her hair in utter frustration. "People leave. They stay in your life, care for a bit, and then get up and walk away. They just leave, Cyril."

He winced slightly at his full name. He wasn't used to her saying that. "Who said I was leaving?"

"Who said that you weren't?" Jacey challenged.

He was silent for a moment. "Why do you doubt me?"

She looked away, not wanting him to see who she was shattering into. "Because doubting people prevents me from being hurt. It lets me warn myself that they are going to leave. You simply got stuck with me."

"But I stayed."

"Because you had nowhere else to go!" Jacey's voice rose at the end. "It scares me, Cyril. It really does."

Cyril looked around, not wanting to say the wrong thing. He ran a hand over the ground, letting what seemed to be sand fall through his fingers.

"Well, this will all go away. I'll get to go home and then I can go back to the people who left me."

He bit his lip, but it was too late, for the words slipped out anyway. "You're the one leaving."

"It's called preventative warfare," Jacey snapped, her voice edgy to hide the realization that she was the one leaving.

"It's called being hypocritical."

She opened her mouth, and then shut it, glancing anywhere but where he was. "I'm not a hypocrite."

"Sure, Jacey. Sure," Cyril mumbled, rolling his eyes.

There was an awkward silence that took over the dark skies, seeping into the already dull apples, the barren ground, the black clouds, and the very air that surrounded the two live beings that sat there. It seemed to be darker than the ominous black that slipped into every crevice that existed in this hell.

The color faded slowly from Jacey and Cyril as they sat there in the silence. The red in her hair dulled to what almost could be passed off as a light brown or a dark shade of auburn. Cyril's already bleak and pale figure seemed to grow even paler, and his eyes dulled to the point where they looked like the eyes of a dead man.

"Jacey," someone mumbled, and she glanced up. Almost all of her wished it was Cyril, but she knew that it wasn't. The stranger from earlier was standing in front of them, with more color than before.

Jacey glanced at the more colorful version of Justin, frowning slightly. "That's my first name," she said simply.

"I know. Jacey Will," the older boy continued. He looked calmer this time, and he wasn't looking behind himself nervously. Perhaps the first time there had been a spirit.

She looked at Cyril, and then back at the other boy. "Can you give us a minute?"

"Sure," the boy agreed reluctantly. "Make it quick. We both need to go back as soon as possible."

Jacey turned to Cyril, bending down and kneeling next to him. She touched his hand with hesitancy that was obvious to him. Her eyes looked a bit pained. Part of her wanted him to argue for her to stay, but she knew she would have to leave anything. It wouldn't change anything. And that was what nearly killed her. This would be the last time she would ever end up seeing Cyril. It was over.

"Go," Cyril said, his voice pained, and there was a lump in his throat.

She tightened her hand on his. "You don't mean that, do you?"

"You need to go. Your heart is hurting, and you're sick. It's better for…" Cyril trailed off, shaking his head.

"Better for me. But that doesn't meant that it is better for you," Jacey pointed out. "I care about you."

His pained and dead eyes met hers for a moment. He held her gaze. "Do you, really?" Jacey cringed at this. She understood what he was getting at. If she truly cared, she would stay. If she cared about him.

"You said so yourself that my heart was sick," she pleaded. "Don't let me leave if you think I don't care. It's not true."

"Whatever. I knew that I would be stuck here. I'm too scared to live, anyway," Cyril muttered, sighing.

Jacey retracted her hand slowly. "I thought maybe you had a reason to live."

"What? You?" He laughed weakly. "I was alive for years because of the ghost of my dead sister. That was what kept me alive, and kept me crazy. It's the only thing that made me think that dying would kill her all over again, too. So I kept her along with me. And now, now that you're here, I thought maybe I had a new reason to live."

She paused, wanting to say that she was there for him. But no words came out.

"But humans are wrong. They make mistakes," Cyril looked at her. His gaze was pointed, as if trying to include her specifically in the group that always made mistakes.

"Don't think of me like that," Jacey said quietly, her voice almost pleading.

He sighed, shrugging. "I don't know what to think anymore. And I don't know why you are still here. After all, you have other and better things to be doing. Go get healed. And just leave. Nothing is going to make you stay. And I'm sure as hell not going to try."

She inhaled sharply. "I'm sorry," she whispered. "But I'm not the bad guy, Cy. I swear that I care. And I'll go on knowing that. I just...I hope that you can learn that it is the truth. That's all that matters. Is that you know the truth."

"Sure, Red," he murmured.

Jacey tilted her head at the nickname. "Let's go," she said quietly to the older boy, standing. Almost all of Cyril wished it was he who Jacey was talking to, but he knew that it wasn't.

The stranger glanced at Cyril, but the boy did not return the gaze. Cyril was biting his lip to prevent himself from saying something stupid, such as 'Jacey, stay.' Despite what he had said, part of him knew what she was saying was true. But he wouldn't speak out. No. She deserved to be healed. She deserved the chance to go home and be healed.

"Come on," Jacey urged the strange man, wanting to go back before her luck ran out. The heart pain would come soon, and she did not want to be the one to blame for her death on this side of the mirror.

Finally, the boy obliged. He tore himself away from Cyril with such difficulty that Jacey worried he would pass out from the strength it took for him to actually walk away. She didn't look back. And because of this, she failed to see Cyril turn into nothing more than a figure of black and white.

The boy beckoned her, and now walked with a sudden urgency. She was grateful for this, but found it slightly difficult to keep up. Her shortness of breath hadn't quite ended yet, and she found a respect for those who had asthma as she struggled to breathe.

"We have to hurry," the boy murmured, his voice trailing behind him with a cold edge to it. He seemed different than before. But this place did change people. He was probably losing himself.

When Jacey finally looked back, she couldn't see the apple tree. She inhaled sharply, feeling more and more lost without the familiar sight of the apple tree and the personality that slipped in between the branches. She looked around, noting his slower pace and copying it.

The boy stopped, halting. He was hunched over, and the color that she was sure she had once seen in him no longer existed. He turned around, on his heel, smirking with obvious triumph. The corners of his mouth curved up and he cackled. It was raspy, as if he hadn't tasted water in days.

"What?" Jacey narrowed her eyes, taking a step back to the safety that no longer was there beneath the apple tree.

There was no answer from the boy as he cackled again, coughing in between his triumphant chuckles.

The boy's name floated to her mind as the color seeped back into her. "Justin, what's going on?"

"Justin?" the boy laughed, hunched over. "My name isn't Justin, doll."

"That's what you said when you came over."

He smirked, his chuckled subsiding. "I have never seen you before in my life. Or, what used to be my life."

She shook her head in confusion, looking around. "What the hell is going on? Who are you?"

"I'm Raymond. Raymond Thompson," he murmured, the smirk still playing on his face. He looked at her as if his name explained everything.

Jacey dug her fingernails into her palm. "How do you remember your name?"

"Because I'm special, too," Raymond snarled. He caught himself after that, trying to take deep breaths.

"'Too?'" Jacey repeated, shaking her head. "What the fuck is that even supposed to mean?"

He smirked. "Do you not know? Did your precious savior not tell you? Or does he not know?" Raymond mused, laughing softly at her.

"Tell me."

Raymond paused, as if debating the options. "You're special. And I'm special. I think that that should have been glaringly obvious by now."

"I'm colorful. What the hell do you do? Make rainbows?" The sarcasm slipped into her voice before she could stop it.

He rolled his eyes, his jaw set. "Aren't you funny? Actually, call me your counterpart."

"What does that mean?" Jacey looked at him in confusion, brow furrowed.

"It means," Raymond explained with extreme impatience, "that I can do the opposite of what you do." Before she could ask what he considered the opposite of being colorful, he decided to show her exactly what the opposite of colorful was.

It was unlike anything she had ever experienced. She looked down at herself, and the colors slowly were being pulled off of her. The colors turned into mist that were absorbed by Raymond. The dead look he had been sporting morphed into something entirely different. The colored mist was absorbed by him, and despite the small amount, it gave him this strange strength and powerful look that she had never seen before. Part of her felt a bit weaker as she lost a small fraction of her own color.

"And that is what I mean," he smirked.

Jacey looked from her to him, eyes wide with shock. "What the hell…" she murmured.

"I am a Furtum," Raymond smirked. "You are a Dator." It sounded as if it was 'dah-tore.'

She shook her head. "What language is that?"

"Latin. I am a Furtum, or a thief. You are a giver, which is a Dator."

"What does that have to do with anything?"

Raymond smiled slightly, but it still had a hint of a smirk. "There's one person born every fifty years. You were born in 1999. The next Dator will be born in 2049. I was born in 1992. The next Furtum will be born in 2042."

"Why?"

"Let's just say that we are just as mortal as everyone else. But we can change other's mortality, not our own."

Jacey frowned. "You're lying."

"The only reason that Cyril isn't dead is because of you, girl. You gave him life. A dateo vitae. Giver of life." He glanced at her, the small amount of color still giving him this air of power.

"But you take colors. Taking colors isn't something that is dangerous," she challenged.

Raymond smirked. "Really? Would you like me to prove you wrong?"

Before Jacey could stop Raymond from his attempt to prove her wrong, she felt something leave her, and a great cloud mist of color exited her body. She collapsed onto her knees, gasping in pain. He paused for a moment, just letting her struggle to breathe before the colors sank back into her body.

"That wasn't even half of your colors. It's so easy to cause pain this way," Raymond smirked, twirling a stream of color mist around his fingers.

She shook her head, still on her knees. "That's not possible."

"I can try it again," he teased, and she shook her head quickly.

"So what does any of this even mean?"

Raymond yawned, looking around. "This is Tenebris et Abeo Positus. The dark and dying places, as we refer to it. The thing about this place is that it steals the reflection's colors so that they really are only a reflection of the person on the other side of the mirror. Colors are the most important thing here."

"Why are colors so important?" she asked, tilting his head slightly.

He nodded slowly, even though a nod didn't exactly answer her question. "Well, each color means something different."

"Okay, so what does each color mean?"

Raymond sighed. "The magic number is six, because there are six colors in the rainbow, and the rainbow colors are the most important."

"Six. Okay." Jacey nodded, taking a step back.

"Red is love. Orange is memories. Yellow is intelligence. Green is hope. Blue is power. Purple is happiness."

She mulled that over, storing it away in her own memories. "Oh. SO what are white and black then?"

"White is death. Black is darkness." Raymond gazed around lazily.

Jacey took the opportunity to take another step back. "Very fitting," she mused.

He nodded. "And we can manipulate colors, too, doll." He let a small amount of green mist leave him, and he twirled it around his fingers.

"Why even have people like us? What if the Furtum and Dator never even cross over to this side?"

"It happens," Raymond admitted with a sigh. "It has happened."

She paused. "How do you know so much about this anyway?"

He nodded slowly, mulling that question over in his head. "I've been here a long time, doll. This place had told me almost all of its secrets. I know how to manipulate it and use its power to my advantage. Color is nutrition here. We don't need to eat. That's one fo the firsts secrets it told me."

"It cannot talk," Jacey challenged.

"But the spirits can," Raymond pointed out. "They respect me for being able to survive here."

Jacey paused, glancing up at him. "So why the hell are you even here?"

"I was on the other side of the mirror, until my reflection pulled me over. I stay here, stealing colors from the living until I can return to my former state and I can cross back over. Killing someone does let you cross back over." Raymond smirked slightly.

"Then why haven't you succeeded yet?" Jacey asked, narrowing her eyes as she stood.

Raymond sighed. "The people that cross over are weak. They don't know what they are doing, and they simply are tormented here. The madness takes over their entire body and brain. By the time they get here, they usually are already colorless. I can only collect so little color from them." He inhaled, filling with a small amount of color. "This is all I have after all my years of work."

"So, you just have to wait," Jacey said after a moment.

"I'm tired of waiting," he snarled. "I want to go back to the life I deserve to live."

She took a step back. "You don't have enough color."

Raymond slowly let a dastardly smile curl on his face. "But you do."

Chapter 31:

A Distant Echo

I can't believe she just walked away.
Shit.
Her name is slipping from me.
All my memories are slipping away.
What the hell?
I can't remember anything.
It's all gone.
That pain comes back to my stomach, and it consumes me.
Sister calls it hunger.
I call it dying.
The pain is too much to bear.
It travels to my heart.
To my lungs.
To my face.
To my neck.
I feel consumed by the pain.
Sister bitterly tells me its heartbreak.
I am breaking.
But I can't remember what a heart is supposed to do.
I ask her.
Sister says she shouldn't tell me.
She says that I'm better off without it.
I shake my head.
I beg her.
In the silence of this place, I am crying for a name.
A definition.

Something tangible to explain the pain.
What hurts almost as much is how the memory of her is starting to slip.
Her face.
Her hair that is—
It's a color.
Red.
Shit.
I almost forgot.
How could I almost forget Red?
Red left me.
Because she was scared and I didn't do shit to help her.
I almost don't blame her.
But this 'heartbreak' makes me blame her.
I want it to go away.
I want it all to disappear.
But I know it won't.
I know with all of my heart that it won't disappear.
Because it's pain.
And this place is meant to cause pain.
I look at Sister.
She says that she can't help me because she has been replaced.
Because Red is my new reason to live.
And so she is nothing anymore.
I tell her it's a lie.
But that's a lie.
I know she's right.
And it hurts even more to know that.
But I don't even know what I am supposed to do now.

I'm no one without Red.

I am nothing more than a shell of a boy with dark imaginings.

I am dark.

I am dying.

And I can't stop what this place is doing to me.

I can't beg this place to stop.

Personality glances at me.

I can feel his gaze on me.

He.

He isn't an it, like Red thought.

If only she knew.

Personality morphs into his true form.

He comes down the tree.

He stands in front of me.

No longer does he look pathetic.

But I know that all he can do is echo.

He looks at me with this gaze of desperation.

"What do you want me to do? I can't follow her."

"Follow," he urges me.

"I can't. She hates me. She left me out of fear."

"Can't hate," he promises.

"She can hate. She was scared to care, so she left."

"Can care," he pointed out.

"If she can care, then why did she leave?"

"Can leave," he said, shrugging with the words he couldn't use.

"She could leave, so she did. I cannot make her stay."

"Make her stay," he suggested.

"I can't!"

He cringed.

"Great. Now I'm the evil one."

"Evil," he said while shaking his head.*

"Well, what do I do now?"

He paused, and then took a deep breath, extending his hand.

"No."

I knew what he was planning to do.

I couldn't let him.

His hand remained outstretched.

"I won't let you give yourself to me."

"Give," he pleaded.*

"All I get is your memories and knowledge. I can't make her stay with that."

"Make her stay with memories and knowledge," he promised.*

"My time is up."

"My time is up," he challenged, his lifeless eyes flaring.*

He was nothing more than a shadow.

That was what he looked like.

And I knew what he wanted to do.

He wanted to give me his memories.

And his knowledge.

He wanted to let me absorb him.

So that I could go to her.

After all, he knew more about her than anyone else.

He knew.

And I wanted to trust him.

Slowly, I reached out my hand.

It was tentative.
He eagerly watched.
He couldn't touch me.
Unless I touched him.
So I did.
I touched my hand to his.
And with that, it happened.
I absorbed the essence of her uncle.
Leroy.

Chapter 32:

Falling Out of Love

"Hey," Randall murmured, slowly walking up behind Connor.

Connor, who was sitting on the bed in Jacey's room, smiled up at her. "Hey, Jay."

Her smile barely faltered at the name, and she sat down next to him. "It's been a while since we could just hang out together. Just the two of us."

"It has been a while," he agreed. She slipped her body under his arm, so his arm was resting around her shoulders.

"Yeah."

Connor glanced at her. "You seem different, Jay. Like, you seem to want me more, now."

"Is that a problem?" Randall's eyes filled with innocence. "I thought you cared about me like that, too, Connor."

"I do. I didn't mean it when I said I didn't love you." He smiled sadly at her, the memory flashing in his mind.

She smiled slightly. "Good." Her lips pressed against his, and he let her slide onto his lap. But once her hands delved under his shirt, he stiffened.

"Uhm," he stammered, cheeks red.

"It's just fun, Connor," Randall promised. "I thought you were always jealous of those guys I hung out with at parties. The ones you had to tell to go away."

He shrugged, rubbing the back of his neck. "Still. It's just not how I thought we would act. I'm not like them."

"Fine." Randall stood, eyes narrowed. "Excuse me for my display of love. I'm going ot go get some air." She rolled her eyes, walking out of the room with loud clicks of her flip-flops.

When she entered the rest room, she glanced in the mirror. It was as if she wasn't even in the room. The mirror was blank, and she had no reflection. Jacey was obviously either dead or somehow managing to survive. Either way, she wasn't a problem.

What Randall wanted was human contact. She wanted someone to actually be with, and entangle her body with. Connor was one of the only viable subjects. She knew about Jacey's life, and how she acted, and who she hung out with. Randall knew what her life was like. The thing was, nothing could make up for what she had gone through when she had first come to this side of the mirror.

"Damn," Randall murmured. How was she supposed to go through Jacey's life like Jacey? She glanced down at her colors, smiling. She had the power. She had the colors, and not even Jacey could take that away. What Randall needed to do was shatter the mirror since Jacey was a rogue reflection. It would prevent her from ever coming back over.

But that dream she had had that first night here had told her something entirely different. Jacey was one of the colored ones. The one who gave colors, according to the dream. And she wasn't bound to just that mirror. She could come through anywhere.

If Randall had known that, she would have pulled Jacey across a long time ago. Of course Jacey would have the luck to be able to cross over wherever she wanted. She could traipse across the two worlds if she so wanted to.

Or could she? After all, the rules still applied. Jacey couldn't cross over unless she destroyed Randall...or killed someone. But it's not like Jacey would ever dare kill someone. And she was so lost that Randall doubted she would ever be able to find herself. Jacey was doomed to die in the colorless land.

"Tenebris," she murmured. Darkness. It was her ally right now. The darkness had always allied with the reflections. It was something that had always been there to help the reflections.

"Abeo," Randall said quietly. Death. It was something that the darkness had used as a weapon. It was what was used against the rogue reflections. When reflections, or newly-turned ones, went rogue, the darkness would drain them of color and kill them. Only if they were deemed a threat. If they were mostly a threat, but questionable, they were turned into a shadow of their personality. After all, not even the darkness could take away all the hope of these rogue people so that they would become reflections.

"Jay, are you okay?" Connor called through the door.

She ran a hand through her hair. "Sure."

"Come on, Jay. Don't be mad. Please?" he sighed and leaned against the door.

She paused, frowning at the reflection that didn't exist. "I don't understand what you want from me, Connor."

"You never have ever talked to me about something like this," Connor pointed out. "We usually just stay friendly."

"Is it bad to change that up?" Randall asked tentatively.

Connor chuckled weakly. "Well, to be honest, yes."

She sighed, again. "Okay. Well, excuse me for caring about someone. Excuse me for actually giving a damn about you, because I apparently have no reason to. I guess I should have thought twice before saying anything. Maybe it's a lost cause."

"Stop throwing me the guilt trip, Jacey," Connor said quietly, a slight growl in his voice. "I hate how you have been doing that recently. It's really horrible."

Randall rolled her eyes. "Man up, Connor. It's not that big of a deal."

She could practically hear him wince.

"I just meant..." Randall trailed off.

"I know what you meant. Whatever, Jay. Being gone really did change you."

She bit her lip. Randall wasn't the same as Jacey, and even Connor was beginning to tell that. "Connor, I didn't mean it like that."

There was no reply from the other side of the door.

"Connor?"

Again, she was met with only silence.

"Come on, don't be like this." Randall opened the door slightly, sighing when she saw that Connor had already left. She peered around the door, exasperated with this boy. Why did Jacey bother to hang around him? It was absolutely fruitless.

Lakewood glanced at her, frowning slightly. "He left."

She rolled her eyes, moving to go to her room.

"Why don't you follow him?"

"He's the idiot that walked away," Randall pointed out.

He sighed. "I wish you would just tell me why you're acting so weird."

"Like you even care," she challenged.

"See?" he murmured, turning and walking away. "I guess you'll just have to believe me."

Randall sighed in frustration, glancing from Lakewood's retreating figure, then to the door, and then at what was supposed to be her room.

"Don't forget about what today is," Lakewood called over his shoulder.

She cursed under her breath. "Oh, yeah."

"Dad will pick you up at five o'clock," he said, shutting his door.

After everything that she had gone through to get here, she realized that she absolutely hated Jacey's life. It was nothing like what Randall wanted. Such a small circle of friends and family that she was always stuck with. Jacey really didn't know what she wanted, but Randall did. Randall was the one in control now.

She had the life. She could do what she wanted, and no one could tell her otherwise. What she would have to do is figure out a way to start a new life and get rid of the idea of Jacey once and for all. She would have to destroy this life and begin her own. Randall would actually get a chance at what she had never been able to have before.

The things Randall could use to her advantage were the other reflections on this side. Ones who knew how to start over. Besides them, she had no chance.

Slipping her phone out of her pocket, she clicked on the contact labeled 'Blue'. It rang four times before the voicemail tone rang in her ear.

"Caesitas," the voicemail murmured. "Livor mortis."

Randall was glad her Latin wasn't as bad as it used to be. She waited for the silence to end until the dial tone echoed in her ear. *Livor mortis* meant the "bluish color of death." *Caesitas* was the color "blue."

"Tu fui ego eris," Randall began with. She switched to English, hoping this would actually work. "Middle mirror of the New York World Trade Center monument. Today. At one in the afternoon."

The phone emitted a ghastly beep, and she winced as the call went dead. Hopefully, one of the members of the caesitas cult.

Randall slipped the paper out of her pocket, glancing at the small writing. It was printed in

Latin and English, with the familiar downwards colored pentagram on the side of the paper.

Rubrum: Creating Love

"*Amor vincit omnia*"

Love conquers all.

Aurantiaco: Living Memories

"*Beatae memoriae*"

Of blessed memory.

Crocus: Limitless Mind

"*Compos mentis*"

In control of the mind.

Herbesco: Blessed Hope

"*Contra spem spero*"

Hope against hope.

Caesitas: Triumphant Power

"Absolutum dominiun"

Absolute dominion.

Purpura: Blessed Smiles

"Arcanum boni tenoris animae"

Secret behind a good mood.

The colored downwards-pointed pentagram, or *deorsum Stella de colos,* was a symbol that was extremely prominent in the dark and dying places. The mirrors that were on the other side were arranged in a pentagram format, and the ground was tinted slightly whatever color the point of the pentagram should be.

Randall remembered that her old mirror where she reflected was in the center of the pentagram. On this, it was black. But the sand was tinted blue. Only she, the original reflection, could actually see that. She wasn't on the line like the rest of them. Her mirror was in the center area, in what seemed to be uncharted territory, in a way.

She had only a little while before she had meet a member of the caesitas cult. But it was time enough. Once and for all, the power of the tenebris would overcome this. Randall could start a new life as soon as she used darkness to destroy her connection to Jacey through the mirror.

Without telling Lakewood where exactly she was going, or if she was leaving, she slipped out of the apartment. Getting to the monument was no problem for Randall. A fifty dollar bill and a taxi could get her anywhere.

Once she got to the monument, Jacey looked at where a guy was sitting by the memorial. He was kneeling, and his head was bowed. But something about him was off. He looked like a typical man in his late thirty's, but there was something about him that just drew her to him. His jacket, of course, was blue. That was the clue. Obvious, and not unique, but it was a dead giveaway. She slowly approached him, not sure if she was wary or nervous or both.

"Aciano," the guy murmured, not bothering to look up at her. "That is my name." She wasn't sure, but his accent hinted at his Italian roots. "You're Randall," he said simply.

She nodded, not surprised at the expanse of his knowledge. He was one of the only ones who could help her now.

"We need to go to the mirror as soon as possible. I think you and Jacey have a conversation worth having," he murmured.

"She isn't at the mirror. How am I supposed to talk to her otherwise?"

Aciano glanced at her, looking bored. His eyes were a startling blue that almost made it look like he had color contacts in. "If she is in the blue section of the pentagram, I an let the mirror see her so she can talk to you."

"What if she is talking, somehow, to someone else?"

"That action freezes all rogue reflections," he explained, voice crisp.

Randall nodded appreciatively. "Okay. It's in there," she said, jerking her head towards the restroom.

Aciano shrugged, standing up. His hair was thin and slightly spiked on his head, and it was a silver color. His eyes, besides the steely blue, were incredibly alert. He was extremely tall, and just looked domineering. He slipped something to her, and she took the gun with wide eyes.

"What the hell?" she muttered.

He smirked slightly. "Just tuck it under your belt. It's fine."

Randall did as he said, sighing. He let her lead, surprisingly, and she was surprised when he stopped behind her before she entered.

"I'll wait outside."

She raised an eyebrow at him.

"If Jacey isn't there in the next minute, it means she isn't in the blue sector," he warned, standing with his back against the wall.

Randall slowly walked inside, shutting the door behind her. She looked at the mirror in the center, eyes widening at the girl that was staring into it, looking extremely pissed off.

"Jacey?" she whispered, walking up to the mirror. Luckily, Jacey hadn't heard. Randall regained her composure, smirking slightly as she stepped in front of the mirror.

Jacey's eyes flickered over Randall, and she growled, "You bitch."

"Me? This is my life, Jacey. You're nothing."

"Shut the fuck up."

Randall chuckled slightly. "I don't have to." She reached up to brush a piece of hair out of her eyes, and Jacey almost did the same. "See?"

Jacey's cheeks flooded with red as she said that. It almost seemed like an instinct.

"It's going to happen soon enough. Being colorful can't save your own skin," Randall challenged.

The other girl glared. "How the hell can I see you? The mirror isn't even close to where I am."

"Call it power," Randall smirked. "I used the power of the pentagram."

Jacey scowled. "What the hell do you want?"

"I'm going to start over. I am going to start over my life."

"You mean my life," the girl on the other side scowled again.

Randall laughed, her laugh more high-pitch than Jacey's. "It used to be your life. Now it's mind. I can do whatever I want. But there are a few loose ends I need to tie up before I can actually do that."

"'Lose ends?' What the hell does that mean?" Jacey asked, frowning slightly.

"It is more of a loose end. You, to be specific," Randall said causally, quirking a brow at Jacey.

Jacey looked at Randall warily. "What about me?"

"You can't cross back over. Ever. I can't allow that."

"What the hell? Why?"

Randall shrugged. "If you cross back over, I am destroyed. I happen to like the life I am about to set up. I don't need you ruining it, Jacey."

"You can't stop me," she challenged.

"I could break the mirror," Randall pointed out, a smirk playing on her face.

Jacey opened her mouth and then shut it, eyes wide. Her face displayed utter panic. "You wouldn't dare."

"You're a liability," the girl pointed out to Jacey. "You are the only risk I have."

"You wouldn't do it," Jacey said, hoping to call out Randall's bluff.

Randall touched the rock that had been in her pocket for the last week. She showed it to Jacey. "Say this flew into the mirror. It would shatter, wouldn't it? Should we test that out?"

Jacey shook her head quickly. "Don't do it. You can't. I mean..." She trailed off, not sure if there was anything she could say.

"I could," Randall said quietly, and she feigned throwing the rock at the mirror. Jacey flinched, and Randall laughed.

"Randall, don't do this. You're not a bad guy."

The girl raised a brow. "You don't know that. You're not me. You are going to be destroyed. Shattering this mirror destroys you."

"How?" Jacey asked, her eyes wide. She couldn't help the fear that was slipping into her expression.

"The connection we have by being on both sides of a mirror like this is crucial. Since we are looking into opposite sides of the same mirror, shattering it destroys your connection to the other side."

Jacey shook her head. "Then every time a mirror shatters, it would destroy the people."

Randall raised her eyebrows at Jacey's perceptiveness. "It regards rogue reflections. Ones who don't obey the rules. Us being on opposite sides of any mirror is a strong enough connection. If you can't find yourself, then you disappear when I shatter this mirror. It's your connection to this side."

"What about our mirror?"

"You're rogue. This connection is something that will destroy our mirror as well."

Jacey frowned. "So I just disappear?"

"Or become a spirit. It depends."

"Our mirror will disappear?"

Randall shrugged slightly. "The connection will. It will be nothing but a window to this side."

Jacey dug her fingernails into her palm. "Why do you have to do that? Why can't you just leave me be and go away?"

"Because I will not take that risk!" Randall nearly shouted. "You could cross back over and ruin everything. I will not let you take my life away."

"It's not your life! You stole what I had!"

"It needs to happen, Jacey. I won't let you steal everything back. I worked for this, and I will not give it up. Not for even you."

Jacey felt her nails dig deeper into her palm. "You bitch."

"I'll do it," she threatened.

"Don't. I'll stay here. I promise."

Randall's eyes widened. "What?"

"I will stay here. I won't try and cross over. Just don't destroy it," Jacey felt pathetic for pleading.

"Why not?" Randall asked, tossing the stone in the air.

Jacey bit the inside of her cheek. "Who said I will ever cross over? I'm too lost. Don't do anything unnecessary."

"True," the girl agreed, nodding slowly.

"I mean, I can't cross over. I can't kill. I can't find myself."

Randall nodded.

"Please."

She slid the stone in her pocket. "Maybe you're right. You're rogue."

Jacey sighed, watching Randall step away. "Have fun in your life."

Randall nodded, turning away. She walked down the small hallway that was directly across from the mirror to the exit.

"Bye, Randall," Jacey murmured wistfully.

She stopped, a small smirk rising on her face. "Oh, and Jacey?" Randall turned on her heel, looking Jacey directly in the eyes. She pulled out the gun, and without the blink of an eye, fired the gun straight at the mirror.

Randall took the time to watch the mirror crack, and to watch the shattered pieces of Jacey's scared expression fall to the ground with a satisfying sound.

Chapter 33:

One More Thing

Callie glanced at the clock, brow furrowed in worry. Justin said it wouldn't take that long. He had come back for Jacey's name, and then he had left again. Surely he had managed to make it back again?

She glanced at the bedroom, frowning at the paper she hadn't noticed on the bed. He must have left it before he left for the second time. She slowly stood, walking over to the bed. Her knees were shaking slightly as she picked up the papers that were there. Messy scribbling covered the pages, and it was all too familiar to Callie. Remembering the last letter she had gotten, her heart twisted as she began to read Justin's letter.

Dearest Cat,

I should have told you all of this before I left for the second time. But they call me a coward for a reason. I was too scared to tell you all of this. It's something that you need to hear from me.

I don't think I have ever loved, or would have ever loved anyone as much as I love you. You changed my world in a way that I didn't know was possible. I thought that I was destined to set fires all my life. I burned all the bridges in my life. I didn't see any other future that was laid out for me besides one with you. When I met you, you became my future.

You are a wonderful girl. Don't let your family tell you otherwise. Like what you tell me, being different is bad. It's something we should appreciate. I know how much stress your parents put on you, but I know that you should not take it to heart. Your mother is scared of differences, and that is something that is quite ridiculous. You think you're bad, but I assure you, Cat, that you are not.

When I first saw you, I didn't see someone damaged. I saw a wonderful mature woman who was different than everyone else. She was unique, and carried herself with pride. She was absolutely beautiful. Her hair fell down in loose waves, and she had a face with bright eyes and a kind smile. There were flaws, but they made her all the more perfect. No part of her was bad. Not even the knowledge that she was damaged, too, would let her image be twisted. Her voice was like an ocean wave that was crashing gently onto me. You were her.

I never thought that we would become something wonderful. I was damaged, too, and I was a risk to society. My parents locked me up out of fear, and I feared that you would be afraid of me as well. It's something that I worried about in the days that preceded me talking to you. I wanted nothing more than to know what you would actually think of me.

Before I talked to you, I actually ended up having a dream about you. I saw you in a white dress, walking down the aisle. Some people say that it's strange and creepy. But I found it fascinating. I watched you get married. I couldn't tell what I was feeling, or why I even dreamed that. You captured all of my attention, Cat. From the moment I saw you. I never thought about your supposed disease.

Then we became friends. Friends. It's such a nice word. Most people were scared of me, and I was fine with that. Do you remember the first thing you said to me? You asked me if I believed in guardian angels. I chuckled at that. If I had a guardian angel, I would have ended up someplace else. You were so shocked. I told you that that was what I believed. You weaved this tale for me about how you had a guardian angel in disguise. Someone human who was always watching out for you. But you wanted to find out who that person was.

To be honest, the first thing I wanted to say was that I could be your guardian angel. But I don't protect people. It's not what pyromaniacs do. We set things on fire and watch them burn. I knew that.

But we became friends nevertheless. We made fun of the doctor who ran small groups, and we talked in the trees outside. It was something that made that hell so much better. You saved me from everything bad that could have possibly happened. You took me away from the dark and led me to the light. It was the best gift anyone could have ever given me.

Something I never realized until later in those weeks of knowing each other was that you weren't damaged like I was. You were rejected by society and your family. I couldn't understand why. The thing was that you were a great person. Hearing voices didn't make you harmful or a burden. So it was hard for me to grasp why you were there.

But I am glad you were there. As bad as it sounds, I would have gotten lost there without you. You saved me, as I said before. I wanted to be there for you every single day. You deserved endless love and support, and I knew that. I wanted you to know that, too.

I think that the day it thundered, when you admitted your fear of thunder, was some day that I will never forget. They revoked the rule for us, so that we could experience people caring, and we could experience love. I know that it is something that would have been the ruin of me if it hadn't happened. You agreed to be my girlfriend, and the happiness I thought I saw in your face was something uniquely you altogether. You felt accepted, and I was glad. You deserved to feel accepted, and I was glad to be the one to accept you. I cared about you so much. And don't ever forget that. No matter what.

We experienced a lot together, despite the short time. My first happy Valentine's day was with you because it was the one time where I didn't have to listen to everyone mope about being single. It was happy because you were happy. That was all that mattered to me, Cat. I wanted you to feel accepted. And loved. And cared for. You were. I wanted to hold you in my arms and never let go.

Fires for me are like oxygen for someone else. It allows me to release all my tension and get happiness. I didn't light fires for money, or for personal gain, or for the sake of ruining someone else. I feel this release of tension when it comes to lighting fires. Something unique. I realized that fires were my only escape. They brought me pleasure, and I figured it was the only thing I could ever rely on to do that in my life. I saw being a pyromaniac as not a maniac, but someone who had nothing else in my life. Someone who had nothing else to rely on for happiness except fires.

The thing is, Cat, that you ended up becoming my fire. I didn't need to release tension with you around. I didn't need to get happiness from matches and lighters because I could simply look at you and it would all begin to make sense. I would be simply happy. It was easy, and it was wonderful. It was better than the stupid medicine they gave me, and I actually began to heal myself. I admit that I was broken and damaged. But you fixed that. And that is a debt I can never repay.

When you ended up missing the dance because I was late, I felt nothing but guilt. I wanted to tell you that I wouldn't have missed it for the world. It was their fault. I expected you to get mad at me, and I expected this serious frustration on your part. But you forgave me. I couldn't believe my luck. You were so willing to forgive me, and you did so with such ease that I was actually shocked. I wanted to pick you up and tell you all of this, but I couldn't. All I could do was tell you your new future.

You agreed to move in with me. Not only did you agree to it, but you also ended up being extremely happy to move in with me. You knew it was strange, and that it was weird, but you said yes anyway. You trusted me enough. You trusted me to take care of you, to not take advantage of you, and not to light such fires that I used to light. I stuck to my promise for your sake. I wanted you to know that I was serious about this, and I wanted to prove myself to the mental hospital and to you. I think I managed to.

We did have that one fight. I was terrified that you were going to walk away. It's scary, and unusual for me, to be the one reliant upon somebody. You walked away when I told you 'I love you' and I almost broke down in tears. I thought maybe that I had been fooling myself all this time. I didn't want to let you go. I wanted you to stay with me and feel my love and feel loved.

But we made it through all that. We had that talk, and it healed anything that might have been splintered in that fight, and I know that that is hard. But we did it. It is quite impressive. Teenage relationships almost never work out. Whether it's because of going to different colleges, or family issues, or moving away. Things happen. I wanted us to be the lucky ones. I wanted to be able to look back on our years and be able to smile proudly. To say that we were the ones who were able to make it.

Things were going really well. In between now and that month, we progressed a lot. We managed to do accept each other more, if that was even possible. More than anything, I wanted to tell you how much I appreciated you. I assumed you knew. I hoped you did. Because now, all I can do is say everything through this letter. There is no taking back the past. I never wanted the memory of us to die. Even if we split apart, I told myself you would always have an important place in my heart.

I had such plans for us, Cat. Those dates we went on and those fun times we had the past three months said a lot. There is nothing wrong with loving someone when we are this young. In fact, it is a gift to find someone who will always care about you. I found you, and you found me. I think that makes us the luckiest people anywhere. Not many people get the chance to love someone and be loved like the chance we had.

Remember that bent spoon you kept? I found it in the washer one day. I took it, and kept it. I should have told you, but I wanted to hold a part of you every day. I remember how we tried to come up with all those uses for bent spoons. I thought of a few more. One is to hold a memory. Another is to use for serving powder sugar. And finally, another is to hold a promise. On the back of this final page is that spoon with a promise inside it. But don't look just yet.

Cat, I wrote this for two reasons. One is because I knew you needed to know this. The second I because I cannot tell you in person. I couldn't bear the thought of telling you the truth. I'm not coming back. I met my old reflection on the other side, and I'm dying. He took my colors, and my life. I can't come back. But please don't ever forget my promise. Please don't ever forget these words. They ring with truth and my love.

Forever is longer than you think, Cat.
Oh, and one more thing.
I love you.
Love,
Justin.

Callie's eyes had been brimming with tears. By the time she got halfway through, she was crying. And now she was downright sobbing. Her fingers shakily took the bent spoon off the tape on the back page. A ring slipped out.

It was a promise. A promise that he loved her. That he loved her forever. It was something she would never forget, not as long as she wore that ring.

Callie slid the promise onto her finger, shaking and nearly in hysterics. But the cold ring and the silence of the room around her reminded her that not even tears could bring Justin back.

Chapter 34:

All the Shattered Worlds

Jacey took a step backwards, running a hand through her hair. The devilish smile that rose onto Raymond's face was etched not with charm, but with what seemed to be almost one-hundred percent evil.

"Oh, darling, you had to know that this was coming," he practically purred. Raymond took a small step forward, and Jacey wasn't sure if he was enjoying the moment because he was driven by madness or if he just was enjoying this because of the sick bastard he was.

She chewed the inside of her cheek, desperate to find a way to escape. He didn't have to touch her in order to steal her colors. And that was what scared her most of all.

"This doesn't have to happen through force," Raymond coaxed, smiling gently, as if they were discussing something as simple as the weather. He took yet another tiny step towards her, the smile still playing on his face.

Jacey couldn't help but raise an eyebrow. "What do you mean?"

"You're a Dator. You could simply give me your colors. It will make everything a lot less painful for you," he said quietly.

"It's not like you don't want me to feel pain," she challenged, not sure of why she was being so snappy with the man who was about to control her pain. What she should have worried about was the shattered mirror because of Randall. But Jacey couldn't help but think about the man that was about to kill her. She had to tackle one problem at a time.

Raymond nodded slowly. "That makes sense," he agreed. "But you should take the chance I am giving you."

"How?" The word slipped out before Jacey could stop it.

He smirked, taking a small step forward. "It's easier than you may think, Jacey. If you'd like, you could try it out on me. You've been doing it unintentionally until now. But you need to learn to control it."

"Teach me," Jacey whispered, desperate for that surety she had never been able to find. This was also another way to stall him from causing unimaginable pain. She didn't move, staring at him directly in the eyes.

Raymond took another step forward. "Think of something happy," he murmured.

Her eyes closed as she flipped through her memories. She grasped hold of a memory that exuded happiness. It was a small one from volleyball, where she had won her first game.

"Now look me in the eyes, and give me the feeling," Raymond coaxed. It was something that he said with such ease, despite how complicated she realized it might be.

Jacey's eyes opened, and the color that was usually hazel was now a vivid purple. The purple actually seemed to come out from her eyes in that same type of mist from earlier. Raymond smiled widely, and it was more of a smirk as he breathed in the purple color.

"See? It's easy," he encouraged her. "It's not hard at all. It is painless."

She nodded slowly, looking at him with her normal hazel eyes. They tingled slightly, as if she was looking at the world through different eyes. Her vision was tinged with purple for a few seconds as the effect faded.

"You can give me all of a color," Raymond suggested, his eyes hungrily searching her eyes, wanting the color.

Jacey closed her eyes to find the memory, finding herself mesmerized by the colors and how they came from the memories. But just as she grabbed a hold of the happiest memories she could think of, which was with her Uncle Leroy, her hazel eye shot open.

"What?" His voice was filled with worry, and it was obvious that he cared more about the colors than her.

"No," her voice rang out in the silence that had existed between then for a few moments. "I will not give you my colors. You can try and take me down but I will not stand by and watch that happen."

Raymond growled at her sudden defiance. "I'm experienced as a Furtum. You should be thankful and you should jump at the chance to not die painfully."

"I'm not going to die!" Jacey's voice rose past a yell, and almost to what could be a scream.

He smirked, and then laughed. His laugh filled the air, and it was quite intimidating. It echoed, and seemed to linger even after he finished. "I can prove you wrong yet again," he said, still chuckling softly.

"I'll go down fighting," she swore, spitting a stream or curses at him. The mirror was shattered, anyway.

"I killed my own reflection today, doll. Don't think I have mercy," Raymond smirked, taking a large step forward.

Jacey scowled, and attempted to swing her fist toward his right cheek. He managed to duck just in time, and he swung his right hand across her cheek with all the strength he could gather. She went down immediately, sprawled across the hard ground. Jacey slid slightly, and abrasions covered her forearms as she used them to attempt to stop herself.

Raymond bent down, squatting next to her. His face, which echoed with insanity, loomed above her. His hand had left a mark on her left cheek, and he smirked at that. He brought his hand up one more time, and Jacey couldn't stop herself from cringing in fear. She hadn't expected the physical pain.

"Get the fuck away from me," Jacey growled, propping herself up. Raymond laughed with that same insanity, gripping her upper arms with a ferocity she had never felt or seen. He quickly brought her to her feet, keeping her pressed against him. His heart was beating quickly, thudding as he planned his next move.

Typically, the Furtum would use Latin to evoke their power. But not Raymond. He was experienced. He could do this with a simple thought. He wondered what he wanted to take away first.

Blue. Power. She deserved no power. Raymond looked her in the eyes. He wanted to see the power drain from her eyes and her body. It was something that would be extremely painful.

A blue mist rose out of Jacey as she shuddered. His grip on her upper arms turned white-hot, and it almost scalded her. The burn mixed with the weakness that snuck into every muscle in her body. Her defiance bubbled inside her, desperate to fight. Jacey cried out, her body practically going limp in his grasp. She felt exhausted, and she hung there like a rag doll. Her mind urged her to fight, but her body couldn't. There was no power left. Her mind began to question if she could even attempt to fight back.

Jacey glared at the ground, her head hanging in a submissive gesture to the lack of blue. Her jeans were now black, as if they had never had any color.

Yellow. Intelligence. She wouldn't become a vegetable without any knowledge, but it took away her common sense. Jacey wouldn't be able to fight. He brought his hands to her waist, holding on tightly to her. She hated the submission. She hated his power. She hated her lack of power. And she hated him.

A yellow mist seeped out of her almost reluctantly. Jacey squeaked, unable to prevent herself from crying out. Her mind went fuzzy, and she couldn't think of anything to do next. Her mind felt like it was collapsing in on itself. It was as if Jacey simply couldn't take the pain at all. The tinges of yellow faded from her limp body, and Raymond smirked. Those were the easy colors.

Purple. Happiness. She had given him a very small amount. Raymond snaked one arm around her, using his now free hand to touch her cheek gently. As he did so, a purple mist rose up out of her cheek. It seemed to come from her pores, as if happiness was nestled in every aspect of her face. The mist was almost a ghost of a smile, as if it represented something that would never exist again.

It was as if a wave of sadness crashed over her due to loss of happiness. She searched in her memories, but they didn't bring back the same happiness as before. His hand was on her cheek again, and she bit back a scream. It felt as if he was dragging something sharp across her cheek, and it was almost unbearable.

Green. Hope. It was almost over, and Raymond knew that. His body vibrated with color, and he surged with this electricity of some sort.

It rose out of her mouth, the green mist. Raymond's mouth hovered above hers, and he inhaled deeply as the mist came to him. Her eyes reflected absolute terror with him standing so close. His lips barely brushed against hers as he murmured something in what she had to assume to be Latin. Her lips felt like they were on fire. And it wasn't a good fire. It was like she was burning to death, and as the last of the green left her, Jacey let out a scream that echoed across the expanse of this hell.

Raymond paused, taking a moment to enjoy his handiwork thus far. Nothing mattered except her colors. Once she had no colors, he would be done with her. He didn't need her, and no one else seemed to need her either. It was a fair deal. After all, he had waited so long for this moment.

Raymond stroked her cheek again, and she screamed at the empty void she felt in her body. She was collapsing in on herself, and Raymond was the only one supporting her. The scream ripped through the air, tearing apart black and white as it reverberated. It soon became nothing more than an echo, just as she would be soon enough.

Chapter 35:

Why Am I Alone?

That scream was all too familiar.
Like the one I heard so long ago.
But I can't possibly remember who let out that scream.
It triggers a memory.
A memory I can't remember.
It is just a figment of my imagination.
Sister winces.
She says that bad things are happening.
I don't really care.
I just want to die.
Another scream rips through the air.
It entrances me.
In fear, I listen to its echo.
Slowly, I feel myself breathe in.
Leroy's essence fills me suddenly.
It's done.
I feel his memories mingle with mine.
I feel...alive.
Jacey.
The name comes up as a sharp memory.
I inhale sharply, looking around.
Why am I alone?
She left me.
I remember that much.
But...it feels different.
It's like an incongruity.
Something that exists—
But it doesn't make sense.

I shouldn't be alone.
I had found someone who gave me a reason
to live.
Sister cringes at this.
I stand, slowly and steadily.
Leroy's essence is urging me forward.
I know where I need to go.
I know where to go.
But Sister stops me.
She slowly reaches out her hand.
She grasps my hand.
I don't understand why she has to do this.
Why now?
Of all times, why now?
My mind swirls as I turn to look at her.
"Don't leave me," she pleads.
Her words fill the air.
Another scream rips through her words.
I need to go.
"I left you."
My words are the truth.
They feel like the truth.
After all, at the restaurant so many years
ago...
I watched her die.
And all I could do was run away.
I was the one who left.
It was all said and done.
Now, I had other business to attend to.
"Don't make the same mistake twice," she
cries.
Her cry hurts my heart.
At her cry, memories flood me.

But it's because Leroy is encouraging me to
remember.
I see myself teaching her to play soccer.
I see myself playing a board game with her.
I see myself holding her after that day the
teacher got...too close.
I see myself murmuring her name as I
pushed her on the wing.
Sister.
Chrissie.
Christabelle.
It hits me hard.
She reaches out to me.
She hands me something.
I've always seen her holding something.
But now she wants me to see.
I take it.
It feels fragile.
This is all I have left.
It's a picture.
Of me and my sister.
Of me and her.
She's wearing a yellow dress.
She's a princess.
Her tiara shines even though the picture is
still.
I stand next to her.
In a tux.
Her Prince Charming.
"You saved me," she whispers.
This is her favorite memory.
I look at her picture.
She looks so alive.

Her eyes are bright and they look deep within me.

She is bright.

She radiates life.

I do, too.

My white-blonde hair is styled.

I look like a prince.

This makes me smile.

Our bright blue eyes match.

It's amazing.

The epitome of life is in this picture.

I glance toward her.

She looks...different.

She is entirely black and white.

There is no color left there.

I look at the picture.

And then back at her.

The difference is unmistakable.

I can't deny the death that now is expressed in her haunted eyes.

I have to remind myself of what happened.

"Come with me."

My voice is no more than a whisper.

"I can't," she says.

And I suddenly come to understand.

Leaving her for Jacey means she doesn't have a purpose.

Her ghost is my imagination.

And now I have a reality.

I have something real.

Something to let me live.

I can't let that go.

Not even for the sister that I left before.

My eyes feel dry.
And as much as it hurts,
I tuck the picture in my pocket.
She understands.
That gesture says everything.
I try not to let the uninvited tears come and
fall.
Her eyes are not as dry.
The tears fall from her eyes.
"Don't stop playing soccer," she murmurs,
voice cracking.
I remember teaching her.
My heart twists inside my chest.
I know what she is feeling
I can see it.
Her pain is my pain.
I have to let go.
The silence is scaring me.
My life is also at stake, I remind myself.
"You'll always be my prince," she says.
I wrap my arms around her.
My mind knows what is needs.
And what it wants.
It always has known.
And that is what hurts most of all.
"And you'll always be my princess."
It's the truest statement I can say.
And it says more than just that.
She looks at me.
Her small arms are around me.
I lift her up.
She is almost weightless.

Because my imagination cannot weigh that much.

Her eyes are filled with pain.

"I understand," she promises.

I know she does.

She knows that I have to do this.

Slowly, I look her in the eyes.

I brush a curl out of her eyes.

Christabelle burrows her head into my neck.

But as she does that, in the silence, it happens.

She begins to fade.

Her body becomes transparent.

I ignore the twisting of my heart.

But I watch.

I hold her tight.

And I watch her fade.

"I love you," she murmurs.

"I love you."

Chrissie's fading eyes glance at me.

"I know," she smiles.

Her smile is sad.

But it's full of life.

And I hold onto that memory.

Her body, as it fades, moves to stand in front of me.

And I run.

Not away from her.

But to something.

To Jacey.

To love.

To life.

My feet keep me from moving.

I know what I am doing.
This had to happen.
I touch the picture in my pocket.
And, this time, I do something I promised myself I would never do.
I keep running.
And I don't look back.

Chapter 36:

Draped in Blue

Randall was stuck in this phase of hyper awareness and she was hyper-aware that her life was going to hell.

But something that Randall trusted were the shattered pieces of the mirror that now lay scattered amongst the ground. She knew that Aciano could be trusted, and that she had to rely on him. She owed a debt to him and the caesitas cult, and it was a debt that was very difficult to repay.

She bent down, gently scooping a fragment of the mirror into her hand. It looked more mortal than ever, despite the fact that it had never had a pulse. Of course, Randall didn't see her reflection in the mirror. One single crack ruins the bond of such a unique mirror set up by a cult. This was irreversible.

The silencer on the gun had worked perfectly. She had barely heard the ring of it as the bullet streamed toward the mirror. To her surprise, Jacey hadn't seen it coming. The look of surprise on her face was priceless, and would forever be imprinted in Randall's mind.

She slipped the fragment into her pocket, tucking the gun into her belt. It wasn't as hard to shoot as she expected. Slowly, Randall turned away from the mirror. Part of her wanted to admire her handiwork, and this was mostly because she knew what was waiting for her when she exited to go see Aciano. All of the cults, especially the caesitas one, demanded something in return for a favor. And knowing the caesitas cult, it would be a debt that was very difficult to repay.

Just as she reluctantly pushed the door to exit the restroom, Aciano glanced at her with wide blue eyes. His eyes were narrowed, as if watching her to make sure she didn't attempt to escape.

"I presume you didn't fail?" he asked. His Italian accent was thicker now, as if he no longer had to hide it. His goatee kept flickering, and it was difficult for Randall to understand what exactly was going on.

Randall bit back the smirk she wanted to display. "Of course I didn't."

Aciano chuckled darkly. "We're going to take you with us this time."

"Excuse me?" she looked outraged. "I have a debt to pay, and there is no reason why I'm going back with you to wherever the hell your cult resides."

"Do you really think you have a choice? You'll pay your debt, one way or another," he murmured, placing his hand on her forearm.

Randall glanced warily at their contact. "What is my debt, anyway?"

"We need information on what's going on in the pentagram's inner pentagon. You can provide us with such information. And perhaps scout for us."

"Be your informative?" Randall asked dubiously. "I don't think so. I may have asked you for help, but you're still the bad guys. You ally with the spirits who try and kill us."

Aciano nodded, not looking surprised or insulted. "I know. But you used to be the reflection of someone very…unique in our world. We need your information."

She felt his grip on her forearm tighten.

"You don't have a choice," he reminded her.

Randall felt her head dip submissively for a moment before she brought her eyes back up to meet his. "That's it?"

"Two weeks of being our informative. That's it. You'll leave tomorrow."

"Fine."

Aciano smirked. "Then you can go start your life or whatever the hell it is that you want to do."

Randall growled under her breath. "Good."

"I recommend you get a new look," Aciano shrugged. "And start over with, well, everything. Figure out a way to make Jacey disappear."

She nodded slowly. "I think I know what I'm going to do."

"Good. And, Randall, try not to fuck this up."

"Whatever, Aciano. You don't own me."

Aciano dug his fingernails into her forearm, smirking at her wince. Without another word, he released her, and stalked away.

Randall made a face at the man as he walked away, and then proceeded to roll her eyes at him. Two years of being an informative was indeed a heavy price to pay, but she could do it. After all, that also meant spending two years with the caesitas cult wherever their base happened to be.

"Bastard," she muttered, rubbing her forearm with a gentle hand. She slowly closed her eyes, thinking of how to make Jacey disappear. The obvious answer was to feign her suicide. It would be risky, and incredibly cliché, but it was one of only ways.

Randall slowly opened her eyes. Maybe there was another way. If she could just talk to Connor about something, then the idea would be fairly plausible. In fact, it would be much more believable than suicide.

But she needed to do this fast, or the idea wouldn't work. She fumbled with her phone, hissing as she cut her finger on the mirror fragment that was in the same pocket. As the phone came out of her pocket, Randall hit the familiar buttons.

"What?" Connor's tone was snappy as he picked up the phone on the first ring.

Randall made a point of sniffling. "I'm sorry. The argument was all my fault, and I feel like an idiot."

He paused, and she could tell he was surprised. "But you never apologize."

"Can't I apologize just this one time?"

"I...I guess," Connor murmured, and there was static as he must have shifted the phone. "It's so unlike you, Jay. It's scary."

Randall ignored the guilt that she hadn't expected to eat out her heart. "But it was my fault.

I mean, you're right. I've been different since I was…"

"I know," he said immediately as she trailed off. As Connor was silent for a moment, Jacey wondered how she could best spring the trap.

"Let's meet up."

Connor was silent again, and she was worried he had hung up on her. "Why?"

He hadn't even asked 'where.' Randall hated the suspicion that he had. It irked her because, although he would never be able to explain it, it risked everything she had.

"Jay?"

"I'm still here," she murmured. "Do we need a reason to meet up? Just, like, an apology lunch."

Connor sighed. "I already ate lunch."

"You have to work with me here, Connor. You weren't usually like this."

"I could say the same to you," Connor challenged.

Randall sighed. "Okay. Then let's meet up and we'll work out something."

There was only silence.

"Pretty please?"

Connor sighed loudly. "The physical appearance of the please does not make a difference, but fine."

Randall nodded, relieved. "Where?"

"The memorial?"

She glanced around. "Uhm, sure."

"Since you're already there," he pointed out before hanging up.

Randall growled in frustration, jamming the phone in her pocket and glancing at her finger, which was still wounded. The bleeding was not a problem, and the cut was minor. She would be fine.

Connor would be a problem, though. He was someone who knew Jacey better than Randall knew Jacey, which was saying something. He could tell that something was off about her. Luckily, the idea of her being Jacey's reflection was something too far-fetched for him to think it up. At least, that was what she had hoped.

She waited for Connor for what felt like forever. In her head, she tried to count. She lost track of the seconds at around two thousand four hundred and ninety one.

When he arrived, Randall was squatting by the section of the memorial that Randall had always seen Jacey at. He came up behind her, kneeling just a bit away.

"Who are you?" he murmured, glancing down as he folded his hands in his lap.

Randall sighed. "I can't tell you." She wasn't sure why she was admitting this to him, or if she was doing something smart. She could only hope.

"Where's Jay?"

"She's not coming back," she whispered, eyes looking haunted as she squatted there. "How did you know it wasn't her?"

Connor glanced her way, but didn't look her in the eye. "First of all, you always kneel when you come here."

"Oh."

"And you're not wearing your necklace."

Randall glanced down. Usually, because she was the reflection, she had a copy of it. But now that she was on this side, she had no copy. Now that he had pointed that out, she felt a bit lighter, like she was missing something.

"Why isn't she coming back?"

Randall didn't want to look at him. "Because I broke the only thing that she could come back through."

"You did it? Why?" His voice was filled with pain and shock.

"Because I was scared. I deserved this, not her. She didn't know who she was, and she was too lost."

Connor winced. "We all are lost every once in a while. She deserved this life."

"No," Randall said a bit loudly. She sighed. "No."

"Some of us needed her," he said wistfully, bringing his brown eyes to meet her hazel ones.

"You need someone who cared about you enough to stay. You need anyone but her..."

Connor tore his gaze away from her. "You don't know that."

"I do."

He sighed. "Fine. Say your lies."

"Connor, I need you to understand that I need to disappear. I need to leave here and never come back."

"Wait," Connor murmured, "that means that, technically, Jacey needs to disappear."

Randall nodded slowly. "Exactly."

"I shouldn't even be fucking helping you. You took her away from me. You are the one who stole all that from me and lied to me," he mumbled.

"There's really nothing else you can do now," Randall pointed out. "Help me make Jacey disappear, and Jacey's family will be able to rest in peace." She frowned. "I mean, be in peace."

Connor opened his mouth, and then closed it. If Randall simply left, Lakewood would be heartbroken at the loss of his sister. He needed surety and clarity more than anything else in the world. And Connor didn't want to watch Lakewood suffer when he could have done something to prevent this pain. Despite the aching in his chest at what had happened to Jacey, he knew that he had to help Lakewood or he would never forgive himself.

"What do I have to do?" he asked, cringing in regret. But he managed to keep his voice steady for the most part as he glanced over at the girl who he really didn't know.

Randall smiled sadly. "It's not that difficult, actually. There was a fire earlier today near here. Some teenagers were having a party. Tell the police that Jacey was there. The DNA is unreadable for the most part, so you should be able to get her name on the list of those who have died."

"Feign her death..." Connor trailed off. "Why not just feign suicide?"

She didn't reply.

"I guess that doesn't sound much like Jacey," he murmured, more to himself than to her.

"Exactly," Randall replied quietly. "Can you at least do that, Connor?"

Connor sighed. "I guess."

"I'll disappear," she promised. "I will leave and never come back. You won't be haunted by me, I swear. Once I leave, I will never come back. You can move on with your life."

He chuckled weakly. "Sure, I will." The sarcasm in his voice was palpable. Randall cringed, but knew that he was telling the truth. Well, the sarcastic truth. Connor's devotion to her was more than obvious, and Randall knew this must pain him.

"Why?" she asked, instantly regretting the question.

Connor looked at her. "Why what?"

"Why are you helping me?"

He smiled, faltering. "Are you *trying* to talk me out of it?"

"No," Randall said quickly. "It's just so strange that you'd agree so quickly..."

Connor nodded slowly, understanding why she would ask. "It must not be obvious," he said, realizing he sounded vague.

"You can tell me," she murmured. "I'm leaving soon, after all."

He glanced at her. "Lakewood," he said simply.

Randall didn't want to jump to any conclusions. "What about him, Connor?"

"Can't you see it?" Connor sighed, laughing weakly. "It's kind of, well, supposed to remain hidden."

She raised an eyebrow. "Do you…"

He nodded.

"Like him?" she asked, looking at him curiously.

"Jacey never knew," was the only thing Connor could manage to say.

Randall rubbed the back of her neck. "Don't feel embarrassed, Connor. I mean, it's not something to be embarrassed about."

"Whatever." His voice was cold, and rough, which obviously showed that he didn't want her to talk about it.

"Well, I have to go now. I…I'll see you…I mean…"

Connor looked hesitant as he brushed his lips against hers, and then turned away. "If I'm never going to see either of you again, then I needed to…"

"I know," Randall said, and she found it all too easy to now ignore the guilt that crushed her heart.

Connor stood, glancing over at the bathroom where he had actually seen Jacey last. His heart felt smaller, and emptier than ever. With a small sigh of pain, he started walking away, leaving Randall there. He didn't want to know who she was, or where she had come from. It didn't matter.

Because even in the wake of all of that, the fact would still remain that Jacey was gone and she wasn't coming back.

Chapter 37:

Searching, Hunting, Seeking, and Never Finding

Orange would be the hardest to take, and Raymond was preparing to attempt it. A small puff of the bright color came out from her eyes. She couldn't bottle the primal cry that managed to escape her. Her eyes were on fire, as memories were ripped away from her. The empty void inside her grew as the moments passed.

Raymond's hands found her eyes, and he slowly forced them to open. Another puff of orange mist, and then a scream followed. Her eyes stared into the sky, unseeing. She couldn't see anything as more and more of her memories were torn from her. She shook, and trembled, unable to stop herself from panicking as she felt the warm memories leave her.

"Get your fucking hands away from her!" The voice echoed, strong and lively. Jacey thought she knew who it came from, but she was lost in the darkness.

Raymond snarled, still holding on to her. "You have no business here!"

"Actually, I do!" Cyril blended in with the darkness, and tried to find a way to show himself. "Who the hell are you, cretin?"

The older boy was turned away from Cyril, fade hidden in shadows. "I'm the one who's going to escape this hell."

"Not if I have anything to do with it," he snarled.

Raymond cackled. "You're black and white. You'll be dead in a matter of moments."

Cyril glanced down. His color was fading, and it was fading fast. But he couldn't let that stop him. Not quite yet.

"Go away. Don't have me be the cause of your death."

"I will as soon as you let her down!" Cyril took a step forward, trying to figure out who the hell was torturing Red. That was the only color he could see in her.

Raymond sighed. He slowly turned, glancing at Cyril. His face was tired, but colorful as he glared. "You'll never learn, will you, little brother?"

The memory tore itself from Cyril's empty void, and his eyes widened in realization. "Ray. You son of a bitch."

"That's no way to talk about your mother," he cackled.

Cyril took a step forward, and a puff of orange smoke escaped Jacey's unseeing eyes once more. "Don't do this, Ray. You...you have good in you." He had always looked up to his older brother, until Raymond had spiraled into a mad arsonist. But he had always had that soft heart for his only older sibling.

"You know that I have to do this in order to get back," Raymond sighed. Cyril may care for him, but he didn't care for Cyril.

"Why?" Cyril's voice cracked, and it was almost drowned out by the painful scream that Jacey emitted.

Raymond smirked slightly. "I don't belong here."

"She had nothing to do with you. You had no right to do this," the younger brother's voice shook as he took a step forward.

"I killed my old reflection to do this! I saw his going towards you and he told me everything. He thought I would spare him. I took his colors. His body lies somewhere over there," Raymond jerked his finger behind him. "They say no one is truly evil, Cyril. They're wrong. But they have a damn twisted version of what evil is. I have self-preservation intents. It just happens that I can't live unless I kill. So that's how it must be."

Cyril glanced at Jacey. "Why her?"

"She's unique. Why do you think she has so much color? If I take her colors, I can go back." Raymond paused. "Let me put it this way: would you rather have her here with you, or have me, your brother, be able to go back?"

"But you killed! You should already be able to get back!"

Raymond chuckled, his voice sour, "Things are different for people like me, who can take colors. We have to be entirely colorful before we can cross over."

"I thought you had good in your heart. You told me before you left that everyone is good somewhere, whether they believe it or not," Cyril pleaded with the man whose eyes reflected nothing but insanity.

"I *lied*," Raymond said slowly, as if making sure that Cyril would understand. He laughed. "I attempted things I shouldn't have. I have burns that I hide."

Cyril tilted his head. "Burns?"

"They're healed for the most part because my reflection healed himself when he was on the other side. But now I have a body littered with burn marks and scars," Raymond scowled, touching his back.

"Those scars remind you of what it is like to do evil," he pointed out.

Raymond rolled his eyes. "Don't try and talk me into being good! It doesn't even work in the movies."

"Ray, you can't do this," Cyril said, his voice quiet. He laid a hand on Raymond's arm.

"Shut up!" Raymond yelled, curling his left hand into a fist and ramming it into Cyril's cheek. Cyril collapsed on the ground, slowly getting back up despite the burning pain in his cheek. Because Raymond was no longer supporting her, Jacey fell onto the ground, twitching.

Cyril stood again, and Raymond brought his fist to his chest, causing the younger boy to fall onto his back. Yet, after a few moments, Cyril shakily stood, glaring at his older brother.

"Give up!" Raymond screamed, and his eyes were afire as he stared at Cyril. "Why the fuck won't you just give up already?"

Cyril shook his head. "You're a fool."

"Don't say you have something worth fighting for. You have nothing! You deserve nothing!" Raymond breathed heavily.

The younger boy's eyes widened. "This isn't just about colors, isn't it?"

"It never was!" the older boy shrieked, unable to control himself. "You don't have to be so damn wonderful. You don't deserve anything!"

Cyril chuckled. "You have nothing to be jealous of."

"Jealous?" Raymond cackled. "No, what I feel is definitely not jealousy."

"Then what is it, Ray?"

The older boy scowled. "I watched you break all those girls' hearts. I watched you take care of Christabelle and be the good role model. I'm tired of the good guy always being loved."

"Have movies taught you nothing?" Cyril taunted.

Raymond curled both his hands into fists once more. "Don't try and tease me. The day I set that fire to the apartment building was the day that I ended up being the bad guy. But you didn't deserve to be Christabelle's role model and big brother. You never deserved that."

"What? Did you want to teach her about arson? Is that what you missed out on?" the younger one glared at the older brother, jaw set.

Raymond approached Christabelle with a bright smile, gazing at her fondly. The fifteen-year old smiled down at the four-year old, who was lying on her bed, talking to the dolls that covered her bed.

"Hey, Christabelle," he murmured, sitting on her bed.

She looked at him almost warily. "Hi." Christabelle tucked a doll behind her back, as if hiding it from Raymond.

"Mom and dad are going to ballroom dance class tonight. I get to watch you tonight."

Her eyes flickered over his face, reading him. "What about Cyril?"

"He's here to," Raymond said quietly, jaw set at the mention of his twelve-year old brother.

"I know," she whispered.

He frowned. "Know what?"

"I watched what you did last night. I saw you light the park tree on fire. Across the street from our house."

Raymond tried to wipe the guilt and surprise off his face. "Oh, Chris, did you have another nightmare?"

"No," Christabelle said, frowning. "And don't call me Chris."

He shook his head. "You're four. Don't get involved in things that you can't understand."

"What does that mean?" she asked, her grip on her doll tightening.

Raymond sighed. "I mean that you need to forget that you ever saw that. It was nothing more than a nightmare."

The young girl stuck her tongue out at him. "Liar, liar, pants on fire!" she called, crinkling her nose.

He resisted the urge to hit her. She was four, Raymond reminded himself. "You're silly," he teased, *the falseness in his voice more obvious than ever.*

"I'm going to tell Cyril," she said, her voice calm.

Raymond reached over, tightening his grip on her wrist. "Don't you dare."

"I will," Christabelle said. *"And if you hit me, I'll tell mom you did it. She'll believe me, I know it."*

For a four-year old, she was pretty damn clever. "Don't say anything," Raymond said. "I know how to light people on fire, too."

"Why do you even fucking care about this bitch?" Raymond asked, gesturing to Jacey. A puff of orange escaped her, followed by an ear-splitting scream.

Cyril glared. "What? Did you expect me to watch someone get murdered? Because I didn't plan on doing that today."

"I'm not going to stop this. You can't do anything. Why did you even follow her?"

The fire in Cyril's eyes was palpable. "I care."

Raymond chuckled. "She can't love someone like you." With that, he bent down, running his hand over her as he pulled red from her. She shook, and trembled, beginning to scream uncontrollably at the immense pain of his hand on her.

"Stop."

The older boy paused for a moment at the authoritativeness of Cyril's voice.

Cyril advanced on Raymond. "Hurt her again. Go on. But I should warn you, there's a reason I've stayed alive all this time and against everything that's been thrown at me, and it sure as hell wasn't luck. So if you think it is at all a good idea to threaten the person I hold most dear in this world, go ahead. See what happens."

Raymond raised an eyebrow at his younger brother. He brought his hand to Jacey's neck, and red clouds began to rise from her and into his arm. The next scream was one that shook the entire realm of the hell they were in, and nearly tore Cyril in two.

It took only a moment for Cyril to jump onto Raymond, knocking him to the ground. Despite his thin stature, he managed to dig his knees into Raymond's rib cage, forcing him to cough and breathe. The black and white figure of Cyril glared down at the more colorful and lively Raymond, who was planning to buck Cyril off.

"I warned you," the younger brother growled. He felt the cold medal against his bare chest, and there was no hesitation as he took off the prized and blood-stained possession.

Raymond smirked. "You can't defeat me. You can't get back. You're too kind to kill, and you're too lost to manage to come back."

"I'm kind enough to rid this hell of evil that is similar to the likes of you," Cyril growled. "I stayed alive for her. I managed to live because of her, and I'm not going to watch either of us die."

Just as Raymond prepared to knock Cyril off of him, turning to the side, Cyril forced the medal strap around his older brother's neck. He took one end of the strap in each hand, twisting them. The twisting motion caused the strap to tighten around Raymond's neck.

"You don't deserve to live," Cyril said, his eyes void of all sanity. But he knew exactly what he was doing, and he wasn't going to stop.

Raymond choked and gasped his face turning blue. He tried to reach his hands up to pull Cyril off, but he couldn't even breathe, let alone move.

"Once upon a time, I was great," Raymond coughed, and Cyril faltered, not wanting to finish the job. "Now, I am nothing. Yet, I am still better than you are."

Cyril shook his head. "In fairytales, good always wins. In this once upon a time, you have lost. I told you, evil never wins. Haven't you heard of happily ever after? It comes to those who manage to overcome their troubles. Those who don't let anything stop them from doing good. And getting rid of evil something good." With a quick jerk of his arms, the strap tightened around Raymond's neck. His older brother's face turned from blue to purple, and then slowly began to become pale.

The face of the younger brother was almost wistful as Raymond went limp. He left the medal where it was, still wrapped around Raymond's neck. He stood, glancing down at his older brother with an expression that couldn't quite be easily identified. Maybe it hurt as Raymond died. But that wasn't really what Cyril was worried about. After all, dying only hurts for a few seconds.

But if hurt for longer than that when Raymond died, then Cyril was okay with that, too.

Chapter 38:

~~Before~~ We ~~Fall~~ in Love

I watched as the colors found their rightful
owner.

Jacey.

Her name was no longer forgotten.

Especially with Leroy in me.

I knelt by her.

My brother was a second thought.

It had needed to happen, I tell myself.

And there are no arguments against that.

Evil.

He was evil.

But that makes me...

The good guy.

I push the questionable thought from my
mind

I can't let that thought be there.

Jacey needs to be my focus.

Her eyes are blank.

Like they are looking into...

Nothing.

They aren't hazel.

They're black.

But slowly...

The colors come back to her.

I assume it's because they were hers in the
first place.

Or maybe she is the one who is truly good.

Not me.

I hope this will fix her.

Because I'm only good at breaking things.
Like hearts.
Or, on one occasion, a bent spoon.
She's still breathing.
My cold hand finds the pulse on her neck.
She's slowly filling with color.
I can feel myself dying.
Inside.
Turning into a spirit.
Raymond was wrong about a lot of things.
But he was right...
I am nothing more than black and white
and—
A little bit of red.
Red.
Love.
Red.
Red.
Jacey.
My mind becomes a blur of those three
words.
I look down at her eyes.
She's blinking.
Seeing.
Her eyes meet mine.
"I didn't see what happened," she murmurs.
I tilt my head.
What kind of sentence is that?
Especially in a time like this.
"But I heard," she whispers, propping herself
up with her arms.
It's amazing what colors can do.
She looks so alive.

So vibrant.
So...much like Jacey.
And that thought makes me smile.
Because I can rely on that.
She notes my cold features.
My black eyes.
My white skin.
My black mouth.
My cold hands.
"You need them," she says.
Her voice is strong.
She knows.
She knows that Raymond is right.
"You need strength," she says.
"Don't worry about it."
I shake my head.
She can't worry about me.
I just watched her almost die.
And I don't want her to die.
Even if it means me dying.
She takes her hand.
And places it over my heart.
I watch.
I don't move.
I don't speak.
I don't breathe.
I can't.
Her pained face nearly kills me.
But suddenly, I can't die.
I don't feel dead inside.
I feel more alive than ever.
Like...I'm colorful.
Color is filling me.

I look at my arms.
And I feel color.
She's barely changing.
Raymond took a lot.
She's only giving me what I need.
So she can do it.
I don't protest.
I revel at her kindness.
My hands grow warm.
I can hear my heart thud against her hand.
It's loud.
But it's there.
And that's all I truly wanted.
A heart beat.
My eyes are seeing the world in this new
light.
I love it.
My eyes look at Jacey.
Jacey.
She's smiling.
Happy.
She gave up colors for me without a second
thought.
"I shouldn't have walked away," she
whispered.
I want to nod.
But all I do is shrug.
"We all make mistakes."
It's the truest thing I can say.
"Thanks for following," she smiles.
"Why wouldn't I have?"
She shrugs.
I know what she's thinking.

She is worried.
Worried about me.
Worried that she had made a huge mistake.
I try and assure her otherwise.
My words stumble out.
But I know what she is thinking.
I understand.
And slowly, my mind is healing.
I guess I am not completely insane.
I have some sanity.
Because of her.
And that is all that I can ask for in a time like
this.

Is sanity.

"The fact that I'm giddy every time I see you,"
she begins.

"Or when anyone says anything about you...
Well, it says something."

"I'd only call it twitterpated at this point, but
I could love you, given time."

My heart nearly stops.

I can't believe these words coming out of her
mouth.

They make me heart feel...
Red.
That's the color.
The 'could' doesn't even bother me.
I'm too happy.
Too ecstatic.
"I believe I will, in fact," she says.
I smile.
A real smile.
Something I haven't done in a while.

Twitterpated.
I like that word.
It means 'love struck.'
Or something close to that.
Almost love.
I can't believe someone could say that to me.
And mean every word of it.
It warms my heart.
And I smile again.
"You should smile more often," she murmurs.
"I'll try."
It's not a serious promise.
But it is a real one.
I intend to keep it.
If it makes her happy, I will do it.
Because it makes her happy.
Her eyes widen.
"What?"
I can't tell if she is happy.
Or scared.
Or something else altogether.
And, yet, she smiled.
"You can leave here," she says.
She almost sounds breathless.
Like she is happy for me.
And I smile.
"We can leave together."
She smiles, but it falters for a moment.
Something's wrong.
"What?"
Jacey shakes her head.
"I'm not leaving. Ever."
I shake my head.

That's not possible, I tell myself.

It's simply not possible that I can leave and she can't.

"Why not?"

My voice is cracking

I can hear it.

I ignore how pathetic I sound.

"She shattered my reflection," *Jacey says.*

I shake my head.

I can't believe it.

I won't believe it.

But then I remember something.

And it seems like the only thing to do.

And I can't stop myself from saying it.

"Use my mirror."

And it means so much more.

Because her eyes widen in realization.

Not only does she understand what it means for me to say that...

She also must realize what has to happen.

"No."

Her voice resonates.

It is firm and clear.

She knows exactly what I need her to do.

I have nothing to go back to.

She has everything to go back to.

I have...

Her.

And that's it.

"You have to."

"I don't have to do anything."

But her voice isn't challenging.

It's sad.

Because she knows what she is rejecting.

"Then I'm not going back."

Her eyes narrow, but the pain still flickers there.

"Don't you dare fucking stay."

I bite my lip.

"You'll die."

I shake my head, and open my mouth to argue.

"I know you will."

She has a point.

She can't give me colors forever.

It's too risky.

Especially if her reflection dies.

"What happened to your reflection?"

I tilt my head.

It's a good question.

"That's a good question."

She knows my reflection is probably having a happy life.

"I'm too lost."

I reach out my hand.

It's tentative.

But a meaningful gesture nevertheless.

And that's what I care about most.

Jacey shakes her head.

"You should go."

Once I cross over, my reflection will be destroyed.

I can start a new life.

Or continue one of my own.

And I can't say anything except—

"This isn't a goodbye."

She tilts her head.

"It's more of a 'see you later.'"

Her eyes crinkle as she realizes what I'm saying.

I can't bear to say goodbye.

So I don't plan to.

I just want to pretend that I'll see her again.

She won't kill me to take my mirror.

So there is nothing left that I can do.

"I'll see you later," *she agrees.*

Her voice is soft, and gentle.

It's the voice of a dying girl.

"We'll meet up sometime," I suggest.

"In San Francisco, California," *Jacey says, eyes brimming with tears.*

I smile sadly.

"No matter what today is, we'll meet up on July seventeenth."

Jacey nods. "At two in the afternoon."

"We'll meet up outside the aquarium by Fisherman's Wharf."

She nods.

"I'd like that."

I wrap my arms around her.

It's not a goodbye hug, I lie to myself.

And as I pull away, my heart feels dead.

More dead than before.

I can feel the tug in my heart.

Raymond's mirror is just around here.

I'll use his.

And my reflection will die.

I see the glimmer just a bit away.

There are no words as I walk there.

And just as I reach the empty mirror, I stop.
I look back.
"July seventeenth!"
I call the date to her.
Jacey is smiling.
But I can see the tears flooding her face.
And as I step through, I can feel the tears on my face.

Chapter 39

Dance Into the Fire

Connor glanced at Lakewood, who was flicking through television channels. He had told the police station, and it had all been settled. Jacey Adams had been pronounced dead on May fifteenth, and the coroner had confirmed that she was one of the victims. Lakewood had just hung up the phone with the coroner, and now was flipping through television channels like...his sister was alive.

"Did you hear about the new mall that is opening down the street?" Lakewood asked Connor, his eyes wide and innocent.

Connor stared at him in disbelief. "No," he said simply, frowning.

"It's pretty cool. They're going to have a supermarket attached and everything." The older boy nodded slowly.

"Really now?" There was no interest in Connor's voice. He shook his head.

Lakewood flicked it to a rom-com, and laughed softly. "I like this movie. Romantic comedies are growing on me."

"Are they now?" Connor's voice was flat as his eyes widened.

The other boy nodded. "Have you ever tried watching one?"

"No." His voice sounded quite annoyed by now.

"This one's pretty decent. It's about a guy who tames spiders for a living, but the girl is afraid of spiders."

Connor shook his head.

"It didn't do too well in theaters," Lakewood noted with a sigh.

The younger boy sighed audibly, now more annoyed than empathetic with the boy who was in denial. "Has there ever been something staring you in the face that you never could really accept?"

Lakewood thought for a moment. "Yeah. Happens all the time."

"Really now?" Connor murmured, hating the sarcasm in his own voice. He felt heartless, but this was ridiculous.

Lakewood shrugged. "Yeah. Kind of like how I realized my dad was a liar. And how my calculus professor doesn't know the answer to number three on the exam. And how I like you."

Connor froze, eyes wider than ever. He stuttered, unable to formulate a response.

Rather than be embarrassed, Lakewood just kind of shrugged again. "It related to the subject at hand, did it not?"

"It...it...it did," the younger boy said slowly.

"Well, it's the truth. I don't really care if it's a secret anymore," his face fell slightly.

Connor nodded slowly. "Why say it now, of all times?"

"Because she's gone. I can't even cry anymore tears. I tried to accept this three months ago and she came back. I felt guilty for it, but I

guess I don't have to feel guilty anymore."
Lakewood sounded tired rather than sad.

"But she's your sister…"

Lakewood shook his head about, trying to
explain what was going on his head. "I tried to be
sad. But I had to accept that three goddamn
months ago. She was different. It's like she never
came back."

"Oh," Connor nodded, his voice small. "That
makes sense."

"Whether or not she actually is gone now,
the truth still stands."

The younger boy felt a blush creep up his
cheeks.

"Sorry."

"Don't apologize," Connor said too quickly.

Lakewood frowned. "Why not?"

"Because then I would have to apologize,
too."

The older boy chuckled weakly. "No…"

"Yes," Connor said quietly.

Lakewood looked over at Connor from his
side of the couch. "But…Jacey…"

"I liked—loved her," Connor murmured
quietly. "Note the past tense."

"What about your family? Your parents?
Your siblings?"

Connor sighed, shaking his head. "I don't
know. Me telling them I was bi would probably be
a shock, but I don't think that they would be that
upset. I mean, the worse they could do is kick me
out of the house."

"Have they ever discussed sexuality with you?" Lakewood ran a hand through his hair, his mind spinning.

The younger boy sighed. "My sister Elizabeth is three years younger than me. She...she asked my dad if girls could marry girls. She said she had seen two girls kissing." He bit his lip, the fears about his dad increasing with every passing moment.

"Daddy, can two girls fall in love?" Elizabeth's fifteen-year old mind was confused from seeing those two girls kissing on their way home from school.

Their dad had paused, thinking about that as he hung his belt with his gun and keys and flashlight in it. "Well, they could, but they shouldn't."

"What do you mean by shouldn't?" Elizabeth asked, frowning. She had never seen such a sight.

Connor glanced up from where he was doing his homework in the corner, watching ht ensuing conversation with interest.

Their dad, Tony, sighed. "See, it says in the Bible that two men, or women, should not wed."

"Where does it say that?" Connor asked, looking at his dad.

Tony looked at his middle son curiously. "Leviticus 20:13. 'If a man also lie with mankind, as he lieth with a woman, both of them have committed an abomination: they shall surely be put to death; their blood shall be upon them.'"

"You have that memorized?" Elizabeth asked, looking bemused.

Their dad nodded. "Yeah, I do. It was part of the sermon from Sunday."

"Why is it an abomination?" Connor asked, interested to hear his dad's opinion. He also feared what would come out of his dad's mouth.

"Well, it wasn't what God intended. He made Adam and Eve because a man and a woman are meant to love," Tony said, frowning.

Connor quirked a brow. "But they still fall in love. A man and a man still end up loving each other. So obviously God did intend it."

"They aren't in love," his dad challenged. "They are confused, and they don't know what they are feeling. Like the rebels of society."

"They have no reason to rebel," Connor almost laughed, but he tried to keep the serious face on.

Tony tilted his head. "They want to be different. They don't want to conform to society, and that's wrong."

"It's not wrong," the teen said, his eyes reflecting fiery anger. "It's who they are. What about the people who love men and women?"

"They don't know who they are. They are lost and they're desperate," Tony chuckled slightly, running a hand over the hair he had left on his head.

Each word felt like a blow to Connor. He winced at the painful words, hoping his dad didn't actually mean that. He shrugged, trying to brush the subject off.

"Why do you care anyway? I thought you were Christian, Connor," Tony said, raising an eyebrow at his son.

"I am," he said, and then shook his head, glancing down at his homework. Connor added in a soft voice, "I thought I was, at least."

Elizabeth didn't look done with the conversation. "But God loves everyone," she said, reciting the childish teachings she had once learned ever so long ago.

Tony glanced at his eldest daughter. "He loves those who are God's children."

"No," she insisted. "He loves everyone. That's what the pastor says."

Their father shook his head. "Okay. Listen to me. The bible says being gay, or loving someone of the same gender is a sin. And it is a sin. It is an abomination to Christians everywhere. It is wrong, and these people are confused. They don't know what is going on with their lives. They are confused. They are lost. They may think they understand God, but they don't. It is something to be looked down upon, and I don't want to hear you challenge it. It's wrong, and you should not be saying such things in our household. I'm forbidding it. You may be curious, but that doesn't mean you question God and the Bible. That in itself is a sin. Don't defend those who are beyond all hope."

"Maybe those who are ignorant about those who are gay are the ones beyond all hope," Connor said, eyes narrowed.

Tony glared in his son's direction. "Why are you defending people who commit sins willingly? They are an abomination."

"Because..." he trailed off, not wanting to upset his dad. "I don't know."

Their dad looked at each of them in turn. "Good. You don't know, and you never will know, okay? Because the answer is as simple as Leviticus 20:13. Do I make myself clear?"

"Yes, Dad," Elizabeth murmured.

Connor wanted to open his mouth and argue the point to hell. But he knew better than to do something like that. He simply nodded, knowing the truth would have to come out sooner or later.

"Let's just say he isn't too fond of the idea. But that doesn't really matter," Connor added at the end, looking at Lakewood. His eyes were wide with hope and a little bit of happiness at the news of who Lakewood liked.

The older boy nodded, his eyes widening with understanding. There were no loose ends here. It was clear cut and smooth. Lakewood moved over, carefully, and placed his hand over Connor's.

Suddenly, Connor didn't feel scared. He didn't feel like this was something he needed to worry about. He intertwined their hands, slowly, eyes bright.

He glanced up at Lakewood and grinned. "So about that romantic comedy..."

JULY

2016

Chapter 40:

Remember the Fallen

Callie couldn't sleep. Of course, she should have been used to that by now. She had been living alone in her and Justin's apartment for almost three months now. Each passing day was a little bit harder. Trent came over every so often, which was nice, but it just wasn't the same. Her teacher had stopped coming last month after proudly handing Callie her high school diploma. Callie didn't quite remember where she had tossed it now.

Sometimes she wondered if she should cross over and attempt to find him. But leaving this place, or the thought of leaving, hurt her heart slightly. Justin existed everywhere here, and it was impossible to leave, and it was impossible to stay.

Jacey had been silent for a couple months now, too. She tried to reach out to Jacey, but it never worked. It was hard enough getting on without Justin, and now she had lost Jacey as well.

Her mother sent a letter, offering to pay for a psychologist. But she didn't need another doctor figure in her life. It wasn't necessary for her to be stuck on some new medication. This was something that not even a psychologist or some shit like that could do.

Callie?

Her heart nearly stopped. It wasn't Jacey, but it did sound an awful lot like Raymond. But the voice was much more gentle, and kind.

It's not Raymond. I swear, the voice pleaded.

"J—Justin?" her voice was tentative. "You're supposed to be dead."

I'm almost there. I chose to be a spirit.

Callie inhaled sharply, remembering what he had said about the spirits. "Why? Why would you do that?" She touched the ring that was on her index finger of her left hand.

I wanted to talk to you.

She inhaled sharply. "I—You would actually do that just to talk to me?"

Of course. I never got the chance to say an authentic goodbye, anyway.

"Why didn't you tell me?" Her voice shook slightly.

It hurt.

"But...how did you know?" Callie pressed her hand to her heart.

Raymond took my colors just as I crossed over. I knew that the instant I went to the other side of the mirror again, I would die.

Callie shook her head. "Then why...why did you go back over? Why didn't you just stay?"

Because I know how much you cared about Jacey. I thought maybe I could save her...

"You..." She trailed off, biting her lip. "You did all that for me?"

It's...it's something you cared about, Cat. Even if it meant leaving you, I thought I could bring peace between you and Jacey.

"I love you."

I have always loved you.

Callie tried to push down the tears. "So this is how you will always be?"

You can talk to me anytime, if you would like.

"Oh…" She trailed off, unsure of where her train of thought was going.

What, Cat?

"It's…it's so hard trying to get on without you. I don't want to hear your voice and never be able to touch you again…or see you…" Callie looked upwards at the man who wasn't there.

I don't have to stay and talk, Cat. I can go.

"I don't want you to leave," she murmured. Her mind was tearing her apart.

You can call me whenever you want, if that works for you. I just want you to be happy. That's all I ever wanted, Cat.

Callie paused. She wasn't exactly sure what she wanted. Talking to Justin wasn't enough, but he had taken that risk for her. He had turned into a spirit so that they could talk to each other and that she could know he was still there.

I'm sorry.

"Don't be sorry," she said sharply, her eyes brimming with salty tears. "It's not something that you should be sorry for. I am…I am sorry."

What do you have to be sorry for, Cat? I'm the one who didn't come back.

She paused, standing up and looking at herself in the mirror. "I'm the one who didn't come. I let you do all the work. And that was wrong. I should have come."

Well, it's too late for that. I did what I wanted to do, Cat. You couldn't stop me from trying to help.

"I could have come with you," she said, her voice small.

No.

His voice was strong as it resonated through her head.

I know what you are thinking, Cat. Don't you dare.

"What? You sacrificed things for me! Why can't I do the same?" She bit her lip, closing her eyes and turning away from the mirror.

Step away from the mirror.

"No."

Callie. I mean it. Don't do this. You'll only hurt me.

She cringed. "How would it hurt you?"

You would be throwing away your life for me. I don't want you to do that. I am not worth your life.

"What if I think you are?" Callie challenged, opening her eyes as she looked in the mirror.

Then you would be wrong. Cat, I need you to live. Please. Don't you dare come over here. This is hell. You have the chance to live a happy life, and you should take that chance. I don't want you to suffer in hell.

"It's not hell if I'm with you," she said, her voice gentle.

People suffer here.

She sighed in frustration. "I don't want you to suffer."

And I say the same about you.

"Justin..."

I'm a lost cause. You're not.

"Maybe there's a way," Callie said, chewing the inside of her cheek.

No. Don't try and get me out of here. I'm different, Cat. I told you that I am lost. It's true. I am never coming back.

She let out a shaky breath. "You told me once that you were here to stay for as long as I would let you. And I'm not ready to let you leave. This is love. It is worth fighting for, no matter what."

Love is about opening yourself up to someone entirely. It's about screaming and shouting at each other, and then just when it seems like it's never going to get better, you realize that to lose one another is worse than whatever you started arguing about in the first place. It's about growing old together and holding your wrinkly hands when you take walks around the neighborhood. I can't be that person, Cat. I never was meant to be in that world, and now I've learned my lesson.

At this point, Callie had succumbed to the tears. She squeezed the promise ring, letting floods of salty tears fall down her face. She knew he was right, and that was what hurt most of all. It hurt to know that there was no truth she could say that could change this.

I'm sorry, Cat. I left again.

"I was the one who walked out on you last time," she said softly, shaking a bit. "It's hard to accept the fact that I will never see you again..."

I'm a spirit, Cat. You wouldn't want to see me like this. I'm not Justin anymore.

Callie shook her head. "You will always be Justin."

I was a reflection. I never belonged on that side. I was a reflection of someone who was evil, and I couldn't change that.

"But you weren't evil," she said gently.

Or was I? I'm a pyromaniac. I set fires. Fires that hurt people. I hurt people, Cat.

"You did not hurt me," Callie said, her voice small, and her eyes reflected a confidence that she didn't feel.

I left. You're hurting now.

She paused. "Why are you trying to convince me that you're evil?" Callie's voice was almost a whimper. She didn't understand what he was doing.

Because you deserve the truth, Callie.

She shook her head. Callie knew that he was trying to get her not to want him. He was trying to get her to move on an accept that he was evil. Part of her almost believed him, but her heart knew the truth.

I'll always be here to talk to you. But you need to move on. Find your true Prince. Get married. Have kids. Hold hands as you walk around the neighborhood.

His voice cracked at the end. Justin was pained by this, too. But Callie knew that he had a point, as much as she hated to admit it.

I will always love you. But don't love someone who is evil. You're so good, and I can't let myself ruin that.

"I love you," she said, her voice strong for a moment as she glanced at the ring.

So, here's to me wishing you a happy life.

Callie wiped away her tears as she glanced in the mirror. Out of the corner of her eye, the mirror flickered. She saw Justin, but it wasn't Justin. Her heart slowly sank with the realization that he was different. But she stood nevertheless, looking directly into the mirror.

I'll be around.

She nodded slowly, taking a shaky breath. "And as will I."

You're still my fire.

Callie tried to bite back tears, and managed to do so after a moment. "You know what I realized? Bent spoons are also useful as a Christmas ornament."

Justin didn't reply. But, somehow, Callie knew that he was smiling.

Chapter 41:

Let's Try That Again, Shall We?

The San Franciscan air was thick and humid. The old clock tower that was somewhere further inland had just tolled two. A boy, who looked to be in his early twenties, was sitting on one of the steps that led to the aquarium. He had been waiting there for two hours now. Some people who passed by gave him a wary glance, as if worried he was dangerous.

He leaned against the wall that was on the left side of the staircase. He sighed, running a hand through his white-blonde hair. It was spiked slightly, and it gave him a more edgy look. He had on what looked like a black blazer, but it had a casual look to it. He was wearing dark jeans that complimented his blazer, and simple sneakers.

His eyes widened as he caught sight of red hair. The woman was walking slowly. Just as he went to stand, the woman's voice rang out. It wasn't her. With that sad note, he settled back into his position on the stairs.

He wasn't sure why he had come. It had been a day set up because he had refused to say goodbye. For the last two months, he had been on his own. He had gone home and collected some of his things, which lay there under a thick inch of dust. His parents were there, but he didn't think randomly appearing was something he should be doing quite yet. After all, they supposed he was dead.

And after using the apartment key his parents had bought him for college, he had resolved to find a job. However, because he lacked a high school diploma, it was rather difficult. Eventually, he landed a job at a local bookstore. It was not quite his taste, but it made decent money.

Cyril glanced at the sky, sending out a silent prayer to whoever was listening. He closed his eyes, hating himself for his high hopes. Why hadn't he moved on in the last two months?

Just as he lost himself in his reverie, a hand rested on his shoulder.

"I don't need anything," he snapped. An old woman had approached him earlier, trying to help what she thought was a homeless teenager. He didn't appreciate the sympathy he didn't need.

The mystery person retracted their hand, but didn't leave. "Are you sure?"

Just as Cyril was about to scowl and come up with yet another snappy retort, his heart skipped a beat. He counted in his head, wondering if he should pinch his arm. It wasn't possible, he reminded himself. This was a lost hope.

"You're such a twit," the soft voice said.

His mouth curved into a smile as he repeated what he had said so long ago. "A twit is defined as a pregnant goldfish. I am neither pregnant, nor a goldfish. I am, however—"

"Gold," Jacey finished. She smiled. "You should find some new comebacks."

Cyril turned, looking at the woman in front of him. He swore she was even brighter and more colorful on this side. His mouth opened and shut, as if unable to function.

She couldn't stop the smile from widening as she waved. "It's been a while." Her voice was gentle, and she looked at him with newfound happiness and hope.

"Jacey..." was call Cyril could manage to say before he wrapped his arms around her in a wistful embrace. She wrapped her arms around his neck, not really wanting to break apart despite the stares.

She pulled back only slightly to look at him.

"How?" His voice was a whisper.

Jacey sighed slightly. "I found something. And it reminded me of my family, and my friends, and...you..." She slipped her hand into the back pocket of her jeans. She tugged out the Polaroid, handing him the old picture of him and Chrissie. "I felt...like Jacey Adams. I can't describe it. Apparently, because I'm a Dator, who gives colors, my old mirror still existed. I just...walked through."

"You found yourself," Cyril smiled.

She nodded. "I went home. Made up some story about how I ran away and now I was back. They all had thought I was dead. So, Randall must be gone now. And, I really have no regret about that."

"It's all back to normal?"

"Yeah."

Cyril grinned, his smile lighting up his eyes. "How do you like California?"

"Getting better and better. It's nice sunshine," Jacey said, winking.

He looked at her, not really sure what to say after all those weeks of hoping hope wasn't lost. It was almost surreal to have her here.

"It was all because of you. You helped me defeat my fears. That's...that's really brave of you."

"You're wrong. I'm not brave. If I was brave, I would let you face these nightmares by yourself. It's the path you chose, and the path you always claim will save you. But I'm a coward, and because of my cowardice I will never give you the glory of having won your battles alone. I'm too afraid to lose you."

Jacey's eyes widened slightly. "The path I chose was you. You have nothing to be sorry for."

Cyril sighed. "Have you heard my reputation? Because I know my reputation. I know what people say about me. The truth is, yes. I've been with a lot of women. But those relationships never...they weren't even relationships. They were just...they were like...it was like I was searching for something that I knew I needed but could never find. I kept hoping the next warm body would have that *something* I was so certain I needed. But I never found it.

Jacey tilted her head, looking awfully unsure of herself and what was going on. "What makes you think *I* have this...thing...you're looking for?"

"I felt it. I felt it when you held my hand in that hell as I recounted how my sister died. I felt it in the way you looked at me and made me remember red. I felt it in the way you stood by me as I watched my brother die. You are everything I've been searching for and I can't possibly go another day without telling you how I feel. We could die tomorrow and I cannot bear the thought of that happening without having said this. I love you, Jacey. I love you so much I can barely breathe." Cyril looked scared after finishing this. But he knew every word he said was true. And even if it scared her away, it had to be said.

She paused. "I can't hesitate anymore. I lost you once, back there."

Cyril sighed, remembering when he had left all those months ago.

"I'm *not* going to lose you again."

He smiled. "So you believe we fit together?"

"I don't know exactly what I believe, but this is what I think I believe: I don't believe in a soul mate, or true love, or one sole kismet or anything. But I do believe in love. I believe that there are many forms of love, and that you can find it anywhere. But above almost all of those loves is the kind of love I feel for you. And that's the kind worth everything I have. The kind worth fighting for," Jacey said. She looked a bit uncomfortable at the awkwardness that was instilled. But she knew herself, now. She understood herself on a whole new level. She had always known this. It was just a matter of how scared she would be to say it.

Cyril smiled softly, despite the unbelievable fact that she was talking to him. That she was saying these things to him, and that she meant all of them. "I'm not one for sappiness, but I have to admit that that was pretty nice."

"What happens now?" Jacey asked, leaning against the wall.

He paused, looking at her. She was wearing jeans, combat boots, and a tank top that was a bit longer in the back. Jacey had been wearing sunglasses, which now rested on the top of her head, on her red hair.

She nudged him gently. "Well?"

"There are a few options," Cyril said, looking thoughtful. "One would be to keep in touch for a bit. Maybe meet up every once in a while."

Jacey's face fell slightly. "Oh. Okay."

"I'm not done," he laughed, smiling widely at her expression. "We could also maybe try things out between us. Or, we could try and go back to our old lives."

She ran a hand through her hair. "Our old lives, huh?"

"I don't know. I could tell my parents that I'm actually alive. You could go back home. You already went home, I assume?"

Jacey nodded.

"I bet they missed you," Cyril said quietly.

She paused. "I missed you, too."

He paused, smiling slightly as they both thought.

"Hey, Cy? Can I ask you something?"

Cyril glanced at her curiously. "Sure, Red. Shoot."

"When I was with Raymond, you came after me. You didn't have any colors, and yet you still remembered my name. You still came after me. How?"

His expression softened. "You know those personalities? Well, when people who have crossed over and then came back, those who have destroyed their reflections, they go to that side when they die. They become those echoes."

"Okay," Jacey nodded, looking a bit confused. She quirked a brow, eyes bright.

"Well, people, reflections, and spirits can all absorb the personalities. Take their knowledge. That personality happened to know you. A lot. The personality gave his essence up so that I could come after you," Cyril rubbed the back of his neck.

She frowned. "Wait...that personality knew me? How?"

"They had crossed over in their life, and then they came back to our side. After they crossed, they knew you. And now they're dead, so they were on that side," he said, his voice gentle, as if worried the news would break her somehow.

Jacey shook her head, a bit frustrated. "But...the only person I knew well who passed was Uncle Leroy. But..." She trailed off, looking at Cyril with wide eyes. "Wait..."

"Yeah," Cyril nodded, a gentle smile on his face. "He helped me save you."

She covered her mouth with her hand, looking a bit shocked. "That was him all along?"

"It was," he said. "How come you and your Uncle were so close?"

Jacey smiled slightly at the bright flash of orange in her mind as she flipped through memories.

"Why did you marry her?" young Jacey asked, gesturing to Aunt Katherine, who was scribbling on a paper, glancing at the computer every once in a while.

Leroy smiled softly. "I loved her."

"But you said we love a lot of people in our life," the young girl challenged, frowning. "How do you know she was the one you were going to marry?"

"Because there comes a point in our lives when we know that the person we love is the person we are never going to stop loving," the uncle said, pressing a key on the piano.

Jacey thought that over for a moment, her young brain unable to comprehend such a grand idea as love.

"See, Jay, it's like a piano song. You feel different. When I hear certain songs, I feel like it's a love song. But one of them is a bit different. You never get tired of hearing it. And it's like that with people. You're going to grow up, and find this one person that is a lot different than the rest of the people," he said quietly.

She nodded slowly. "But then I'll have to be old. Because I'll have to love a lot of people."

"Not necessarily," Jacey's uncle laughed. "You might meet that person when you're young, or maybe when you're mom's age. It might be when

you're my age, but we never know when it will happen."

Jacey smiled slightly. "I want to be loved like how you love Aunt Katherine."

"And you will be," Leroy promised her, tapping her on the nose. "Any boy would be lucky to be able to love you for their whole life."

"It's like magic," she mused.

"Why is it like magic?" Katherine asked the girl, smiling up from where she was by the computer.

Jacey thought about her words carefully, like she always did. "Because someone is meant to be with you for a long time. And they fit with you, like a puzzle piece. It's magic because not everyone is good at puzzles."

"That's a good point," her aunt said, laughing softly. "I never thought of love like a puzzle."

The young girl smiled proudly. "I'm not very good at puzzles, though," Jacey said after a moment, frowning. "Does everyone find love?"

"No," Leroy said with some reluctance. "But I think that you will. In fact, I believe you will. You are such a strong girl, and you're going to grow into a wonderful woman. You will find love because no one else will be able to not see how amazing you are. I guarantee it, Jay. I can't wait to watch you grow up and become that strong woman."

Jacey smiled, glancing in the mirror. She took a moment, trying to see the woman that her uncle was talking about. Part of her could see it, but it *seemed more like a dream than anything else. Katherine smiled, turning back to the computer.*

"Just you wait, kiddo," Leroy said, grinning down at his niece. "You'll find love, and you'll know when it's the one. Just go with your gut."

Jacey glanced up at Cyril, snapping out of her pensive state. "He was the one who always talked to me about love."

"I hate to ask," he said softly, "but how did he pass?"

She sighed. "Did you ever hear of the September eleventh terrorist attacks on the World Trade Center in New York?"

"Yeah," Cyril murmured, biting his lip at the tragedy he knew was about to be relayed.

Jacey had told the tale enough times that she had learned how to ignore the lump in her throat. It was something that she hoped she could ignore this time, as well. "He worked in the second tower, on the forty-first floor. When his building was hit, he managed to get down to the third floor, they think. And as the tower collapsed, he went down to the first floor or second floor and jumped. The debris crushed his legs, paralyzing him. They found him, transported him to the hospital, and they claimed him to be in a coma. They told us that he would never wake up."

"Oh," he murmured, eyes wide.

"They were right," Jacey said, her voice sounding empty.

Cyril bit his lip. "It's nice that you two were really close, though," he said quietly.

"Yeah," she said, smiling sadly. "He was the one who taught me my first few lessons of piano. He's the reason I continued piano. And one of the only reasons why part of me didn't give up on love."

"You gave up on it?" he asked, tilting his head to the side. "Why?"

Jacey shrugged slightly. "I compared true love to a puzzle. Two pieces that fit together. The thing was, I was never very good at puzzles. I figured that there are some people better off alone. I assumed that I was one of those people."

"But you had all those boys back home, didn't you?" Cyril asked, wincing slightly at the things she had told him about her school. Then again, he had been the male version fo that at his school.

She laughed, but it was empty. "There is a fine line between love and lust."

"Have you ever considered that people aren't always going to leave?"

Jacey paused. "No. Actually, I haven't."

"Well, maybe you should," Cyril said, eyes softening slightly as he looked at her.

"What do you mean?" Jacey asked, frowning slightly. "What are you suggesting, Cy?"

He stood, extending his hand. "I've been informed that I'm a bad influence. Want to come along and be corrupted?"

Jacey glanced up at him, eyes shining slightly. Once upon a time, she would have laughed at his offer. She would have assumed he was going to stab her in the back and walk away like everyone else. But not now. Not when it came to Cyril. He was...that one piano song that was a bit different than the rest. She took his hand without hesitation. "Why, I thought you'd never ask." Jacey smiled up at him.

Anyone else who saw probably wouldn't believe their eyes, but the fact was that there was red mist that encircled their hands as they walked.

DECEMBER
2030

CHAPTER 42:

THIS IS NOT A LOVE SONG

He was going to kill that cricket. This time for certain. It mocked Connor every time he slept, and it was impossible to get any sleep. He had given up on sleeping, at least for tonight. After all, it was already four in the morning, and it was doubtful that he would get much sleep. He had work to do today, and his alarm was set for seven anyway. Three hours of lost sleep could be made up for, especially given that today was Friday.

The shower clicked on, and Connor realized that Lakewood was probably getting ready for work by now. He groaned at the continuous humming of the cricket, wishing he could just take a shotgun to its head. But Connor had never been a good shot, even though his father had attempted to teach him. It was simply impossible for him to have a good aim. Connor called his lack of ability to shoot a talent that consisted of stopping violence. His father called it a lack of talent and hand-eye coordination. Perhaps it was a bit of both, to be honest.

"Damn cricket," Connor muttered, grasping a flashlight. Instead of shining it where he thought the cricket would be, he chucked the flashlight extremely hard. It hit the wall with a loud crash, and the room was silent for a few moments. Connor punched the air in victory and lied down. Maybe three hours of sleep would be nice.

The chirping noise echoed through the room with a new ferocity as Connor lied down. He growled to himself, covering his ears with his pillow. The shower clicked off, and the dripped wet head of Lakewood peered through the door crack.

"Everything alright?" he chuckled, glancing at Connor.

Connor peeked out at Lakewood. "I want that cricket dead."

Lakewood laughed, rolling his eyes. "It's a part of nature. I'll find him when I get home from work." He closed the door behind him, humming softly as he dried his hair.

The younger man hated the idea of bugs, and he frowned in the cricket's general direction. He slid out of bed, deciding to get to work earlier than usual. He hadn't been called in recently, except the three in the morning incident yesterday. His desk job at the Manhattan Police Department was actually pretty interesting given the crime rates in New York.

His phone made a siren noise, which was his ringtone for when the office called. He pressed the phone to his ear, willing himself to be more awake.

"Connor Tarrentine's line, what's going on?" Connor sighed.

"We found a skull buried beneath the front yard of 1109 Bradbury Street in Manhattan. We need you down here to take it to the lab," Leah's voice sounded tired, like it usually did when she called him in this early.

Connor nodded. "Okay. I'll be there shortly. I think that it is just around the corner."

"And that Johnson case should be wrapped up today, too. Don't forget." She clicked off her line.

It was typical for forensic chemists to be called in at any hour in the day. He had woken Lakewood many times getting up at midnight, one in the morning, or three in the morning. Sometimes he left at midnight and didn't come home until midnight of the next day. Sleep was not something guaranteed in his line of work.

"Are you leaving?" Lakewood asked, coming out of the restroom with a frown. "Did they call you in?"

Connor nodded, glad he had showered the night before. He shrugged off his old shirt that he had slept in and tugged on the collared shirt he had lied out on his dresser last night.

"What happened?" the older man dried off his hair, rubbing the goatee that was starting to grow on his face. He would have to shave soon.

"They found a skull on Bradbury Avenue and they need me to come and take it to the laboratory." Connor pulled on slacks, buttoning them after tucking his shirt in. He carefully looked in the mirror, tying his tie neatly after a few moments of concentration.

Lakewood sighed. "And didn't you say something about the other case that you have to wrap up today?"

"Yeah. I should be home late tonight, but I don't know..." he trailed off, sitting down and putting on black socks and dress shoes.

"Tomorrow is the day before Christmas Eve," Lakewood frowned. "You have that day off, right?"

Connor shook his head. "No. I only have Christmas off."

"Okay. Well, I'll drop Emily off, then. Try and come home. Dad is going to pitch a fit if we're not at Christmas Eve," the older man slipped on a shirt and tie, frowning. A lot had changed between the two of them over the past years. They were beginning to develop their relationship more and more. Emily was the biggest step. Their three-year old was took a lot of their time, but it had really helped them bond.

"I'm sorry. The crime rates in this city are ridiculous."

Lakewood shrugged, glancing around at their small home. "Well, good luck. I have a minimum day today at the university, since it is just teacher planning. And I have no school tomorrow or the day after. We still doing Christmas dinner?"

"Yeah, I think so. Is Jacey flying in from California, then?" Connor tilted his head looking at Lakewood as he ran a brush through his hair.

"I think so. So it would be Jacey and her family, dad, mom, and us. Is your family coming?"

Connor laughed softly, making sure not to wake Emily. "No. My siblings all live in random places across America now. It's not worth the hassle. We can video chat or something."

"Are you sure?"

"Well, there's Annie, who lives alone with her two-year old son in Nevada. Brooke moved to England with her husband. Elizabeth still lives in Long Island, alone. Liam still is with mom and dad, and James lives in Albany," Connor said, counting off his fingers.

Lakewood whistled. "Wow. Well, maybe Liam and Elizabeth could come over," he suggested.

"Maybe," the younger man nodded. "I'll call them. But I doubt it. They're still a bit touchy about everything."

"Which one was the one who cursed me out for making a devil out of you?" Lakewood asked, biting back a chuckle.

"James," Connor said. "He's the religious nut in our family. I mean, most of us are Christian, but he's a bit...eccentric. Even Dad admits that, and Dad is really strict on religion."

Lakewood nodded. "Your dad accepted us, eventually."

"Thanks to Annie for that. She's the one who made that happen. She's pretty damn good at persuasion." Connor opened a locked drawer, taking out the gun and strapping it to his belt.

His partner shook his head. "I still don't understand why you have one of those. You don't need a gun. You're a forensic chemist, not a cop."

"I go to crime scenes. They aren't the safest places in the world, Lake. I want to be prepared in case I need it."

"Who the hell taught you to shoot a gun anyway?" Lakewood asked, his expression dubious.

Connor grinned. "Your sister. Who else would be able to teach me that?"

Lakewood had never bothered to ask before because he wasn't sure he wanted to know the answer. But when Connor answered, he laughed, covering his mouth so he didn't wake Emily.

"She's a good shot," the man appraised. "You should be proud of Jacey."

The other man nodded, a wide grin still on his face. "I can't believe her. She really is doing what she always wanted to do."

"I should probably get going soon. Leah will wring my neck if she thinks I fell asleep and I end up coming late," Connor said, slipping keys into his pocket.

Lakewood nodded. "I'll go grocery shopping today, if you want."

"Thanks so much, Lake," Connor said, smiling softly. "Tell Emily I'll be home tomorrow sometime for sure. I'll try and stop by here and drop off dinner for you guys."

The older man smiled, checking the baby monitor to make sure Emily slept through their conversation.

"See ya," Connor murmured, squeezing Lakewood's hand before heading out of their bedroom.

Lakewood called out softly, "Love you!"

Just as Connor left, Lakewood sighed. He frowned as his phone rang, picking it up.

"Love you, too," Connor laughed.

CHAPTER 43:

SILLY STRING AND WEDDING RINGS

Jacey reached over to the backseat, holding out the bag of cheese crackers to silence the ruckus that was going on in the backseat. The chaos continued, and the bag of crackers was launched, spilling all over Jacey's lap from where she sat in the passenger seat of the white car.

"Joy, we're almost to the hotel. Can you please give Charlie the juice box?" she asked, her voice rising slightly with authoritativeness. It wasn't as much of a question as it was a nice way of ordering her seven-year old to give her five-year old the last juice box. It was another two minutes to the hotel they were staying at in Manhattan. This was a rental car, after all, and she was not going to pay for it to be cleaned when they were only borrowing it for the week.

"I think it would be smart of you to listen to your mother," Cyril called over his shoulder, smiling at Joy and laughing softly.

Jacey gently pushed Cyril's shoulder. "I'm trying to issue a threat."

"Key word being 'try', Red?" he asked, winking at her as he turned the corner.

She shook her head, chuckling slightly. "Shut up," she murmured, quiet enough so the kids wouldn't hear, but loud enough so that it wasn't just a mumble.

Joy slowly held the juice box out to her brother, who was sitting next to her. Charlie snatched the juice box, carefully taking a sip. He watched his older sister with careful eyes, smiling in a way that almost made it seem like a smirk. It was quite classic, and Jacey bit back a laugh as she glanced in the rearview mirror at her children.

Cyril pulled into the hotel, and gently parked the rental car in the small parking lot. He looked over at Jacey, placing his hand over hers.

"Thanks for agreeing to come to my family's Christmas," Jacey murmured, smiling slightly at him. The sound of seatbelts being unbuckled was the only other noise heard.

He smiled crookedly. "No problem, Red." He squeezed her hand before slipping out of the car. "Charlie!" he laughed, helping the small boy clamber out of the car.

Jacey got out of the car as well, opening the right side door of the backseat, and offering her hand to Joy.

"Mommy, why am I never in the mirror?" she asked, her curious eyes searching her mother's face.

That had been a question Cyril and her had discussed, but had never been able to come up with a suitable answer for their children. "I'll tell you when you're older," Jacey promised. She reached down, tucking a strand of her daughter's white-blonde hair behind her ear. Joy frowned, sighing slightly.

"Come on," Jacey coaxed. "Let's go get ready for Christmas Eve dinner. You get to see Emily."

Joy perked up at this, taking her mother's hand and pulling her toward the hotel. Jacey laughed, shutting the door behind Joy and carefully holding her hand as they walked across the parking lot and into the hotel.

"Room seven hundred and seven," Cyril said, waiting for her by the elevator. Brown-haired Charlie was perched happily on his daddy's shoulders, smiling triumphantly. His hazel eyes watched Joy as he held the juice box higher, laughing slightly.

Jacey took the card key from Cyril's hand, entering the elevator with Joy. Cyril ducked, and Charlie laughed as he clasped his arms around his dad's neck so that he didn't fall off.

"We have to be there in five hours for the dinner at Connor's place," Jacey reminded Cyril, leaning against the wall.

Cyril nodded. "We can put the kids down for a nap and just relax for three hours or so," he suggested, looking a bit exhausted.

"I don't need a nap!" Charlie insisted, frowning.

Jacey reached up and tapped her son gently on the nose. "If you want to stay up late tonight, then you need a nap, Charlie."

"And that includes you, Joy," Cyril said, smiling down at his daughter. She reminded him of Chrissie more and more as she grew up. He looked a lot like her, and he had definitely taken after her more and more.

Joy pouted, silently crossing her arms. She was the quieter one of their family, for sure.

The elevator dinged and the doors opened. Cyril ducked again, and ran forward down the hallway, smiling while Charlie laughed.

Jacey picked up Joy with only a little difficulty. Joy clung to her mother's neck, sighing slightly as she looked around.

"What's going through your mind, angel?" Jacey murmured, running her hand through her daughter's long curls.

Joy looked at her mother with such a serious face. "You and Daddy fight sometimes, but you still say you're happy. Why?"

"Oh," Jacey murmured. She realized that the small argument her and Cyril had had yesterday had stayed in her daughter's mind. "See, when you love someone a lot, you manage to work through your problems. It can be really hard, but that's what love does."

The young girl was silent, just nodding as she ingested the information. Jacey set her on the ground when they reached the hotel room, where Cyril had propped open the door. Joy ran inside, tackling her dad who was kneeling over the suitcase the porter had brought up.

"Oomph!" Cyril exclaimed, laughing as he pulled his daughter into a warm embrace. He pointed to the bedroom on the right. "You'll sleep in there, on one side of the bed. Charlie will sleep on the other."

"But Charlie snores in his sleep!" Joy said with indignation, but marched into the room at her father's glance.

Cyril stood, running a hand through his hair. He glanced at Jacey, sighing with a small smile. "I'll be right back. Our room is in there." He jerked a hand toward where the other bedroom was. He flashed a crooked smile at her, stepping into the kids' room with a smile.

Jacey slowly walked into the bedroom, letting her hair fall loose down her shoulders. She didn't really want to do anything but relax for the next few hours. That redeye flight may have been cheap, but it had taken a good chunk out of her sleeping hours. The issue was, the clock read noon, but it felt like nine in the morning to Jacey.

She entered the bathroom, gazing appreciatively at the decent restroom. Her eyes flickered to the mirror, which didn't show her reflection. Then again, her reflection had been dead for quite some time now. If Jacey remembered correctly, it had been fourteen years since she had lost her reflection. And it wasn't something she wanted back, actually.

Jacey raised her left hand to the mirror, pressing her hand against the cool mirror. No longer did she have to worry about being pulled over to the other side. And now that she was on this side, colors weren't as of much importance compared to the other side. But, somehow, as a Dator, Jacey felt colors almost like someone with synesthesia might. It was like a confusion of the sentences.

Even from the restroom, Jacey could hear Cyril laughing as he read their kids a childhood book. They always seemed to like the rhymes, especially Joy.

"It's again, not a-gain, Daddy!" Joy laughed, and Jacey couldn't help but smile at the pronunciation change.

Jacey glanced down at the two rings on the ring finger of her left hand. The engagement ring Cyril had given her ten years ago was one with a silver band and a princess cut diamond. Her wedding ring was a simple silver band with diamonds and rubies embedded into the band. She smiled slightly, the memory flickering in her mind like a streak of bright orange and red.

Jacey was sitting by Cyril on her bed at home. He was about to leave for his part-time job, and was finishing slipping on his shoes.

"You know, Jacey, I don't really like your name."

Jacey looked slightly indignant. "Excuse me?"

Cyril shrugged slightly, finishing tying his left shoe. "Your name. Particularly your last name. It sucks."

"What's wrong with my last name?" Jacey almost snapped, her lack of sleep not really helping the situation.

He glanced over at where his jacket lied over the chair. He slid it on. "It doesn't suit you. You should change it."

"Change it?" Jacey exclaimed, her eyes narrowed in absolute fury. He was never like this around her. Her eyes warily followed him to the chair, where he was zipping up his jacket casually. "To what?"

Cyril was silent for only a moment. "Thompson." He picked up his phone and walked out of the room.

"Thompson?" Jacey looked bemused. Her eyes then widened in absolute shock. "Did you just..." Her voice was nearly a whisper.

She called after him, breathing heavily.

"Did you just propose?"

"Don't walk away!"

"Are you smirking?"

"Come back here!"

She ran after him, running a hand through her hair. Her mind was spinning, and she couldn't really comprehend what was going on. When she entered the living room, he was on one knee in front of the door, a small ring box propped open in his hands.

"So..." Cyril said, a smile creeping up on his face. "About changing your last name..."

Jacey inhaled sharply, covering her mouth with her hands. She took a few tentative steps forward, eyes brimming with tears. Despite how close they were over the past four years, she hadn't seen this coming.

"Red, will you marry me?" His voice was strong, and he made it clear that he was absolutely sure that he knew what he was doing. The silver band and the diamond that was attached glittered as she walked closer to him with every step.

All Jacey could do at first was nod. As she came directly in front of him, her mouth opened slightly. "Yes," she whispered. "Yes, I will."

Cyril's smile brightened as he slipped the ring onto the hand that she slowly outstretched. She was breathing heavily, and tears were freely flowing down her face. Cyril stood, wiping her cheeks with a gentle hand. He carefully wrapped his arms around her, wanting her close.

"Yes," she couldn't help but whisper again, her arms slowly wrapping around his neck.

January fifteenth. It was a day she would literally never forget. Jacey smiled as she touched the ring, pulling herself out of her reverie. The memory was one of the strongest she still had. It was more orange than most of her memories. She smiled, stretching her neck to relax herself. He was someone who she knew would never leave. He had proved himself to her and she had done the same for him.

"Hey," Cyril murmured, sliding his arms around her waist. She inhaled sharply in surprise. Since neither of them had a reflection, he often snuck up on her, and he prided himself in that ability.

Jacey laughed, leaning her head back against her chest. "Joy asked me why none of us have reflections."

"She's so inquisitive," he laughed softly, pulling her backwards and away from the restroom. "What did you say?"

"I said I would tell her when she was older," Jacey shrugged. "I didn't really know how to best explain it. And I don't really get why Charlie and Joy don't have reflections, either."

Cyril sat down on the bed, and Jacey sat next to him, looking at him. He ran a hand through his hair. "You know how I never let you eat those apples?"

"Yeah," Jacey frowned.

"Each of those apples is a child. Those apples multiply and bloom in a matter of seconds. When it comes time, the apple falls. It turns into a spirit and floats over to where its mirror is. But it happens extremely quickly. That's why we never saw it or noticed it," Cyril sighed. "I was there long enough to figure it all out."

She ran a hand through her hair. "But then they should have had an...apple..."

"Not necessarily. It has to do with the seeds. The seeds of us disappear when the reflections did. So since there were no seeds left near or on the tree of us, I guess that's why..." he trailed off.

Jacey touched his shoulder, slowly unbuttoning the first two buttons of his shirt. She pushed the right side of his shirt back, running her hand over the scar. "I'm so sorry all of this had to happen." She was referring to not only the incident when he was fifteen, and the gunshot wound, but also about everything that happened beyond the mirror.

"I'm not," he said simply.

"What?"

He placed his hand over her hand which rested on his bare shoulder. "I'm not sorry that all of this happened."

She frowned. "Why?"

"Because I still have you, don't I?"

Jacey smiled softly, pecking his lips gently. "Indeed, you do, Cy."

Cyril smiled widely, gently brushing his fingers over the rings on her left hand. "And now we have our own family and our own lives. Despite all of the fuckery we had to live through."

"There's a reason Yin and Yang are dancing together at the end of the day, and I think I'm beginning to figure it out. It's because we manage to make it work," Jacey smiled. "I look forward to every tomorrow. I come home from the office, put away my FBI badge, and get to be a mom."

He smirked, kissing her cheek. "And a wife, Red."

"I guess that, too," Jacey laughed. "When I thought about love, I thought about a storm. I thought about chaotic mess, passionate madness and thunder and lightning and fire and wind and pain. But I guess it's not always like that. You're not always like that. And...well, I'm getting to be ok with it."

"I am, too," Cyril murmured. He looked at her, and just as they leaned in, Charlie's voice could be heard loud and clear from where he now stood in the doorway.

"Ewwwww!" Charlie shrieked, running out of the room. "Joy, mom and dad are kissing again!"

Jacey laughed as Cyril stood to go calm their children. Just as he passed by her, she grasped his tie gently and pulled his lips to hers.

CHAPTER 44:

COUNTING MIRACLES, NAMING WONDERS

I look at her.
She's sleeping.
Charlie and Joy tire both of us out.
The clock tells me we still have two hours before we have to leave.
I'm kind of excited.
This tradition of going to Connor and Lakewood's place is...nice.
I feel like a part of the family.
Like I belong.
Her dad respects me.
Her brother has accepted me.
And even Connor understands my place in her life.
It all starts to make sense.
Joy is so much like Chrissie.
But at the same time they are so different.
I see the same person...
But a different one.
Joy doesn't speak her mind often.
Chrissie did.
Joy thinks before speaking.
Chrissie just spoke without thinking.
Joy is mature for her age.
Chrissie lived in a world of fairytales.
Joy is trying to understand love.
Chrissie feared it.

But they both are determined.
They want to understand everyone.
They both look similar.
Passion burns in their soul.
I can see it in their eyes.
Of course, I haven't seen Chrissie for fourteen years.

...Technically, for nineteen years.
I remind myself that she was a ghost.
I'm thirty-one now.
And adult.
A father.
A husband.
Jacey is twenty-nine.
And I couldn't imagine never seeing her.
I love her.
Like red.
And that's what I call her.
Because she is my red.
She gave me red.
And that's the strongest bond between us.
Charlie is a talkative child.
He looks a lot like his mother.
I know that he will be strong.
He cares about everyone.
The other day, another little girl fell down in the airport.
He ran over.
And he helped her up.
Jacey has a fondness in her heart for the both of them.
They're both so unique.
And it's been such a long fourteen years.

I've been married for ten years.

Our tenth anniversary was on April tenth of this year.

I took her on a trip to California's greatest landmarks.

She loves traveling.

And she gave me two things.

A watch that opens to show the picture of Chrissie and I.

And as if that wasn't enough, a photo album.

Of us.

Of our family.

With quotations alongside each picture.

I love it.

Some place to flip through memories.

I pull the scrapbook out of my suitcase.

I had to bring it.

It's important.

I open to the first page.

She went to finish her senior year of high school.

Somehow.

And this was her and I, with her holding her diploma.

The next picture makes me smile.

My cheeks flush slightly.

Our first kiss.

Callie took the picture.

I remember it like it was yesterday.

She looked at me, and she had told me she loved me.

And I said that I knew that already.

Jacey had pushed me slightly, and it had gone silent.

Callie was in the next room.

She had stopped by.

And she took a picture of what happened next.

I laugh softly at the next one.

Our technical first date.

She looks so beautiful.

In her red dress.

I gave her a rose.

It was plated in silver.

Back at our home in San Francisco, it is on her nightstand.

She loves it.

I said it represented something eternal.

All she could do was smile.

And it is me giving it to her.

The next is my first day of college.

And hers.

We both went to University of Los Angeles.

It was a long commute.

We moved into the dorms, and moved out of our apartments.

She was smiling widely.

Majoring in criminology changed her life.

I majored in physical education, and minored in psychology.

Since I now play soccer professionally, I don't really need to worry about that.

Her dad paid for college.

For the both of us.

Claimed it was an apology gift.

I still want to pay him back.
I see the next photo.
Of her with her ring.
The day we got engaged.
I love that day.
That ring makes me smile.
The next was us graduating.
My smile widens.
The next is her first day of work.
She scares me sometimes.
Being an agent is scary.
Sometimes, they don't come home.
I can't bear the thought of Red not coming back.
It pains me.
She swears she is careful.
And that she is doing what she wants to do.
But I always call her.
Whenever I can.
To tell her I love her.
I never want to miss that opportunity.
In this picture, she's gussied up in her gear.
Bulletproof vest.
Gun.
Belt.
And I admit to myself that she does look pretty damn good.
The next picture is us.
Together.
Her in a white dress, and me in a tuxedo.
The day we got married.
I said my vows with more passion than I had ever had in my life.

Her smile made me so happy.
They say the story ends there.
The story ends when the conflict ends.
But isn't that the purpose of an epilogue?
It tells you that everything turned out the way I should.
It gives you a sense of peace.
And I know that this story is far from over.
Because love doesn't end.
Even after death.
I know what happens to us after.
People like us go to the other side of the mirror.
Like her uncle Leroy, who had once been where we were.
He became a spirit.
And we'll become the same.
Forever.
I meant it when I said it to her.
Charlie and Joy...
I don't know if they will become spirits, too.
But I can't wait to watch them grow up.
After tonight...We'll go home.
And life will continue.
I would say that things were about to calm down.
But there was one more thing that we had to our life events.
And then things could calm down.
In our Californian home.
I'm not done looking through the pictures.
But I close the book.
The memories are vivid in my mind anyway.

I slip it back into the suitcase.
My eyes are bright.
And for the moment...
All I can see is red.

Chapter 45:

Seeing Red

"Oh, hush, you!" Jacey laughed, taking a sip of wine as she rolled her eyes at Connor. "It should be illegal to tell childhood stories at family dinners. Especially with children present."

Connor laughed, bouncing the young Emily on his lap. "Come on, Jay, that's a classic."

"The stories I could tell about Lakewood, though," Jacey challenged with a small laugh, glancing at her much older brother.

Lakewood's eyes went wide as he choked on his own wine. "Let's not tell those stories."

"Oh, come on," she laughed. "When I was ten and Lakewood was about fifteen, I caught him dressed up in one of dad's suits. He then stripped down to nothing but dad's boxers and pretended to be Superman."

Connor burst out in laughter, and Richard Adams looked extremely appalled. He looked at his son, barely able to bit back a laugh. "In my good suits?" he exclaimed.

Lakewood turned a dark red, laughing through his embarrassment.

"You have a strange family," Cyril joked, leaning over and sliding down onto the couch next to Jacey.

Jacey laughed, pulling Charlie onto her lap as he squealed. "Lakewood also was the one who found the pineapple-infused jelly the day before

Thanksgiving and he hid it in his room. But then he *forgot* where it was."

"We found it in his room a month later," Richard roared with laughter.

Lakewood looked desperate to get the subject off of him. "Well, we can't forget the Easter where dad forgot..."

"Oh!" Jacey laughed, understanding that he couldn't say it all in front of Emily, Charlie, or Joy.

Richard laughed again, the wine obviously affecting him a lot more. "I made up for it, though!"

"Hiding real eggs and having us break them open without knowing does not count!" she said with a bright smile.

Lakewood nodded, chuckling. "Our apartment smelled like rotten eggs for forever," he complained, winking at his father with a bright smile.

"I heard that Richard also let young Jacey answer the phone once, and she said 'I love you' to the government official," Cyril chimed in, and Jacey turned dark red as everyone laughed.

Charlie tugged on the end of his mom's shirts. "Mommy, can we open presents now?"

"Yeah!" Joy agreed, tickling Emily with a bright smile. She looked extremely happy, and her eyes were bright.

Connor picked Emily up, moving over to the tree. "Emily, can you help me?"

The three-year old nodded, smiling as she looked around.

"This one is for Lakewood," Connor murmured. "Go give it to daddy." Emily grasped the present, toddled over to Lakewood, and placed it on his lap before racing back. It continued on like that until all the presents were passed out.

"This is for Auntie Jacey."

"This is for Joy."

"This is for grandpa."

"This is for Uncle Cyril."

"This is for Charlie."

"This is for Joy."

"This is for you."

"This is for Auntie Jacey."

Eventually, the conversation turned back to childhood stories as the endless presents were passed out by Connor and Emily.

Finally, when it wall was done, Charlie began to tear into the nearest present.

"Woah," Jacey laughed, tugging the present away. "Let's see who this is from, pumpkin." She glanced at the tag. "It's from Connor and Lakewood, Charlie."

Charlie grinned at his uncles, continuing his endeavors to rip off the paper with extreme ferocity. His eyes widened at the box of blocks, pumping his fist into the air in triumph.

Cyril smiled while Charlie and Joy began to build amongst the torn wrapping paper. He glanced at one of him and Jacey's presents, fingering the bow. Connor threw him a sideways smile.

As he tore off the wrapping paper gently, his eyes widened. It was a small clock that was inside a tall glass dome. The clock had Roman Numerals, and a picture of him and Jacey on the face of the clock. Supporting the clock were two columns that had Joy and Charlie's pictures.

"Connor...Lakewood..." Jacey murmured, smiling softly. Connor winked, leaning back in his chair with a victorious grin on his face.

Cyril placed it behind them, smiling slightly. Beneath the clock were two pillow cases. One was a girl holding a can and a string to her mouth, talking into it. The cord, since the pillow cases were side by side, looked like it was connected to the can and string that the boy was holding, listening into it.

"That was my idea!" Lakewood claimed, smiling widely at Jacey. She had asked for new pillow cases, and this was, well, adorable.

Joy was looking around, and had already placed the two books she had gotten in a neat pile with the other ones she had brought to dinner. She looked patient and calm as she sat there.

"Grandpa got something for you, Joy," Richard murmured. "Let me go get it."

Jacey watched her dad stand. "Dad...what did you do?" She asked him with wary eyes and Cyril grinned.

"It's okay," he reassured his wife, placing his hand over hers. She watched Cyril carefully, and then looked around for her dad.

"A puppy!" Joy shrieked, jumping up from where she had been calmly sitting.

Jacey hit Cyril's leg lightly, looking shocked. "You let him buy us a dog?" she exclaimed. But she was smiling softly.

Cyril grinned sheepishly. "It'll be okay. I thought you said you wanted a dog, anyway."

"I did," she admitted, leaning back in her chair, a soft smile gracing her features.

Joy took the tiny husky pup in her arms, holding her tightly. The puppy licked her cheek, and she giggled hysterically. Charlie carefully circled the two, unsure whether the dog was friend or foe.

"Here, Red," Cyril murmured, pushing over a box to her. She frowned, looking at it. "It's from me," he told her, smiling slightly.

Jacey slowly opened the box, finding a small red velvet box and a long black velvet box. She flipped open the red box first, inhaling quickly and smiling widely. It was the newly released silver dollar from that year. She collected quirky coins, and even had a 1978 silver dollar. She reached over, squeezing his hand.

Cyril pushed the small velvet box over to her, and she opened it with care. A heart locket was revealed, embedded with small rubies.

"Thanks, dear," she murmured quietly, smiling.

Cyril grinned. "That's not it." He reached over, opening the heart locket to reveal pictures. On one side of the heart, the side backing the front, was Cyril's picture. On the other side, the side backing the back, was Joy's picture. There was a small heart that had two sides within the heart. On one of those sides was Charlie's picture. And the final side held the ultrasound picture.

Jacey wrapped her arms around his neck, smiling widely. When he pulled away, he carefully clasped the necklace around her neck.

"You're the best, dear," she said quietly.

Connor smiled at the two. "Hey, lovebirds, we're about to open your present."

Cyril laughed, and Jacey pushed him gently, trying to bite back a laugh herself. Lakewood roared with laughter at the matching Superman pajamas.

"Nice one, sis," Lakewood chuckled.

"Look beneath," Cyril added, high-fiving Jacey with a wide grin.

Connor pulled away the pajamas with a laugh, and then smiled, going quiet at the picture frame beneath. It was a picture of a dog pile of Lakewood, Connor, and Emily, and was one of the cutest pictures Jacey had ever seen. She smiled at their reaction. Lakewood squeezed Connor's knee, and kissed Emily on the head.

"Thanks," Connor said sincerely, going over to Jacey and hugging her tightly. He hugged Cyril, too, smiling softly still. "It means a lot."

"We have a present for all of you, technically," Jacey said with a wide smile. Cyril smiled as well. She was going to announce that they were going to have everyone over for New Years', which was their surprise for the night.

Jacey glanced over at Cyril, and her smile softened. "First, we're going to invite everyone to our home for New Years', should you like to come."

"'First?'" Cyril asked, looking slightly confused.

Jacey nodded, looking slightly nervous. She looked around at each person, giving them a unique smile. "You all have been really supportive. You never gave up on me, or on Cyril and I. I have enjoyed having a family, and I know that they are my first priority. When I first had Joy, you guys were there for me every step of the way. You flew out to us at three in the morning on a redeye flight when I went into labor."

"We're grateful you didn't give up on us, either, Jay," Lakewood said with a wide grin. She had given a speech similar to this last year, and had given each of them a family portrait.

She nodded slowly. "Well, I figured you all deserved to know that our family is growing."

Everyone's face morphed into one of absolute shock as they tried to comprehend exactly what she saw saying. Cyril looked the most surprised, looking up at Jacey, who was standing next to him.

Jacey nodded, eyes brimming with happy tears. "I'm going to have another child."

SEPTEMBER 2040

Chapter 46:

Red Sky Warning

Charlie watched his older sister enter the restroom at Yosemite, staying by Swinging Bridge. He stood on the edge of the bridge, like some tourists had before him, and jumped into the cold water below.

"Mom, I want to do what Charlie did, too!" Scarlett said, pulling on her mother's arm. Jacey and her youngest daughter, who was ten, were wading around the shallow end of Merced River.

Jacey squeezed her daughter's hand. "Maybe. It's a bit too high."

"Please? Pretty please?" the young child jumped up and down.

Cyril came up behind the two of them, tapping Scarlett's head gently. "The physical appearance of the please doesn't make a difference," he reminded her.

Scarlett frowned, plotting her next move as she tried and failed to skip stones.

"Where's Joy?" Jacey asked, looking around a bit nervously.

Cyril placed his hand on her shoulder. "She's in the restroom. She's seventeen, Red. She'll be okay."

"Yeah," Jacey tried to convince herself. She slowly glanced over at Cyril, and smiled slightly.

Charlie swam over to where his mom, dad, and younger sister were. For a fifteen-year old, he was pretty fit. He had brown curls that covered his head, and they had recently cut them so they didn't hang over his eyes. He was a swimmer, and Cyril and him had been learning how to surf together. His eyes were a bright hazel, and he smiled at his mother.

"Hey, Charlie," Cyril said, grinning. Yes, Cyril was now forty-three, and Jacey was forty-one. They were old, and in ten years, Jacey presumed they could even be grandparents. Thinking back on everything that had happened in the dark and dying places felt like forever ago.

The teenage boy floated on his back. "When are we going to dinner?"

"Soon," Jacey promised, and watched Scarlett as she walked over to where Charlie was. Charlie stood up, helping his younger sister who couldn't quite reach the bottom of the floor of the Merced River.

"Maybe we can go to the ice cream place in Yosemite Village," Cyril suggested. This was Jacey's second time being in Yosemite, and the kids' first time being there.

Jacey nodded, grinning. "Sounds great, dear."

"Where *is* Joy?" Cyril asked, frowning. "It's been quite a while now since she went to the restroom."

His wife nodded, looking a bit worried. "I'll go check," she said.

"I want to come!" Scarlett said, wading over quickly to her mother with Charlie's help.

"Okay," Jacey agreed, grasping her youngest child's hand as she made her way over Swinging Bridge and over to the small restroom.

She knocked on the door she had seen Joy walk into. "Joy?" she called through the door.

"What?" her eldest daughter called through the door.

"Just making sure you're okay," Jacey said quietly.

Joy chuckled slightly. "I'm fine, mother," she promised. She opened the door, smiling at her mother. "See? Totally fine."

"Good," Jacey said, looking at her eldest daughter with a smile. Joy had certainly grown up over the past ten years. She was a few inches shorter than Jacey, and looked quite mature. Her white-blonde hair color had remained over the years. She had bright blue eyes, still, and this time had her hair pinned up in a messy bun. She wore a short skirt and tank top to cool off. It might have been September, but California got quite hot.

"Dinnertime?" Joy asked, smiling at her mother with a smile that most seventeen-year olds wouldn't have ever given their mother, especially with the stress of senior year looming over the family. They didn't want to reply on Richard Adams, given his ailing health due to the problems that had developed from the alcohol.

Scarlett nodded, grasping her sister's hand. "Let's go tell dad we're hungry," she said, pulling Joy's hand with an impressive strength.

As they walked over Swinging Bridge, Jacey watched as Charlie and Cyril met up with her two girls. The kids jumped excitedly, most likely at the prospect of ice cream, and raced across the bridge.

Cyril watched carefully as the kids ran in front of them along the sidewalk. It wasn't that long of a walk to Yosemite Village from there, and he caught up with Jacey, who was just behind the kids. Joy had taken responsibility like usual, and was carefully watching Charlie chase Scarlett.

"It's nice to be here as a family," Jacey said, interlacing her hand with Cyril's left hand. "Isn't it, dear?"

He gazed over at her. "It is, Red."

"They're growing up fast," she commented, laughing softly as they watched their kids run about.

Cyril nodded. He paused before looking over at her with care. "Do you ever think about back when we were younger? And everything that happened on the other side?"

"Too often," Jacey said quietly, sighing. "Practically every night." She bit back the memory of last night, when Cyril had woken her, telling her she had been calling out for him. Just like that nightmare she had had back on the other side of the mirror.

"It really affects people," Cyril said. "Like Callie."

Jacey shook her head, biting back the image. "Suicide. I couldn't believe my eyes. She...she was so strong."

"But we did it. And against all odds," he reminded her, squeezing her hand gently. His eyes crinkled as he smiled, eyes brightening when he looked at her.

She nodded, smiling a bit at that. "Remember that meeting in San Francisco?"

"I told you I was a bad influence," Cyril winked, his teenage charm coming back to him despite how old he actually was.

"I agreed to be with you," Jacey said, touching her ring finger with her index finger of her left hand.

He whistled. "Pretty damn impressive that I managed to ensnare you," he teased.

"For twenty years of marriage," she agreed, laughing softly. "That's a long time."

"We've still got a lot of time ahead of us," Cyril said, a soft smile gracing his face. "A lot of time, Red."

Jacey and him were silent for a bit as they walked to Yosemite Village, approaching the ice cream shop.

"Dinner first!" Cyril announced, and Scarlett let out a loud 'Awh!'. Joy tugged on the hand of her younger sister, pulling her away from the ice cream shop and toward the deli next door.

Charlie sauntered in between the line of family: just in front of his parents, and just behind his sisters.

"You okay, Charlie?" Jacey asked, ruffling the hair of her teenager.

He shrugged, smiling at his mother. "Yeah. Just thinking."

"About that girl?" his mother teased, unable to stop herself from referencing the girl who had complimented Charlie on his flips off of Swinging Bridge.

Charlie rolled his eyes. "Dad, make her stop!"

Cyril shrugged. "She's relentless, Charlie. I wish there was something I could do."

"See? I'm just too powerful," Jacey teased, watching her fifteen-year old run up to talk with his sisters up ahead as the family entered the deli.

"Go sit with the kids. I'll order," Cyril said, squeezing her hand.

Jacey let go of his hand. "Thanks, dear," she said, heading over to the table that Joy, Charlie, and Scarlett were already settling down.

"Dad better not get me anything with cheese," Scarlett said, sticking her tongue out at the thought of the slimy melted cheese that came on sandwiches. She wasn't picky, except for the fact that she hated cheese of all kinds. Pizza night didn't exist at their house because of Scarlett.

Cyril came up with the readymade sandwiches them, placing them in front of each member of his family with care. He slid into the bench seat next to Jacey, watching Scarlett carefully inspect her own for cheese. When she was pleased with her search, she bit in.

"Tomorrow we'll hike some," Jacey said.

Charlie grinned. "Can we go to Yosemite Falls?"

"I suggest Bridal Veil falls," Joy said, chipping in to the conversation, which was unusual for the quiet girl.

Cyril grinned. "Why not all of them?"

Chapter 47:

Blurring Eyes, Last Goodbye

Joy sat on the counter, pressing the phone to her ear.

"When are you coming back?" the voice on the phone asked, sighing slightly.

She leaned against the wall, glancing at the mirror that she wasn't in. "In three days. It's not that bad here, you know. I kind of like Yosemite."

"What's it like?" the boy on the phone asked.

Joy sighed happily. "It's quite beautiful. Bridal Veil Falls was absolutely wonderful. It's this thin waterfall that looks just like a bridal veil. El Capitan was pretty cool, and I took so many pictures. It's just so amazing."

"I'm glad you're having fun, Joy," he said, and she should tell by his voice that he was smiling.

She smiled as well. "I am. I can send you pictures if you want, Matt."

"Sure," Matthew said, his voice quiet. "I'd like that."

"I guess I'll talk to you tomorrow?" Joy asked, making sure that he did want to talk to her tomorrow as well.

He paused. "Yeah."

"Talk to you later, dear. Sleep tight," she smiled softly, cheeks tinged with a bright shade of pink.

Matthew was silent for a few moments. "You too. Night."

The line clicked dead, and Joy placed the phone down with a small sigh of happiness and frustration. It was hard, and she wasn't quite used to the new dynamics of this relationship compared to her last one.

After all, that's what relationships were. Mom said that each relationship was a test to see if they would be the one for her. And each time, Joy found herself falling a bit too hard for whoever she was with.

Joy.

Her name meant joyful.

But it didn't have to be true.

Mom's name meant beautiful.

It was true, according to her pictures.

However, mom was the lucky one.

The one who managed to find herself. Somehow.

Matthew was...quieter. Mom had always told her that dad used to be shy, similar to that. But the used the word 'introverted', not 'shy.' Mom had continued to explain that dad hated the word shy because he wasn't shy. He simply didn't care for social interaction as much as some people in her family.

Joy was quiet around her family, but it was a bit different around her friends. She was the loud one of the group. No, she wasn't liked by everyone, but that didn't really matter to her. In fact, she dismissed the idea that she should be annoyed by someone's reaction to her being negative.

Matthew didn't really like the idea of PDA, or public displays of attention. Some people disregarded them for that. She didn't really think it mattered, for what mattered was how much he cared. When they were alone, or with close friends, they would hold hands, or gently push each other's feet. It was something they did, and it didn't bother Joy like it used to. It simply took getting used to.

Her family valued love a lot, and that much was obvious. Mom had always been close to dad, and had constantly talked about her Uncle, or Joy's great uncle.

Joy glanced in the mirror. Like always, a shadow flickered for a moment, and then disappeared. It was a mystery that her mom and dad had never explained to her. She wanted to be like the other kids who could look in the mirror and fix their hair. Joy wanted to be like the other people. The shadow was risky, and it used to scare her when she was younger. It was a powerful being that Joy didn't want to be connected to.

She sighed, shaking her head as she glanced into the mirror once more. Where she was seemed darker, as if something should be there. No one in her family had a reflection, and Joy figured it was because of her parents. Grandpa had a reflection, and so did Uncle Lakewood and Uncle Connor.

Carefully, she pushed the phone away from the sink. Looking close at the mirror, Joy tried to see herself. She willed herself to be seen in the mirror. Nothing happened. Not even a flicker of an image. She sighed with utter disappointment. Perhaps, Joy had hoped, something would have come to life from where she was. She had prayed that, possibly, it would have come to life. Her reflection, that is.

Joy glanced at her bracelet. It had a green band and an Italian flag charm. She unhooked it, setting it down on the counter. She felt emptier with it off, and it was hard for Joy to set it down. She had taken it off, figuring maybe there was something preventing her from being seen. Maybe she was linked to the people who didn't have reflections, and they had prevented her from seeing herself in the mirror.

But reflections were part of science. There wasn't a person that was a reflection, it was a trick of the light and the bends in the mirror. No magic, and nothing supernatural. It seemed, to Joy, to be something unexplainable.

She pressed her hand against the mirror, which was cool to the touch. Joy paused, shaking her head. Only her hand was there.

The shadow flickered in front of her, becoming more solid with every passing moment. Joy watched eagerly, wondering if her reflection was finally coming into existence.

Whatever it was in front of Joy in the mirror was smirking. It started to look like her, but it was a her without color. It reached out, and its hand went through the mirror. Its black hand wrapped around her wrist, and Joy felt herself being pulled through the mirror.

Into hell.

Chapter 47:
The End of an Epilogue...And the Beginning of the War

Joy glanced in fear at the rectangle that was looking into her old life. A black and white version of her was slowly filling with color as it smirked, slipping her bracelet on.

"This once was your parents' battle," the girl whispered, her lips curving upwards in a more pronounced smirk.

The real Joy shook her head, taking a step back. Her mom had once said something about this being over. About the fight being done.

The other girl ran a hand through her white-blonde hair, and stared Joy directly in the eyes, refusing to break away.

"So they thought this was over, eh?"

"They were wrong."

"This is only the beginning."